"With a readable style, deep engagement with other scholars, and an impressive grasp of the particulars of the ancient cultural situation, Keith offers a stimulating and creative proposal about the origins of tensions between Jesus and the scribal elite. Keith emphasizes Jesus's social status as a key contributing factor in these tensions. Along the way, Keith addresses questions about the historicity of the Gospels' portrayal of controversies with scribes and Pharisees, and a number of other issues, making this study well worth reading."

—**Larry Hurtado**, New College, University of Edinburgh

"Chris Keith is one of the leading scholars of literacy in Christian antiquity, especially as it relates to the historical Jesus. In this new contribution, he makes his views accessible to the nonspecialist who is interested in knowing, was Jesus a well-educated teacher who could read and write? And if not, why did he fall afoul of the powerful scribes—the readers, writers, and teachers of his world—leading to his demise? Clearly written and coherently argued, this will be a book for scholar and layperson alike."

—**Bart D. Ehrman**, University of North Carolina at Chapel Hill

"This is a fresh and fruitful approach to a key aspect of the historical Jesus by one of the more creative younger scholars in the field."

—**Richard Bauckham**, University of St. Andrews;
Ridley Hall, Cambridge

"This well-written study by Chris Keith puts Jesus as a public teacher into new light. The attention this book devotes to Jesus in relation to the social context of his day not only challenges assumptions about what it means for Jesus to be God's Messiah and Son of God but also offers a fresh way to understand what it meant for Jesus to have given instructions at all and to have debated them with his Jewish contemporaries. Readers with any interest in the historical Jesus will have a hard time putting the book down."

—**Loren Stuckenbruck**, Ludwig-Maximilians-Universität München

"Building on extensive research in oral culture and collective memory, Chris Keith helpfully contextualizes Jesus's debates with the scribes and other experts on the Jewish Scriptures within the media culture of Roman Palestine. His readings of the Gospels offer new insights on those texts and on Jesus's teaching career, adding greater clarity to the ways that Jesus confronted the religious authorities of his own time and, ultimately, the reasons for his death."

—**Tom Thatcher**, Cincinnati Christian University

"In *Jesus against the Scribal Elite*, Chris Keith provides a distinctive angle to the controversy narratives by focusing on how the scribal elites perceived Jesus's literacy and authoritative status. Keith's research complements older approaches to the controversy narratives and their focus on the law, miracles, and exorcisms. The book is convincing, carefully argued, well documented, and remarkably easy to read. It will surely prove its worth both in the classroom and in the ongoing quest for the historical Jesus."

—**James Crossley**, professor of Bible, politics, and culture,
University of Sheffield

"In this book, as lucid and accessible as it is compelling, Chris Keith exposes the issues that lay at the very heart of Jesus's engagement with the scribal elite. This is written for upper-level students, but scholars too will find much to consider in this excellent treatment."

—**Helen Bond**, Centre for the Study of Christian Origins,
University of Edinburgh

"This work is a well-researched, well-written, and significant contribution to the discussions of literacy and conflict in Jesus's ministry and to discussions of the nature of the Gospels. Even if one disagrees with some of the conclusions, it offers a new perspective worthy of analysis and reflection."

—**Klyne Snodgrass**, North Park Theological Seminary

"Well informed by current academic discussions of historical Jesus research, memory, orality, and literacy, Chris Keith adds a very important social dimension to understanding the conflicts between Jesus and other teachers of his day. This fascinating book makes a new and welcome contribution to the discussion."

—**Craig S. Keener**, Asbury Theological Seminary

"Christianity was birthed from debate, conflict, and bitter rhetoric. *Jesus against the Scribal Elite* offers a realistic, often disturbing portrait of how this all began. Built from sound scholarship and great respect for the biblical Gospels, this book confirms what most New Testament scholars already know: Chris Keith is the best and brightest scholar of Christian origins in the field."

—**Anthony Le Donne**, University of the Pacific

JESUS AGAINST the Scribal Elite

JESUS AGAINST the Scribal Elite

The Origins of the Conflict

Chris Keith

Baker Academic

a division of Baker Publishing Group
Grand Rapids, Michigan

© 2014 by Chris Keith

Published by Baker Academic
a division of Baker Publishing Group
P.O. Box 6287, Grand Rapids, MI 49516-6287
www.bakeracademic.com

Printed in the United States of America

Library of Congress Cataloging-in-Publication Data is on file at the Library of Congress, Washington, DC.

ISBN 978-0-8010-3988-1 (pbk.)

14 15 16 17 18 19 20   7 6 5 4 3 2 1

To Anthony Le Donne and Christopher Rollston,
no strangers to teaching, conflict,
or Jesus

veritas vincit

Contents

Preface

The publication of this book brings me both joy and sadness in light of what has transpired between its conception and completion. It began life as the 2011 Frederick D. Kershner Lectures in New Testament at Emmanuel Christian Seminary (then Emmanuel School of Religion). The lectures offered me the opportunity to complete the final stage of a three-part research project. In my first monograph, *The* Pericope Adulterae, *the Gospel of John, and the Literacy of Jesus* (Leiden: Brill, 2009), I asked whether John 8:6, 8 is a claim that Jesus was literate and concluded that it was such a claim. In a subsequent monograph, *Jesus' Literacy: Scribal Culture and the Teacher from Galilee* (London: T&T Clark, 2011), I asked whether the historical Jesus really was literate and concluded that he did not hold scribal literacy. My further conclusion, however, was that the matter is not as straightforward as one might think, and was not straightforward in Jesus's day either. The present book takes the conclusions of *Jesus' Literacy* to the controversy narratives, which portray Jesus's spirited debates with the leading teachers of his day, and addresses their interpretation and historicity. As such, a few of the chapters in this book function as something of a popularization of *Jesus' Literacy*'s main argument, a more accessible version for students and general readers. On occasion I have repeated a paragraph or two and gratefully acknowledge the permission of T&T Clark. I am grateful to Emmanuel Christian Seminary for the opportunity to develop these thoughts in a nascent form and for their hospitality while I was there. I am also grateful to the John Templeton Award for Theological Promise, given by the Forschungszentrum Internationale und Interdisziplinäre Theologie at the University of

Heidelberg, for the funds that enabled my acceptance of the invitation to deliver the Kershner Lectures.

As befits its focus, however, I wrote this book amid controversy. The first controversy was the unexpected dismissal of my friend and colleague Anthony Le Donne from Lincoln Christian University, which directly led to my departure from that institution. The second controversy was Emmanuel Christian Seminary's dismissal of Christopher Rollston, also a colleague and friend and one of several Emmanuel faculty members who hosted me in my time there. I do not think it necessary to rehash the details of these unfortunate situations. Neither can I ignore them entirely, however. I will simply state that neither Anthony's nor Chris's scholarship warranted the reactions they received. Commendably, they conducted themselves with a professionalism and grace that was not always shown to them. Both have emerged as honorable men, and I am one of many people, in both the church and the academy, who hold these men in the highest esteem. To them I dedicate this study.

I have accrued many debts in the process of writing this book, foremost to my family. My beautiful wife, Erin, is my best friend and possibly the only person in the world who could tolerate being married to me. I am forever grateful for her love and support. My children, Jayce and Hannah, provide the highlights of my day, whether we are wrestling, reading, playing Angry Birds on the iPad, watching UofL games, or sneaking cookies behind Mom's back. I cannot imagine life without all three of them.

I thank Anthony Le Donne and Anders Runesson for reading portions of this study in draft form and saving me from many mistakes. Anders also graciously provided prepublication copies of essays. I extend thanks also to Tom Thatcher and H. Gregory Snyder. They have been great friends to me, but my debt goes beyond that. Those familiar with the literature will have little difficulty recognizing their influence on my conception of Second Temple scribal culture and Jesus's place within it. Two excellent librarians helped me acquire resources when needed: Leslie Starasta of Lincoln Christian University and Anne Hutchinson at St. Mary's University College, Twickenham. Frank Dicken helped me acquire resources as well. It has been wonderful to work with Baker Academic and especially my editor, James Ernest. His reputation precedes him, and for good reason. I thank Michael Robinson for his work on the indexes.

Finally, I must mention my grandmother, Louise Keith, who passed from this life at the age of 93 only one month before I finished this book. With the exception of the last few years, my grandmother at all times was a tornado of activity. She was especially proficient at encouraging her grandchildren in their various pursuits. I have few doubts that she would raise a suspicious eyebrow at some of my thoughts concerning Scripture in this book. But in the end I think she would like it and take it in stride. Its main concerns—Jesus and conflict—were two of her favorite things.

Easter morning
March 31, 2013
London

Abbreviations

Bibliographic and General

AAW	Approaching the Ancient World
ABRL	Anchor Bible Reference Library
ABS	Archaeology and Biblical Studies
ACAF	Ancient Context, Ancient Faith
ANRW	*Aufstieg und Niedergang der römischen Welt*
AT	author's translation
BASP	*Bulletin of the American Society of Papyrologists*
BCE	before the Common Era
BG	Biblische Gestalten
Bib	*Biblica*
BRS	Biblical Resource Series
BS	Biblical Seminar
BTB	*Biblical Theology Bulletin*
BThSt	Biblisch-theologische Studien
BZNW	Beihefte zur Zeitschrift für die neutestamentliche Wissenschaft
CBQ	*Catholic Biblical Quarterly*
CCSS	Catholic Commentary on the Sacred Scripture
CE	Common Era
CEB	Common English Bible
CM	Christianity in the Making
ConBNT	Coniectanea biblica: New Testament Series
COQG	Christian Origins and the Question of God
CRNT	Conversation on the Road Not Taken
ECLS	Early Christian Literature Series
EDB	*Eerdmans Dictionary of the Bible*
EDEJ	*Eerdmans Dictionary of Early Judaism*
EKKNT	Evangelisch-katholischer Kommentar zum Neuen Testament
ESCO	European Studies on Christian Origins

ESV	English Standard Version
FC	Fathers of the Church Series
FRLANT	Forschungen zur Religion und Literatur des Alten und Neuen Testaments
GBS	Guides to Biblical Scholarship
GRBS	*Greek, Roman, and Byzantine Studies*
ICC	International Critical Commentary
JBL	*Journal of Biblical Literature*
JCM	Jews, Christians, and Muslims from the Ancient to the Modern World
JDS	Judean Desert Studies
JECS	*Journal of Early Christian Studies*
JGRCJ	*Journal of Greco-Roman Christianity and Judaism*
JQR	*Jewish Quarterly Review*
JRASup	Journal of Roman Archaeology: Supplementary Series
JSHJ	*Journal for the Study of the Historical Jesus*
JSNTSup	Journal for the Study of the New Testament: Supplement Series
JSOTSup	Journal for the Study of the Old Testament: Supplement Series
LCL	Loeb Classical Library
LHJS	Library of Historical Jesus Studies
LNTS	Library of New Testament Studies
LXX	Septuagint (Greek translation of the Hebrew Scriptures)
MS(S)	manuscript(s)
MT	Masoretic text
Neot	*Neotestamentica*
NICNT	New International Commentary on the New Testament
NIGTC	New International Greek Testament Commentary
NIV	New International Version
NovT	*Novum Testamentum*
NPNF[1]	*Nicene and Post-Nicene Fathers*, series 1
NRSV	New Revised Standard Version
NTGJC	New Testament Gospels in Their Judaic Contexts
NTL	New Testament Library
NTS	*New Testament Studies*
NTTSD	New Testament Tools, Studies and Documents
OBO	Orbis biblicus et orientalis
OCPM	Oxford Classical and Philosophical Monographs
OHJDL	*The Oxford Handbook of Jewish Daily Life in Roman Palestine*
PAWB	Potsdamer altertumswissenschaftliche Beiträge
PG	Patrologia graeca
PL	Patrologia latina
PNTC	Pillar New Testament Commentary
RFCC	Religion in the First Christian Centuries
RLS	Rockwell Lecture Series
SBEC	Studies in the Bible and Early Christianity
SBLSP	Society of Biblical Literature Seminar Papers
SBLTCS	Society of Biblical Literature Text-Critical Studies
SBLTT	Society of Biblical Literature Texts and Translations
SBT	Studies in Biblical Theology

SCC	Studies in Creative Criticism
SemeiaSt	Semeia Studies
SGJC	Shared Ground among Jews and Christians
SJ	Studia judaica
SJC	Studies in Judaism and Christianity
SL	Scribner Library
SNTI	Studies in New Testament Interpretation
SNTSMS	Society for New Testament Studies Monograph Series
SPNT	Studies on Personalities of the New Testament
TENTS	Texts and Editions for New Testament Study
TNIV	Today's New International Version
TSAJ	Texte und Studien zum antiken Judentum
TTGP	T&T Clark Guides for the Perplexed
UBCS	Understanding the Bible Commentary Series
UJT	Understanding Jesus Today
VPT	Voices in Performance and Text
WUNT	Wissenschaftliche Untersuchungen zum Neuen Testament
ZNW	*Zeitschrift für die neutestamentliche Wissenschaft*

Hebrew Bible

Gen.	Genesis	Song	Song of Songs
Exod.	Exodus	Isa.	Isaiah
Lev.	Leviticus	Jer.	Jeremiah
Num.	Numbers	Lam.	Lamentations
Deut.	Deuteronomy	Ezek.	Ezekiel
Josh.	Joshua	Dan.	Daniel
Judg.	Judges	Hosea	Hosea
Ruth	Ruth	Joel	Joel
1–2 Sam.	1–2 Samuel	Amos	Amos
1–2 Kings	1–2 Kings	Obad.	Obadiah
1–2 Chron.	1–2 Chronicles	Jon.	Jonah
Ezra	Ezra	Mic.	Micah
Neh.	Nehemiah	Nah.	Nahum
Esther	Esther	Hab.	Habakkuk
Job	Job	Zeph.	Zephaniah
Ps(s).	Psalm(s)	Hag.	Haggai
Prov.	Proverbs	Zech.	Zechariah
Eccles.	Ecclesiastes	Mal.	Malachi

Greek Testament

Matt.	Matthew	Luke	Luke
Mark	Mark	John	John

Acts	Acts	Titus	Titus
Rom.	Romans	Philem.	Philemon
1–2 Cor.	1–2 Corinthians	Heb.	Hebrews
Gal.	Galatians	James	James
Eph.	Ephesians	1–2 Pet.	1–2 Peter
Phil.	Philippians	1–3 John	1–3 John
Col.	Colossians	Jude	Jude
1–2 Thess.	1–2 Thessalonians	Rev.	Revelation
1–2 Tim.	1–2 Timothy		

Old Testament Apocrypha and Pseudepigrapha

Jub.	*Jubilees*	1–4 Macc.	1–4 Maccabees
L.A.B.	*Liber antiquitatum*	*Sir.*	Sirach
	biblicarum	*T. Levi*	*Testament of Levi*

New Testament Apocrypha and Pseudepigrapha

Inf. Gos. Thom.	*Infancy Gospel of Thomas*	*Ps.-Mt.*	*Gospel of Pseudo-Matthew*
Prot. Jas.	*Protevangelium of James*		

Rabbinic Tractates

The abbreviations below are used for the names of the tractates in the Mishnah (indicated by a prefixed *m.*), Babylonian Talmud (*b.*), and Palestinian/Jerusalem Talmud (*y.*).

'Abot	*'Abot*	*Meg.*	*Megillah*
B. Bat.	*Baba Batra*	*Sukkah*	*Sukkah*
Ketub.	*Ketubbot*	*Yoma*	*Yoma*

Dead Sea Scrolls and Related Texts

CD	Cairo Genizah copy of the *Damascus Document*
4Q213 (4QLevi[a] ar)	Aramaic *Testament of Levi*
4Q266 (4QD[a])	*Damascus Document*[a]

Josephus and Philo

Ag. Ap.	Josephus, *Against Apion*	*Hypoth.*	Philo, *Hypothetica*
Ant.	Josephus, *Jewish Antiquities*	*J.W.*	Josephus, *Jewish War*

Legat.   Philo, *Legatio ad Gaium*   *Prob.*   Philo, *Quod omnis probus liber sit*
Life   Josephus, *The Life*

Classical and Patristic Writers

1 Apol.   Justin Martyr, *Apologia i*
Att.   Cicero, *Epistulae ad Atticum*
Cels.   Origen, *Contra Celsum*
Comm. Ezech.   Jerome, *Commentariorum in Ezechielem*
Comm. Matt.   Origen, *Commentarium in evangelium Matthaei*
Cons.   Augustine, *De consensu evangelistarum*
Dial.   Justin Martyr, *Dialogus cum Tryphone*
Eph.   Ignatius, *To the Ephesians*
Faust.   Augustine, *Contra Faustum Manichaeum*
Hist. eccl.   Eusebius, *Historia ecclesiastica*
Inst.   Quintilian, *Institutio oratoria*
Magn.   Ignatius, *To the Magnesians*
Oct.   Minucius Felix, *Octavius*
Or.   Libanius, *Orationes*
Paed.   Clement of Alexandria, *Paedagogus*
Peregr.   Lucian, *De morte Peregrini*
Strom.   Clement of Alexandria, *Stromateis*
Vis.   Shepherd of Hermas, *Visions*

Introduction

The Teacher from Galilee and the
Origins of Controversy

Most of Jesus' Jewish contemporaries rejected him, but they could not ignore him. (Barry Schwartz)[1]

The Pharisees came and began to argue with him. (Mark 8:11)[2]

How did the controversy between Jesus and the scribal elite begin? We know how it ended—in Jerusalem, Rome involved, Jesus's battered body hanging on a cross. But how did it start? What first put Jesus on the radar of the Jewish authorities? What made Jesus, unlike thousands and thousands of first-century Palestinian Jews, a threat to Jewish leaders? This book argues that an answer to that question must go beyond typical explanations such as Jesus's alternative views on Torah or his miracle working and consider his status as a teacher. As a preliminary step in that direction, let us go to Matt. 23 and see what Jesus looks like when he is addressing rival teachers and sounds so angry that he might explode.[3]

A Real Mad Jesus and His Rivals in Matthew 23

Toward the end of the first century CE, the author of the Gospel of Matthew presents a claim of Jesus that appears nowhere else in the canonical Gospels. After criticizing the scribes and the Pharisees, Jesus instructs his followers to refer to him—and him alone—as their teacher.

1. Barry Schwartz, "Where There's Smoke, There's Fire: Memory and History," in *Keys and Frames: Memory and Identity in Ancient Judaism and Early Christianity*, ed. Tom Thatcher, SemeiaSt (Atlanta: Society of Biblical Literature, 2013), n.p.

2. Unless otherwise indicated, all Scripture quotations are from the New Revised Standard Version.

3. The majority view among scholars is that Matt. 23 reflects the realities of later Christians in conflict with non-Christian Jews, not the realities of Jesus's life. Later in the book, I will argue that wholesale dismissal of the controversy that this text and others reflect is unwarranted, despite any exaggeration of the hostilities by Matthew.

> Then Jesus said to the crowds and to his disciples, "The scribes and Pharisees sit on Moses' seat; therefore, do whatever they teach you and follow it; but do not do as they do, for they do not practice what they teach. . . . They do all their deeds to be seen by others. . . . They love to have the place of honor at banquets and the best seats in the synagogues, and to be greeted with respect in the marketplaces, and to have people call them rabbi. But you are not to be called rabbi, for one is your teacher, and you are all students. And call no one your father on earth, for one is your Father who is in heaven. Nor are you to be called instructors, for you have one instructor, the Messiah." (Matt. 23:1–10; modified from NRSV; cf. Luke 11:42–52)

Perhaps more than any other passage in the New Testament, this text turns on the identity of Jewish teachers: who they are; what they look like; the titles they receive; the honor they are (or are not) due; and especially, where Jesus stood among them. For Matthew, Jesus stood above all other teachers to the extent that no one else even deserved the title of teacher.

Yet, this claim that Jesus alone should be Christians' teacher makes sense only in a context where there were other options. This text further reveals, therefore, Matthew's conviction that Jesus made these claims in something of a competitive market wherein Jewish teachers vied with one another for followers, honor, and status. And when it came to his competitors in this pedagogical market, Jesus apparently did not mince words. In Matt. 23, Jesus proceeds to direct toward the scribes and Pharisees a blistering critique in prophetic fashion. He rains down condemnatory "woes" (23:13–29) upon those whose pedagogy he views as an external veneer of religiosity and thinly veiled showmanship, hiding internal decay and lawlessness.[4] Consider these highlights from Matt. 23:

> "Woe to you, scribes and Pharisees, hypocrites! For you lock people out of the kingdom of heaven!" (Matt. 23:13)

> "Woe to you, scribes and Pharisees, hypocrites! For you cross sea and land to make a single convert, and you make the new convert twice as much a child of hell as yourselves." (23:15)

> "Woe to you, blind guides." (23:16)

> "You blind fools!" (23:17)

---

4. This type of polemical language was typical of ancient rhetoric generally and sectarian Judaism specifically. See Luke Timothy Johnson, "The New Testament's Anti-Jewish Slander and Conventions of Ancient Rhetoric," *JBL* 108.3 (1989): 419–41; J. Andrew Overman, *Matthew's Gospel and Formative Judaism: The Social World of the Matthean Community* (Minneapolis: Fortress, 1990), 16–23. More broadly on the topic, see Craig A. Evans and Donald A. Hagner, eds., *Anti-Semitism and Early Christianity: Issues of Polemic and Faith* (Minneapolis: Fortress, 1993).

"Woe to you, scribes and Pharisees, hypocrites!" (23:23)

"You blind guides!" (23:24)

"Woe to you, scribes and Pharisees, hypocrites!" (23:25)

"You blind Pharisee!" (23:26)

"Woe to you, scribes and Pharisees, hypocrites! For you are like white-washed tombs, which on the outside look beautiful, but inside they are full of the bones of the dead and all kinds of filth." (23:27)

"Woe to you, scribes and Pharisees, hypocrites!" (23:29)

"You snakes, you brood of vipers! How can you escape being sentenced to hell?" (23:33)

"Upon you may come all the righteous blood shed on earth." (23:35)

Matthew 23's Jesus is not a vacation Bible school Jesus or seeker-sensitive Jesus. That Jesus's hair is nice and combed. His robes are sparkling white, and his face is aglow as he hovers about six inches off the ground. He hugs people a lot, speaks in calm tones, and pats little children on the head as he tells his audience, only four chapters earlier in Matthew's Gospel, that the kingdom belongs "to such as these" (Matt. 19:14; cf. Mark 10:14//Luke 18:16). The Jesus of Matt. 23 is of a different sort. He is fired up and within a word or two of unleashing some profanity in the style of a high school football coach. This Jesus's hair is untamed. His clothes are beaten and tattered from a semitransient lifestyle. His face and neck are reddened by the Palestinian sun, and his feet are blistered, cracked, and calloused. There is a wild look in his eyes, sweat pouring down his forehead, and spit flying off his lips when he yells, "Woe to you, scribes and Pharisees, hypocrites!" (Matt. 23:13, 15, 23, 25, 27, 29; cf. 23:16). His message ends not with a head pat to a child and an aphorism about the kingdom, but with tales of murder and bloodshed (23:34–37).

When you finish reading Jesus's tirade against the scribes and Pharisees in Matt. 23, you might need a deep breath. Those who have grown all too accustomed to the teddy-bear Jesus may need to reassess wholesale their idea of Jesus. At the very least, we can point to this text and affirm that, when early Christians such as Matthew commemorated Jesus's life in the form of narrative Gospels, they portrayed a Jewish teacher who was embroiled in heated controversy with other Jewish teachers and gave as good as he got.

The Teacher from Galilee and Other Teachers

An Overview

The central argument of this book is that the two concerns that surface in Matt. 23—(1) Jesus's status as a teacher and (2) his conflict with scribal authorities—are intrinsically related, with Jesus's status as a teacher being a central factor in why the conflict with the scribal authorities arose. Readers may think that I have just stated the obvious, so let me be clear. My argument is that, in addition to, but distinct from, the content of his teaching (what he taught) and the style of his teaching (how he taught), Jesus's very status as a teacher was controversial. The scribal authorities likely disagreed with what he taught and how he taught it, but a central part of the problem was that, from their perspectives, Jesus did not have the right to be teaching in the first place.

In this vein, important factors such as social class and literate education[5] stood at the cradle of the controversy over Jesus of Nazareth.[6] I will argue that Jesus was not a member of the authoritative scribal elite class, but acted in some ways as though he were, and managed to convince some of his audiences that he was.[7] Among other reasons, this blurring of social categories prompted attempts to expose him publicly as clearly not part of the authoritative elite, thus beginning a controversy that soon spiraled beyond these initial concerns and ever closer to a Roman cross outside Jerusalem during Passover.

---

5. I use the phrase "literate education" to signify specifically the acquisition of reading and writing abilities. Almost all Jews of Jesus's time period received instruction on the law and the past of their people, which one could describe as "education." If nothing else, this education was acquired weekly in synagogue. As the next chapter will observe, however, very few Jews in this period attended a formal school and learned to read and write. It is therefore necessary to distinguish between a general education that was culturally acquired and a literate education that was acquired in a classroom context.

6. I will shortly note how these issues are often overlooked. For exceptions to this scholarly neglect, however, see H. Gregory Snyder, *Teachers and Texts in the Ancient World: Philosophers, Jews and Christians*, RFCC (New York: Routledge, 2000), 188–89, 222; Tom Thatcher, *Jesus the Riddler: The Power of Ambiguity in the Gospels* (Louisville: Westminster John Knox, 2006). Also emphasizing the role of social class in Jesus's relationship to the authorities is Richard A. Horsley, "A Prophet like Moses and Elijah: Popular Memory and Cultural Patterns in Mark," in *Performing the Gospel: Orality, Memory, Mark*, ed. Richard A. Horsley, Jonathan A. Draper, and John Miles Foley (Minneapolis: Fortress, 2006), 172–90.

7. Importantly, I am not arguing that this perception of Jesus was ubiquitous. To the contrary, it was precisely the fact that others perceived Jesus as clearly *not* a scribal-literate teacher that created the context for controversy and rejection. See further chaps. 2 and 4.

The Historical Origins of the Conflict and Scholarly Neglect

Although this book is designed for upper-level students as an introduction to the early period of Jesus's ministry, it also has within its purview a scholarly contribution. Students and scholars alike will best understand its argument against the backdrop of previous assessments of why Jesus and the authorities viewed each other as threats.

Scholars refer to the accounts of the controversy between Jesus and the scribal authorities as the "controversy narratives" or "conflict stories." Although the conflict itself is a perennial topic among Jesus scholars, the historical origins of the conflict receive substantially less attention. Indeed, to my knowledge, this is the first book-length treatment of the origins of the controversy between Jesus and the scribal elite.

There are at least two reasons why the controversy's historical origins are routinely overlooked. The first is a sustained history of scholarship that insists that the controversy narratives have no historical value for the time of Jesus because they are the products of Christian debates with non-Christian Jews at the time of the Gospels' authorship, reflecting only this later time period. I will deal with this topic more thoroughly in chapter 6, but some brief comments are in order now. I agree that the controversy narratives as they appear in the Gospels are, to one extent or another, clearly a product of the time(s) in which they were formed and committed to writing. I also agree that there was conflict between Christians and non-Christian Jews that impacted that form.

I disagree, however, that these points lead necessarily to the conclusion that the controversy narratives are without historical value for the time of Jesus. The fact that a narrative carries symbolic value in a later period (such as Jesus in the controversy narratives symbolically representing later Christians and his enemies in the narratives symbolically representing their enemies) does not automatically render that narrative ahistorical or useless for historical research. While indicting this type of overly skeptical Jesus scholarship, Schwartz provides an apt counterexample from American history: "John F. Kennedy's birthplace, Boston, connects him to the beginning of the American Revolution, but this hardly means that he was not born in Boston."[8] As Alexander says, "The historicality of the material itself has to be assessed on other grounds."[9] In line with these statements, and against a strong tradition

---

8. Barry Schwartz, "Christian Origins: Historical Truth and Social Memory," in *Memory, Tradition, and Text: Uses of the Past in Early Christianity*, ed. Alan Kirk and Tom Thatcher, SemeiaSt 52 (Atlanta: Society of Biblical Literature, 2005), 49.

9. Loveday Alexander, "Memory and Tradition in the Hellenistic Schools," in *Jesus in Memory: Traditions in Oral and Scribal Perspectives*, ed. Werner H. Kelber and Samuel Byrskog (Waco: Baylor University Press, 2009), 152.

of scholarly skepticism, this book will provide "other grounds" for making such decisions and ultimately argue that there are good reasons to believe that Jesus had the types of debates with scribal authorities that the Gospels claim he did. I will thus locate the origins of the controversy narratives in the life of the historical Jesus and affirm that the conflict had the general shape ascribed to it in the Gospels, at least in the early period of Jesus's ministry. I also note that I will not be arguing for the historicity of every account of controversy, or even for any one in particular. Rather, I will affirm that debates of the sort occurred.

The second reason that the historical origins of the controversy are routinely overlooked is more innocuous. In short, scholars are more interested in how the conflict these narratives portray led to the arrest, trial, and crucifixion of Jesus. That is, they are interested in the controversy as a point of origin itself, the beginning of a larger series of events that ended in Jerusalem. This approach is natural and largely a result of the Gospels themselves. The narratives of the Gospels tip toward Jesus's final days in Jerusalem in numerous ways,[10] such as the sheer percentage of the total Gospel narrative that the end of the story occupies (Jesus's final trip to Jerusalem onward ranges from a substantial 23 percent of Luke's Gospel to a whopping 48 percent of John's Gospel)[11] or the authors' usage of techniques such as the slowing of narrative time in order to highlight the Passion narrative.[12] The narratives are weighted toward the resolution of the conflict, and scholarly interest has naturally followed suit. Thus, one popular introductory textbook discusses the Gospel reader's knowledge that the conflict in its early stages is "life-threatening, because the fate of Jesus . . . is in the balance."[13]

10. In reference to the Gospel of Matthew, Dale C. Allison Jr., *Studies in Matthew: Interpretation Past and Present* (Grand Rapids: Baker Academic, 2005), 217, says, "In many ways the entire narrative leans forward, so to speak, to its end." Consider also N. T. Wright, *The New Testament and the People of God*, COQG 1 (Minneapolis: Fortress, 1992), 202: "The gospels read the debates between Jesus and the Pharisees as foreshadowings both of the 'trial' of Jesus himself and of the missionary concerns of the early church." Martin Kähler, *The So-Called Historical Jesus and the Historic Biblical Christ* (Philadelphia: Fortress, 1964), 80, famously described the Gospels as "passion narratives with extended introductions."

11. Modern chapter-and-verse divisions of the narratives were not part of the original text. They are still useful for understanding this point, however. The block of text extending from Jesus's (final) trip to Jerusalem to the resurrection narratives occupies 28.5 percent of Matthew's Gospel (8/28 chapters, starting at Matt. 21:1), 37.5 percent of Mark's Gospel (6/16 chapters, starting at Mark 11:1), 22.9 percent of Luke's Gospel (5.5/24 chapters, starting at Luke 19:28), and 47.6 percent of John's Gospel (ca. 10/21 chapters, starting at John 12:12).

12. Elizabeth Struthers Malbon, *In the Company of Jesus: Characters in Mark's Gospel* (Louisville: Westminster John Knox, 2000), 14–15; David Rhoads, Joanna Dewey, and Donald Michie, *Mark as Story: An Introduction to the Narrative of a Gospel*, 3rd. ed. (Minneapolis: Fortress, 2012), 46–47.

13. Rhoads, Dewey, and Michie, *Mark*, 85. In a related sense but with reference to Matthew's Gospel, Allison, *Studies*, 217, notes, "Already in [Matthew] chapter 1 . . . the prophecy that Jesus

This statement is correct, but it reflects strictly the knowledge of *readers* of the Gospels, since they typically already know how the story ends before they begin and, at the least, experience Jesus's life through the scripted narrative dynamics of the Gospels. The real life of Jesus and his contemporaries was not a scripted narrative in this sense, however. As lived experience, the beginning of Jesus's story was not yet intertwined with its end. There is, therefore, no reason to assume that in the early months the parties involved in the controversy knew any more than the Gospels portray them as knowing. In that early stage, they likely did not view Jesus's conflicts with other teachers as a life-or-death situation.[14] Along these lines, we can further assume that the conflict between Jesus and these authorities was not born in the fury that it eventually reached. Even further, we can assume that Rome was not initially involved. In other words, the conflict must have developed and progressed through periods of lesser and greater hostility as Jesus interacted in any number of social circumstances with scribal authorities of various kinds (Pharisees, Sadducees, scribes, priests, etc.) and in different locales (Galilee, Jerusalem, the market, the temple, etc.).[15] The authorities' conviction that Jesus must be eliminated was reached over time, with that final Passover serving as the zenith of concerns that were initially less flammable.

Jesus, Teaching, Healings, and Exorcisms

Not all scholars have overlooked the origins of the conflict between Jesus and the scribal elite, however. Scholars who, like me, affirm some level of historicity in the controversy narratives typically account for the emergence

---

'will save his people from their sins' (1:21), although unelaborated, moves one to think of his salvific death on behalf of others (20:28; 26:28)."

14. Even at the narrative level, some of the human characters surrounding Jesus, especially the disciples, routinely fail to grasp the significance of events. On the disciples in particular, see Larry W. Hurtado, "Following Jesus in the Gospel of Mark—and Beyond," in *Patterns of Discipleship in the New Testament*, ed. Richard N. Longenecker (Grand Rapids: Eerdmans, 1996), 19–21; Elizabeth Struthers Malbon, "Fallible Followers: Women and Men in the Gospel of Mark," in *In the Company*, 42–45 (repr. from *Semeia* 28 [1983]: 29–48).

15. In terms of the Gospels' portrayal of such shifts, an example is the role of the Pharisees in the conflict. Whereas Pharisees play a major role in the early controversies, they almost disappear in Jerusalem during the arrest, trial, and crucifixion, where the priestly aristocracy takes the lead role. In the Gospels of Matthew, Mark, and Luke, the Pharisees are nowhere to be found in the accounts of Jesus's arrest, trial, and crucifixion. They make no appearance in Mark after Mark 12:13–17 and no appearance in Luke after Luke 19:39–40. After Jesus's entry into Jerusalem, Pharisees appear once more in Matthew's Gospel, in the account of the authorities' response to the empty tomb (Matt. 27:62). John places Pharisees among those who come to arrest Jesus (John 18:3), but they do not appear in the narrative after that passage.

of those initial concerns with some combination of at least three factors: Jesus's healings and other miracles, Jesus's exorcisms, and the content of his teaching. Although he is by no means alone, Keener's exhaustive (831 pages!) treatment of Jesus and the Gospels provides an excellent example of this theory for how Jesus gained attention from the authorities. In discussing Jesus's eschatological teaching, Keener says, "Jesus must have calculated such warnings to dislodge his hearer's comfort and security, and must have been aware that it would provoke hostility from the elite. . . . Healings and exorcisms could point people to depend on God rather than the old order for their fundamental needs."[16] Note in particular that, according to Keener, Jesus "provoke[d] hostility from the elite" on account of the content of his teaching (eschatological "warnings") and his "healings and exorcisms." Keener places the accent on the content of Jesus's teaching one page later: "One can well imagine how Jesus' frequently non-Pharisaic approach to the law would have brought him into conflict with Pharisees."[17]

Later in the volume, Keener has an entire chapter titled "Conflicts with Other Teachers." In this chapter, he says,

> Although Jesus' teachings fit their Palestinian Jewish environment, that Jewish environment included a range of perspectives. . . . If Jesus taught some ideas that differed from those of some other teachers of the law, we would expect some disagreements. . . . If Jesus' other activities (such as healings) augmented his popularity beyond that of most other teachers, others may have viewed him as undermining the sound teachings they were laboring to cultivate among the people.[18]

Here again one sees the combination of what Jesus taught with his miraculous activity as an explanation for the emergence of disagreement between him and scribal authorities. Only a few pages later Keener specifically addresses the question "Why then would conflict arise between [Jesus and the Pharisees]?" He appeals to social conflict theory, claiming, "What we can know of Jesus' actions suggests that his ministry would have generated at the least vigorous debate with many of his Pharisaic contemporaries."[19] By "Jesus' actions," he seems to mean Jesus's criticisms of the Pharisees, since he goes on to say, "Jesus was not alone in criticizing some fellow Jews for hypocrisy" and points to evidence in rabbinic Judaism and the Dead Sea Scrolls.[20]

16. Craig S. Keener, *The Historical Jesus of the Gospels* (Grand Rapids: Eerdmans, 2009), 38.
17. Ibid., 39.
18. Ibid., 223.
19. Ibid., 231.
20. Ibid.

I choose Keener as a representative of a large swath of Gospels scholarship because his book is recent and a particularly clear example of the intertwined miracles-exorcisms-and-Torah-teaching theory for why Jesus became a threat for the authorities. Others affirm similarly, although many scholars highlight one factor in particular.[21] And for the sake of clarity, I do not necessarily disagree with Keener. Any one of these factors, or any combination of the three, can explain why there was conflict to a degree. Other scholars are also likely right that there were additional factors, such as Jesus's open table fellowship with known sinners or his known association with John the Baptist, whom Herod Antipas had killed.[22]

My claim is not that these suggestions are wrong; it is that they have left out a crucially important factor. That factor is Jesus's reputation as a teacher. Keener assumes this issue, but does not address it directly, when he attributes the source of conflict to Jesus's "frequently non-Pharisaic approach to the law" and the fact that Jesus's ideas differed from "some other teachers of the law," as well as when he compares Jesus's criticisms of the scribal authorities to the types of criticisms one finds in rabbinic Judaism or the Dead Sea Scrolls.[23] No doubt these statements are correct to an extent, but their underlying assumption is that Jesus functioned on the same, or at least similar, reputational level as that of the Pharisees, Qumranites, and the rabbis of the post-70 CE period. Under this theory, Jesus, as a widely accepted teacher of the law, simply differed in opinion or approach from "other teachers of the law."[24] Stated otherwise, this theory seems to assume that Jesus and the authorities' debates were like debates between the aristocratic Sadducees and more popular Pharisees[25] or the intra-Pharisaic debates between the more lenient school of Hillel and

21. For example, Morton Smith, *Jesus the Magician* (Wellingborough, UK: Aquarian, 1985), 16, 142, saw Jesus's miracle working to be the decisive factor. Joseph Klausner, *Jesus of Nazareth: His Life, Times, and Teaching*, trans. Herbert Danby (London: George Allen & Unwin, 1928), 278, saw healing on the Sabbath as "what . . . mainly aroused the indignation of the Pharisees." Günther Bornkamm, *Jesus of Nazareth*, trans. Irene McLuskey, Fraser McLuskey, and James M. Robinson (New York: Harper & Row, 1960), 97, thought Jesus's approach to the law was most significant: "Significant above all . . . is the open conflict with the law which causes the mounting antagonism of the Pharisees and scribes." See the collection of opinions in E. P. Sanders, *Jesus and Judaism* (London: SCM, 1985), 1–3, 23–58. Historically, the most prominent explanation for the conflict has been Jesus's approach to the law.

22. Helen K. Bond, *The Historical Jesus: A Guide for the Perplexed*, TTGP (London: T&T Clark, 2012), 128–32. See also Marcus Borg, *Conflict, Holiness, and Politics in the Teachings of Jesus*, new ed. (Harrisburg, PA: Trinity, 1998), 88–134, on Jesus's table fellowship as opposition to the Pharisees.

23. Keener, *Historical*, 39, 223, 231, respectively.

24. Ibid., 223.

25. Josephus, *Ant.* 13.5.9 §§171–73, describes the disagreements between Pharisees and Sadducees.

more stringent school of Shammai;[26] that the criticisms exchanged were like the criticisms that the Qumranites aimed toward the priests in Jerusalem[27] or any number of criticisms recorded in the rabbinic corpus between various rabbis, including Pharisees and Sadducees.[28]

Although there are many ways in which Jesus's debates with the scribal authorities were indeed similar to these other debates, the conflict with Jesus was more complex and ultimately dissimilar when it came specifically to the status of the parties involved. These other debates within the Judaism of Jesus's day were akin to public debates between two university professors who disagree, although both are credentialed with PhDs and recognized as experts in their fields. Some texts in the New Testament portray Jesus's debates with the authorities along these lines, but other New Testament texts portray them quite differently. They describe a situation that is more like a scheduled debate between two university professors when only one has arrived on time. While waiting for the other expert to arrive, the school's janitor—without credentials or recognized authority and armed only with his reputation for janitorial services—strides to the podium, takes the tardy expert's place, and commences the debate by correcting publicly a point or two in the punctual professor's research and publications. The analogy breaks down on multiple levels, but the important point remains—the ensuing discussion between the recognized expert and the recognized janitor would involve not only the janitor's ideas and criticisms but also his qualifications for voicing them in such a context in the first place.

In the following pages, I suggest that what Keener assumes—Jesus's reputation as an authoritative teacher of the law—was itself debated in Jesus's time and a key component of the controversy between Jesus and authorities such as the Pharisees. Furthermore, I suggest that controversy over Jesus's status as a teacher in fact provides the foundation for why his miraculous activity, exorcistic activity, and even the content of his teachings proved worthy of the authorities' attention. This point merits reflection in light of the facts that Jesus was not the only miracle worker in Second Temple Judaism,[29] not the

26. See further Paul Mandel, "Hillel," *EDEJ* 742–43; idem, "Shammai," *EDEJ* 1224–25.

27. On Qumran as an extension of priestly education, including the possibility that some of their texts were from the temple in Jerusalem, see David M. Carr, *Writing on the Tablet of the Heart: Origins of Scripture and Literature* (New York: Oxford University Press, 2005), 219–20, 233.

28. See Jack N. Lightstone, "The Pharisees and the Sadducees in the Earliest Rabbinic Documents," in *In Quest of the Historical Pharisees*, ed. Jacob Neusner and Bruce D. Chilton (Waco: Baylor University Press, 2007), 255–95.

29. On other Jewish miracle workers, such as Honi the Circle Drawer and Hanina ben Dosa, as well as the distinctive aspects of Jesus's reputation as a miracle worker, see Bond, *Historical Jesus*, 104–5.

only exorcist in Second Temple Judaism,[30] and certainly not the only teacher in Second Temple Judaism whose teachings disagreed with the Pharisees. One could justly describe all Jews in the Second Temple period who were not Pharisees—that is, the majority of Second Temple Jews—as holding a "non-Pharisaic" approach to the law. To say it another way, we may grant that Jesus's healings, exorcisms, and particular perspective on Torah would have garnered him attention from the scribal authorities, but *only under the circumstance that Jesus's opinion mattered in the first place.* And with regard to the circumstance that Jesus's opinion did matter, unlike that of thousands and thousands of other Jews in the Second Temple period, we may ask the simple but poignant question "Why?" Why did the authorities care at all what Jesus thought or did? Why did they not dismiss him as a harmless madman? Or why did they not dismiss him in the style of the Pharisees of John 7:49, who dismiss the opinion of "this crowd" by claiming that it "does not know the law"?

This question, and the earlier analogy of a janitor in an academic debate, is particularly acute if one accepts that Jesus was himself a member of the manual-labor populace, as claims the synagogue audience in Mark 6:3 that rejects him as a synagogue teacher by identifying him as a carpenter (cf. Matt. 13:55, "carpenter's son"; see further chap. 2). Surely there were many carpenters in Second Temple Judaism who held a variety of perspectives on the Torah, most of which affected the scribal authorities about as much as a bricklayer's opinions on global warming affect policy makers in Washington, DC. The Second Temple scribe Jesus ben Sira (second century BCE) exhibits just this type of dismissal of the manual-labor class. Similar to the Pharisaic dismissal of "the crowd" and their opinions in John 7:49, Sirach claims explicitly that carpenters (Sir. 38:27) and all others who "rely on their hands" (38:31) *cannot* become wise in the law (38:24–39:1). With opinions like this in the elite class, why did the authorities not just ignore Jesus's opinions as beneath them? To further an observation at the beginning of this chapter: Why did the authorities consider Jesus not just a threat, but a threat that had to be engaged?

The Structure of the Argument

The structure of this book reflects its proposed answer to this overlooked line of inquiry: namely, that Jesus was not a scribal-literate authority but was nevertheless perceived as one on some occasions. Chapter 1 lays the groundwork

---

30. Craig S. Keener, *Miracles: The Credibility of the New Testament Accounts*, 2 vols. (Grand Rapids: Baker Academic, 2011), 2:781–87; Anthony Le Donne, *The Historiographical Jesus: Memory, Typology, and the Son of David* (Waco: Baylor University Press, 2009), 142.

for asking what kind of teacher Jesus was by first presenting what kinds of teachers there were. Generally speaking, there were authoritative members of the minority scribal elite class who had received a literate education, and then there was, well, everyone else. The important question, both then and now, is whether Jesus was a teacher from the scribal elite class. Chapter 2 turns to see how the Gospels address this very issue and observe that, within those first-century accounts of Jesus's life, there are differing opinions. The Gospels of Mark and Matthew portray Jesus as a teacher outside scribal circles, while Luke portrays him as a member of the scribal elite; meanwhile John's Gospel reports simply that Jesus's literate education and scribal status were matters of debate among his audiences.

Chapter 3 serves as a brief interlude and looks at how scholars approach the "historical Jesus" when the Gospel testimony about him contains contradictions, as it does in this case. I argue that any proposal must account for the emergence of both the Markan and Lukan images in the first century CE, rather than simply choosing one image over the other. On this basis, chapter 4 then answers the question of Jesus's identity as a teacher. I argue that Jesus was not a member of the scribal elite, but that he was likely often perceived as one as a result of placing himself in social positions associated with scribal authority and literate education.

Chapter 5 surveys the content of the controversy as portrayed in the Gospels. Although there are nuances here and there, the controversy between Jesus and the authorities in these stories revolves around two thoroughly intertwined issues: the interpretation of Scripture and (Jesus's) authority. Chapter 6 then addresses the conflict's historicity, origins, and nature. I argue in favor of the Gospels' claims that Jesus and the scribal elite were in conflict over Scripture and authority. I further argue that the origins of this conflict are, to a large extent, attributable to Jesus's debated status as a teacher. In this light, the controversy narratives reflect the scribal elites' attempts to expose Jesus publicly as an imposter to the position of scribal authority. Concluding remarks on the relationship between the beginning of the conflict and its end close the book.

The overall aim of this book is to give introductory and advanced readers a more nuanced sense of how Jesus fit within the social and political matrices of his day, especially in the early period of his ministry. His reputation as a teacher contributed heavily to the whirlwind of controversy that he inhabited.

1

Teachers in the Time of Jesus

Scribal Literacy and Social Roles

"But you are not to be called rabbi, for you have one teacher." (Matt. 23:8)

According to Matthew, Mark, and John, Jesus's followers often referred to him as "rabbi," a word used in Aramaic and Hebrew that technically means "my great one" but functioned as an honorific title for pedagogical figures.[1] Thus John 1:38 translates the transliterated *rabbi* for its readers as "Teacher" (*didaskalos*).[2] *Didaskalos* appears in all four Gospels in reference to Jesus.[3] The Gospels, therefore, collectively affirm that those around Jesus recognized him as a rabbi and teacher, and there is no reason to doubt this portrayal. "It is more than a safe bet that Jesus was a teacher."[4] Some scholars even claim that "rabbi" is "the best historical designation for Jesus."[5]

Unfortunately, however, the appearances of such phrases in the Gospels do not offer much specificity about his pedagogical identity beyond the fact that Jesus garnered such titles. Certainly both terms referred specifically to teachers of Jewish texts and traditions. They were, however, also rather general and

1. Matt. 26:25, 49; Mark 9:5; 11:21; 14:45; John 1:38, 49; 3:2; 4:31; 6:25; 9:2; 11:8. *Rabbi* never appears as a title for Jesus in Luke's Gospel.

2. See also John 20:16, which translates the related term *rabbouni* also as "Teacher." *Rabbouni* occurs elsewhere in Gospel tradition only at Mark 10:51.

3. Matt. 8:19; 9:11; 10:24, 25; 12:38; 17:24; 19:16; 22:16, 24, 36; 23:8; 26:18; Mark 4:38; 5:35; 9:17, 38; 10:17, 20, 35; 12:14, 19, 32; 13:1; 14:14; Luke 6:40; 7:40; 8:49; 9:38; 10:25; 11:45; 12:13; 18:18; 19:39; 20:21, 28, 39; 21:7; 22:11; John 1:38; 3:2, 10; 8:4; 11:28; 13:13, 14; 20:16.

4. Dale C. Allison Jr., *Constructing Jesus: Memory, Imagination, and History* (Grand Rapids: Baker, 2010), 24. Consider also Keener, *Historical*, 186, who notes that Jesus's identity as a sage is something "the majority of scholars today accept regardless of their views on other issues." Further, Leander E. Keck, *Who Is Jesus? History in Perfect Tense*, SPNT (Columbia: University of South Carolina Press, 2000), 65, claims, "To a considerable degree the history of the quest [of the historical Jesus] is the quest of Jesus the teacher."

5. Bruce Chilton et al., "Rabbi as a Title for Jesus," in *A Comparative Handbook to the Gospel of Mark: Comparisons with Pseudepigrapha, the Qumran Scrolls, and Rabbinic Literature*, ed. Bruce Chilton et al., NTGJC 1 (Leiden: Brill, 2010), 561. In sharp contrast, Martin Hengel, *The Charismatic Leader and His Followers*, ed. John Riches, trans. James C. G. Greig (Edinburgh: T&T Clark, 1981), 50, argues that on account of the lack of clarity for the meaning of "rabbi," "we should desist altogether from the description of Jesus as a 'rabbi.'"

covered a spectrum of meanings. In the first century CE, "rabbi" did not have the formal meaning that it would later gain in reference to the great rabbis in post-70 CE Jewish literature.[6] In Jesus's time, it was simply "a kind of unofficial title"[7] or "a loose designation for a teacher."[8]

In addition, although Jesus is a "rabbi" and "teacher" throughout the canonical Gospels, those terms can carry different connotations for different Gospel authors. In Matthew's Gospel, for example, "rabbi" can be a negative title. Matthew 23:7 refers to pretentious scribes and Pharisees who love to be called "rabbi"; so 23:8 forbids Jesus's true followers from referring to themselves with the title. The only occurrences of "rabbi" elsewhere in Matthew's Gospel are dark, as Judas addresses Jesus as "rabbi" twice in contexts of his betrayal (Matt. 26:25, 49). Matthew instead often uses "teacher," and in his Gospel it refers exclusively to Jesus. The Matthean characters' exclusive usage of "teacher" for Jesus can, however, as in all the Gospels, be sincere (or neutral) or insincere as part of an attempt to trap Jesus.[9] Like Matthew, Mark places "rabbi" on the lips of Judas at the moment of betrayal (14:45) but, unlike Matthew, also places it on the lips of Peter (9:5; 11:21). Mark uses it only for address by Jesus's disciples, then, and only by the lead disciple and by the betrayer. Luke avoids "rabbi" altogether, preferring, like Matthew, to refer to Jesus the pedagogue as "teacher." In contrast to Matthew, however, in Luke's narrative "teacher" is not an exclusive title for Jesus. He shares it with those discussing the law in the temple (Luke 2:46) and John the Baptist (Luke 3:12).[10] John refers to Jesus as both "rabbi" and "teacher," but in John these are not titles unique to Jesus. He shares the former with John the Baptist (John 3:26) and the latter with Nicodemus, to whom Jesus himself applies the title "teacher" sarcastically (John 3:10).

Therefore, neither the historical context nor the literary usages of the pedagogical titles of "rabbi" and "teacher" for Jesus clarify the precise type of rabbi or teacher that Jesus was. Was he more like the "teachers" in the temple (Luke 2:46), the eccentric rabbi/teacher John the Baptist (Luke 3:12; John 3:26), or

6. Chilton et al., "Rabbi," 560–61, 565; Hengel, *Charismatic*, 42–43; Joachim Jeremias, *Jerusalem in the Time of Jesus: An Investigation into Economic and Social Conditions during the New Testament Period*, trans. F. H. Cave and C. H. Cave, 3rd ed. (London: SCM, 1969), 236; Hershel Shanks, "Is the Title 'Rabbi' Anachronistic in the Gospels?," *JQR* 53.4 (1963): 339–41; W. Dennis Tucker Jr., "Rabbi, Rabboni," *EDB* 1105–6. See also Richard Kalmin, "Rabbis," *EDEJ* 1132–34.

7. Shanks, "Is the Title," 340.

8. Tucker, "Rabbi," 1105–6.

9. For insincere references to Jesus as "teacher," see Mark 12:13–14//Matt. 22:15–16//Luke 20:21; Mark 12:19//Matt. 22:24//Luke 20:28; John 8:4–6.

10. Cf. also the "teachers of the law" (*nomodidaskaloi*) in Luke 5:17.

the Pharisee Nicodemus (John 3:1, 10)? Or was he something else entirely? Jesus may have acted "typical for a rabbi in his day,"[11] but what in the world does that mean?

Literacy, Authority, and Scribal Culture in the Time of Jesus

Although one can be sure that Jesus was a teacher, there remains the task of determining what type of teacher he was and, further, what that means for the interpretation of the Gospels' portrayals of his interactions with other teachers. Scholars have attempted a more nuanced understanding of Jesus as a teacher with a variety of methods. Some scholars compare him to contemporary figures such as the Pharisees Hillel and Shammai,[12] Honi the Circle Drawer or Hanina ben Dosa,[13] or the Teacher of Righteousness, Theudas, or Jesus ben Ananias.[14] Others study the style or content of Jesus's teachings.[15] Still other scholars approach Jesus's teaching career by attempting to identify the right general label, such as Cynic, charismatic, sage, wisdom teacher, social prophet, apocalyptic prophet, storyteller, and so on.[16]

These approaches contribute to our understanding of Jesus as a teacher, but they will not be the approach taken here. Rather, I will approach Jesus as a teacher, and the Gospels' portrayals of Jesus as a teacher, by focusing upon

11. Ian Paul, "Introducing the New Testament: New Testament Story," in *The IVP Introduction to the Bible*, ed. Philip S. Johnston (Downers Grove, IL: IVP Academic, 2006), 152.

12. Harvey Falk, *Jesus the Pharisee: A New Look at the Jewishness of Jesus* (New York: Paulist Press, 1985), esp. 111–47; Hyam Maccoby, *Jesus the Pharisee* (London: SCM, 2003), 180–95; cf. Chilton et al., "Rabbi," 563–64.

13. Geza Vermes, *Jesus the Jew: A Historian's Reading of the Gospels* (Philadelphia: Fortress, 1973), 69–78; idem, *Jesus and the World of Judaism* (London: SCM, 1983), 7–11.

14. Scot McKnight, *Jesus and His Death: Historiography, the Historical Jesus, and Atonement Theory* (Waco: Baylor University Press, 2005), 177–87. Pheme Perkins, *Jesus as Teacher*, UJT (Cambridge: Cambridge University Press, 1990), 1–22, covers many of these teachers in brief.

15. Among many others, Borg, *Conflict*; Perkins, *Jesus*, 38–61; Robert H. Stein, *The Method and Message of Jesus' Teachings*, rev. ed. (Louisville: Westminster John Knox, 1994); Thatcher, *Jesus*.

16. This approach has been particularly popular in the so-called Third Quest for the historical Jesus. For a review of scholarly opinions, see Mark Allan Powell, *Jesus as a Figure in History: How Modern Historians View the Man from Galilee* (Louisville: Westminster John Knox, 1998), 51–166; Ben Witherington III, *The Jesus Quest: The Third Search for the Jew of Nazareth*, 2nd ed. (Downers Grove, IL: IVP Academic, 1997), 58–232, summarized succinctly on 233–48. For Jesus as a storyteller, see Gary M. Burge, *Jesus, the Middle Eastern Storyteller*, ACAF (Grand Rapids: Zondervan, 2009), 15–29. Cf. the cogent statement of Keener, *Historical*, 187: "It is unlikely that Galilean Jews who saw themselves as faithful to God's law would have made a hard-and-fast distinction among categories like charismatic sage, teacher of wisdom and teacher of Scripture."

a more rudimentary question that other studies often overlook. In Second Temple discussions about teachers and textual authorities, there is a divide between those who can access (study, read, copy) the holy text themselves, and those who must have others access it for them. That is, there is a difference between those who hold scribal literacy and those who do not. Often the ancient sources identify the nonscribal group as manual laborers. As I mentioned at the end of the introduction, this issue is significant when it comes to considering Jesus. In light of the fact that early Christians remembered Jesus as a teacher *and* a manual laborer (Mark 6:3//Matt. 13:55),[17] the pertinent question for understanding Jesus's pedagogical identity is "Was Jesus the type of Jewish teacher who held scribal literacy?" Before turning to how the canonical Gospels answer that question in the next chapter, this chapter will further introduce the significance of scribal literacy and its social manifestations for pedagogical authorities in the time of Jesus.

Scribal Authority: Six Key Factors

Literacy—in general, the abilities to read and write—may seem, or even be, a boring topic to readers in the industrialized world. In these contexts, widespread and publicly funded education systems ensure that reading and writing skills are typical for citizens and, in most cases, remarkable only in their absence. Over the last twenty or so years, however, literacy has become one of the hottest topics of discussion among historians of the ancient world. This renewed interest in ancient reading and writing is due in large part to classicist William V. Harris, who initiated nothing short of a sea change in our understanding of how literacy functioned in the ancient Hellenistic and Roman Empires with the publication of his groundbreaking *Ancient Literacy* (1989).[18] Since the publication of this volume, a flood of further research has revealed that literacy and scribal culture in the time of Jesus were substantially more complex than previously thought and intricately related to the sociopolitical structure of Palestine. At least six aspects of this complexity are significant for

17. Manual labor and scribal-literate authority are not necessarily mutually exclusive categories in Judaism (*m. 'Abot* 2.2), but they can be (Sir. 38:24–39:11). See further the notes under "Clarifications on Scribal Literacy" below and chap. 2.

18. William V. Harris, *Ancient Literacy* (Cambridge, MA: Harvard University Press, 1989). For a collection of early responses to Harris, see Mary Beard et al., *Literacy in the Roman World*, JRASup 3 (Ann Arbor, MI: Journal of Roman Archaeology, 1991). On the widespread acceptance of Harris by scholars in Biblical Studies, along with a few detractors, see Chris Keith, *Jesus' Literacy: Scribal Culture and the Teacher from Galilee*, LHJS 8 / LNTS 413 (London: T&T Clark, 2011), 73–75.

the Gospels' portrayals of Jesus as a teacher in conflict with other teachers: majority illiteracy, degrees of literacy, reading and writing as separate skills, multilingualism, scribal literacy, and the social perception of literacy.

Majority Illiteracy

First, Harris's most famous argument is that nothing like mass literacy existed in the ancient world. He claims, "The likely overall illiteracy level of the Roman Empire under the principate is almost certain to have been above 90%."[19] A central contributing factor to 10 percent overall literacy is that there is no unambiguous evidence of a widespread publicly funded elementary education system that would teach reading and writing skills to the majority of an agrarian population, whose lives would rarely require their usage. Students of early Christianity perhaps did not need Harris to point out this fact. Origen's third-century defense of Christianity against the critic Celsus, which I will discuss further in subsequent chapters, states bluntly that most people were illiterate. When Celsus claims that Christianity is successful mostly among illiterates, Origen defuses the charge by stating that most people in general held that status, not just Christians: "It was inevitable that in the great number of people overcome by the word, because there are many more vulgar and illiterate people than those who have been trained in rational thinking, the former class should far outnumber the more intelligent."[20]

Twelve years after Harris, Hezser published a massive and detailed study that took Harris's research interests and focused specifically upon Roman Palestine.[21] She found that, if anything, illiteracy was more common in this context, the context of Jesus. She claims 3 percent literacy or slightly higher.[22] Furthermore, she observed, as had Harris for the empire in general, that there was nothing like a formal network of elementary schools in Palestinian Judaism that would have educated the populace in literate skills. Stated otherwise, the common assumption that Jewish children received a literate education in the synagogue has been built upon multiple premises, which are now rejected. First, scholars have discredited the "abecedary-school connection" that saw alphabet lists as clear evidence of an elementary education system.[23] The ma-

---

19. Harris, *Ancient*, 22.

20. Origen, *Cels.* 1.27 (Chadwick).

21. Catherine Hezser, *Jewish Literacy in Roman Palestine*, TSAJ 81 (Tübingen: Mohr Siebeck, 2001).

22. Ibid., 496.

23. In particular, see James L. Crenshaw, *Education in Ancient Israel: Across the Deadening Silence*, ABRL (New York: Doubleday, 1998), 62–63, 100–108; Menahem Haran, "On the Diffusion of Literacy and Schools in Ancient Israel," in *Congress Volume: Jerusalem 1986*, ed.

terial evidence could just as well have come from specialized scribal training, apprenticeships, trained scribes practicing letters or sharpening their implements, or any number of other possibilities. In other words, no one doubts that someone was writing, but it is almost impossible to settle who was writing, why they were writing, and what level of proficiency they possessed. Second, the rabbinic evidence for teachers and synagogue schools is notoriously unreliable as evidence for the first century CE.[24] Although these traditions make claims for Second Temple realities, the rabbinic texts containing them actually come from somewhere between the third and sixth centuries CE.[25] Furthermore, only one text, *y. Meg.* 73d (3.1), actually refers to synagogue schools, and it is clearly exaggerated.[26] There are no other "sources which could support the notion of a Jewish school system in Second Temple times."[27]

It is worth pausing to underscore precisely what this information does, and does not, indicate. It does not indicate that Jews received no general instruction in their past, identity, or Torah. In light of the long-standing tradition in Judaism that fathers are responsible for teaching the law to their children,[28] it seems safe to assume that at least some Jewish fathers succeeded. Even if they failed, Jews would have received general instruction in these matters at synagogue, where public reading and expounding of the law occurred. This information does not indicate that there were no Jewish schools at all. Sirach references a "house of instruction" (*byt mdrš*; LXX *oikos paideias*), a secondary school, in the second century BCE (Sir. 51:23). This information also does not indicate that there was no literate education at all. Some Jews learned to read (such as the father of 4 Macc. 18:11), and among those a few even learned to write. This information furthermore does not indicate that

---

J. A. Emerton (Leiden: Brill, 1988), 81–95; Christopher Rollston, *Writing and Literacy in the World of Ancient Israel: Epigraphic Evidence from the Iron Age*, ABS 11 (Atlanta: Society of Biblical Literature, 2010), 91–113. The major proponent of the "abecedary-school connection" is André Lemaire, *Les écoles et la formation de la Bible dans l'ancien Israël*, OBO 39 (Fribourg: Éditions Universitaires, 1981), 7–33.

24. See *b. B. Bat.* 21a; *y. Ketub.* 32c (8.11); *y. Meg.* 73d (3.1).

25. See especially Hezser, *Jewish Literacy*, 46–48.

26. Thus *y. Meg.* 73d (3.1) places 480 synagogues, each of which had primary and secondary schools, in Jerusalem prior to 70 CE. Karel van der Toorn, *Scribal Culture and the Making of the Hebrew Bible* (Cambridge, MA: Harvard University Press, 2007), 24, refers to *y. Meg.* 73d (3.1) as "exaggerated even for a much later date"; similarly, Martin Hengel, *Judaism and Hellenism: Studies in Their Encounter in Palestine during the Early Hellenistic Period*, trans. John Bowden, 2 vols. (Philadelphia: Fortress, 1974), 1:82; Hezser, *Jewish Literacy*, 47, 50.

27. Hezser, *Jewish Literacy*, 47. Further, "Altogether, then, the Talmudic texts cannot be taken as historical sources but must be considered anachronistic and idealistic depictions of a Jewish educational system in pre-70 times." Hezser thus places the rise of synagogue schools in the Amoraic period (third–fourth century CE) (54).

28. Deut. 6:2, 7; 4 Macc. 18:10; *Jub.* 8.2; 11.16; Philo, *Hypoth.* 7.14; *L.A.B.* 22.5; *b. B. Bat.* 21a.

the teaching of reading or writing *never* occurred in *any* synagogue *ever* in Second Temple Judaism. We simply do not have enough information about literate education in general or synagogues in general to know these things with 100-percent certainty.

What this information does indicate is that those individuals who went to school for any period of time and received any literate education at all were atypical and in the stark minority. The extant evidence simply cannot support the supposition that schools were widely available or that there was any organized system of education in Jesus's time. It also cannot support the idea that literate education occurred in synagogues. There is no actual evidence of this practice until centuries later. The majority of Second Temple Jews learned about the holy texts, but only a few could access those texts for themselves. Thus, although Josephus's claim for universal literacy among Jewish children (which never mentions the context in which this instruction supposedly occurred) may reflect, to a limited degree, the reality for the privileged and urban class from which Josephus derives,[29] there is no reason to affirm it as reality for the rest of the poor and agrarian population. Crenshaw is right to dismiss it as "exaggerated apologetic" for the sake of his Roman readers.[30]

Those interested in the world of Jesus and the earliest Christians cannot afford to take these conclusions lightly. For generations many Gospels scholars have assumed that literate education and its accessibility in Jesus's time were similar to our own time, especially by frequently making the assumption that Jesus attended elementary school in the Nazareth synagogue.[31] They have

29. Josephus, *Ag. Ap.* 1.12 §60; 2.25 §204. Similarly for Philo, *Legat.* 16.115–16; 31.210. Elsewhere Josephus identifies himself as coming from a priestly family in Jerusalem (*Life* 1–2 §§1–7).

30. Crenshaw, *Education*, 6. Likewise, David M. Carr, "Literacy and Reading," *EDEJ* 888–89.

31. Among many, many others, William Barclay, *The Mind of Jesus* (New York: Harper & Row, 1961), 8–9; Markus Bockmuehl, *This Jesus: Martyr, Lord, Messiah* (Downers Grove, IL: InterVarsity, 1994), 38; C. J. Cadoux, *The Life of Jesus* (Gateshead on Tyne: Pelican, 1948), 37; Bernard J. Lee, *The Galilean Jewishness of Jesus: Retrieving the Jewish Origins of Christianity*, SJC, CRNT 1 (New York: Paulist Press, 1988), 126–27; Alan Millard, *Reading and Writing in the Time of Jesus*, BS 69 (Sheffield: Sheffield Academic, 2001), 146; Armand Puig i Tàrrech, *Jesus: A Biography*, trans. David Cullen, Sid Phipps, and Jenny Read-Heimerdinger (Waco: Baylor University Press, 2011), 185–87; Rainer Riesner, *Jesus als Lehrer*, WUNT 2.7 (Tübingen: Mohr Siebeck, 1981), 232; idem, "Jesus as Preacher and Teacher," in *Jesus and the Oral Gospel Tradition*, ed. Henry Wansbrough (London: T&T Clark, 2004), 191; idem, "Jüdische Elementarbildung und Evangelienüberlieferung," in *Gospel Perspectives*, vol. 1, *Studies of History and Tradition in the Four Gospels*, ed. R. T. France and David Wenham (Sheffield: JSOT, 1980), 218. Cf. Maurice Casey, *Jesus of Nazareth: An Independent Historian's Account of His Life and Teaching* (London: T&T Clark, 2010), 158–64, who does not claim that Jesus learned to read specifically in a synagogue but does affirm, "When they grew up, Jesus and Jacob [James] will have become, like Joseph, adult male Israelites who read from the Torah in Hebrew on the sabbath and at major festivals" (161). Cf. also Perkins, *Jesus*, 1, 15, 21–23.

simply been wrong. There is no reliable evidence for such a claim. And even
if there were two, three, or four times as many literates in the time of Jesus
as Harris, Hezser, and others estimate, that still leaves one with a majority
illiterate populace. Most people in the time of Jesus could not read or write.

Degrees of Literacy

Second, "literacy" itself was not a monolithic category but rather existed in
degrees and variations. Most people were illiterate agrarians working the land
in some fashion, but even among the literate, abilities differed from person to
person depending upon a variety of factors, principally social/financial status,
profession, and language. A vineyard tenant did not need to read as much as
a village scribe, and a village scribe did not usually need to be able to write
as much, or in the same language, as a Torah scribe. In short, the few who
received a literate education typically learned only what skills their position
in life required of them and rarely more. There were many individuals whom
scholars refer to as "semiliterate": "persons who can write slowly or not at all,
and who can read without being able to read complex or very lengthy texts."[32]
These persons straddled the line between literacy and illiteracy. In their cases,
answering the question "Was she or he literate?" is a difficult task. The ability
to write one's name ("signature literacy") was not comparable to the ability to
author *Jubilees* or copy a scroll of Exodus. Similarly, the ability to recognize
a name on an ossuary (burial box) or Caesar's name on a monument was not
comparable to the ability to read Aramaic, Hebrew, Greek, or Latin literary
works, much less in public (see below regarding 4Q266 under "Scribal Literacy
and Synagogue Roles").

Separate Literate Skills of Reading and Writing

Third, the two literate skills—reading and writing—were separately acquired
and utilized. In addition to the fact that not everyone was literate, not everyone
who could read could also write.[33] There is no clear evidence that writing was

32. Harris, *Ancient*, 5. Several formulae appear in ancient papyri that identify such individuals
as "slow writers." See Thomas J. Kraus, "(Il)literacy in Non-Literary Papyri from Graeco-Roman
Egypt: Further Aspects to the Educational Ideal in Ancient Literary Sources and Modern Times,"
in *Ad fontes: Original Manuscripts and Their Significance for Studying Early Christianity—Selected Essays*, TENTS 3 (Leiden: Brill, 2007), 110–11; repr. from *Mnemosyne* 53 (2000): 322–42;
as well as his "'Slow Writers'—ΒΡΑΔΕΩΣ ΓΡΑΦΟΝΤΕΣ: What, How Much, and How Did They
Write?," in *Ad fontes*, 131–47; repr. from *Eranos* 97 (1997): 86–97.
33. Rafaella Cribiore, *Gymnastics of the Mind: Greek Education in Hellenistic and Roman
Egypt* (Princeton: Princeton University Press, 2001), 177; M. C. A. Macdonald, "Literacy in an

even part of Jewish literate education in the first century CE, which appears to have focused instead on Torah-reading abilities.[34] Clearly, some pedagogical structure trained Jewish scribes in the ability to write and copy ("grapho-literacy"), a fact to which the manuscripts they produced attest. And, as the Gospels and other texts show, some of these scribes even used those abilities to become Scripture authorities, although not all Jewish scribes were Scripture authorities.[35] But these Torah scribes appear to have attained grapho-literacy through apprenticeships or special scribal training, not as part of "normal" literate education, which itself was "normal" for only a fraction of the population. Thus, although many Jews may have been able to write their names, the ability to compose literary texts was exceedingly rare and the possession of few.

Occasionally scholars object to the foregoing arguments by pointing to the widespread awareness of, usage of, and dedication to texts in Second Temple Judaism.[36] Such an objection, however, confuses textuality and literacy, since one's ability to use a text does not automatically imply an ability to read or copy that text, much less in its original language or to a high degree. Babatha daughter of Simeon, a twice-married landowner from the time of the Bar Kokhba revolt (132–135 CE), died alongside marriage deeds, court minutes, property registrations, loan records, and so forth that also mention her illiteracy.[37] Similar formulas, noting that one person had to sign for another due to his or her illiteracy, appear throughout the papyrological record.[38] The illiterate individuals (*agrammatoi*) referenced in these papyri were nevertheless clearly familiar with and committed to texts and textuality, demonstrating that literacy and textuality are not the same phenomenon. Alternatively, one may note similarly that fervent dedication to Scripture among Christians or Jews today does not automatically enable them to read the biblical languages. Even the ability to read a short section of a text does not indicate the ability

---

Oral Environment," in *Writing and Ancient Near Eastern Society: Papers in Honour of Alan R. Millard*, ed. Piotr Bienkowski, Christopher Mee, and Elizabeth Slater, JSOTSup 426 (London: T&T Clark, 2005), 52.

34. Hezser, *Jewish Literacy*, 88; Catherine Hezser, "Private and Public Education," *OHJDL* 471; Chris Keith, *The Pericope Adulterae, the Gospel of John, and the Literacy of Jesus*, NTTSD 38 (Leiden: Brill, 2009), 72–79; Keith, *Jesus' Literacy*, 100–104.

35. Christine Schams, *Jewish Scribes in the Second Temple Period*, JSOTSup 291 (Sheffield: Sheffield Academic Press, 1998); also Keith, *Pericope*, 103–6.

36. For example, Casey, *Jesus*, 160; Paul Foster, "Educating Jesus: The Search for a Plausible Context," *JSHJ* 4.1 (2006): 11–12.

37. Naphtali Lewis, Yigael Yadin, and Jonas C. Greenfield, eds., *The Documents from the Bar Kokhba Period in the Cave of Letters: Greek Papyri*, JDS (Jerusalem: Israel Exploration Society, 1989), 4, 24, 67, 60, 99.

38. Rita Calderini, "Gli ἀγράμματοι nell'Egitto greco-romano," *Aegyptus* 30 (1950): 14–41; Kraus, "(Il)literacy," 110–11.

to read further, as is revealed by the common example of the young man who learns to read a portion of Hebrew text for his bar mitzvah but is incapable of understanding what he is reading and incapable of reading anything else. Furthermore, the ability to speak a language does not necessarily imply the ability to read or write that language, as illiterates in many societies today demonstrate. First-century Jews could, therefore, be highly devoted to Scripture and simultaneously reliant upon local authorities to copy, read, and interpret the texts for them.

Multilingualism

A fourth factor demonstrating that "literacy" is a general and imprecise word in practice is that Jesus's sociohistorical context was multilingual. To the questions "Was she or he literate?" and "How literate?" one must now add "In what language(s)?" In first-century Palestine, Aramaic was the everyday language of Jews.[39] Short Hebrew phrases appear on ossuaries (bone boxes), ostraca (broken pieces of pottery), and in other contexts, but literary Hebrew, including Biblical Hebrew, was restricted to the scribal-educated elite, particularly in and around Jerusalem.[40] Virtually the only first-century Jews who were reading and writing/copying lengthy documents in Hebrew, including the Scriptures, were the elite minority. Greek was the lingua franca of the empire, and Latin was the language of the Romans. Both these languages were also known and used in Palestine, then, with Greek being more widespread than Latin but probably less widespread than Aramaic. Several New Testament texts reflect the multilingual context of early Christians. For example, John 19:20 notes that the *titulus* over Jesus's head on the cross "was written in Hebrew, in Latin, and in Greek." Similarly, according to Acts, Paul spoke to the Gentile tribune in Jerusalem in Greek (21:37), but addressed the Jews present "in the

39. On languages and their usage in the time of Jesus, see the classic study of Joseph A. Fitzmyer, "The Languages of Palestine in the First Century A.D.," *CBQ* 32 (1970): 501–30; repr. in *A Wandering Aramean: Collected Aramaic Essays* (combined ed. in *The Semitic Background of the New Testament*, BRS [Grand Rapids: Eerdmans, 1997]), 29–56, and the more recent thorough study of John C. Poirier, "The Linguistic Situation in Jewish Palestine in Late Antiquity," *JGRCJ* 4 (2007): 55–134.

40. As a helpful analogy, think of Latin in today's world. It is not uncommon to come across Latin in a variety of contexts today (military and school slogans, classics departments, tombstones, tattoos), but its societal function in this regard does not mean that it is a "live" language that people actively use on the street. Similarly, Hebrew was present in Second Temple Judaism, even at the popular level (and probably more than Latin is today since Hebrew and Aramaic are both Semitic languages with much overlap), but does not appear to have been an active language in the manner that Aramaic was. I thank Anders Runesson for his encouragement to clarify this point.

Hebrew language" (21:40). (In John 19:20 and Acts 21:40, "Hebrew" likely refers to Aramaic; that is, the language that Hebrew people spoke.) Gamble aptly describes the complexity of the literacy landscapes of first-century Judaism and early Christianity: "A Christian in first-century Palestine might have been thoroughly literate in Aramaic, largely literate in Hebrew, semiliterate in Greek, and illiterate in Latin, while a Christian in Rome in the late second century might have been literate in Latin and semiliterate in Greek but ignorant of Aramaic and Hebrew."[41]

Scribal Literacy

Fifth, in addition to low literacy rates, and in conjunction with the existence of a variety of literate skills in different languages, the aforementioned issue of scribal literacy is particularly important for understanding portrayals of Jesus as a teacher in the Gospels. In Jesus's context, scribal literacy refers to the state of literacy held by those (comparatively) few literate-educated interpreters of the Hebrew Scriptures. These were individuals who could read the text in its original language and whose knowledge of the text translated into interpretive authority.[42] Scribes, some of whom were responsible for copying the texts, undoubtedly held scribal literacy, but the term applies to other groups as well, such as priests, Pharisees, Sadducees, teachers of the law. Although perhaps not having attained the grapho-literacy of scribes, these groups could at least read the text.

Related to this point, one should not confuse literate skills in general with scribal literacy in particular. A Palestinian Jewish scribe who was responsible for drafting divorce contracts, land contracts, tax records, livestock sales, court proceedings, and other documents in Greek or Aramaic was more literate than the vast majority of his contemporaries.[43] But his social status could not compare to that of a scribe, Pharisee, or priest who specialized in the Hebrew Scriptures.

41. Harry Y. Gamble, *Books and Readers in the Early Church: A History of Early Christian Texts* (New Haven: Yale University Press, 1995), 3. On Jesus's context in particular, see Sang-Il Lee, *Jesus and Gospel Traditions in Bilingual Context: A Study in the Interdirectionality of Language*, BZNW 186 (Berlin: de Gruyter, 2012).

42. Mark Allan Powell, "Do and Keep What Moses Says (Matthew 23:2–7)," *JBL* 114.3 (1995): 431–32, correctly notes in this regard "the social and religious position that [scribes and Pharisees] occupy in a world where most people are illiterate and copies of the Torah are not plentiful." Powell's efforts to distance this social position from their "roles as teachers" (431) is strained, however, since the two were thoroughly intertwined. See Snyder, *Teachers*, 165–89.

43. For example, the scribes responsible for the Babatha cache; see Lewis, Yadin, and Greenfield, *Documents*. This is not to claim that such scribes could not also have facility with the Hebrew Scriptures, but one must note that these types of bureaucratic documents are not in general what one finds in, for example, the scribal text-centered community at Qumran.

Scribal literacy in Roman Palestine was tied to social power in a manner that other literacies were not because of its symbiosis with sacred texts.[44] Josephus provides an example of the social power associated with scribal literacy among first-century Jews when he describes his acquisition of literate skills in Greek. He notes that his Greek is imperfect because Jews as a people do not privilege knowledge of foreign languages, but rather scribal literacy: "They give credit to those alone who have an exact knowledge of the law and who are capable of interpreting the meaning of the Holy Scriptures."[45] By reading the Scriptures and teaching on them at synagogue, festivals, and other gatherings, scribal-literate individuals provided points of access to those texts for the majority of illiterate adherents for whom the text was all but inaccessible.[46]

Scribal-literate provision of access to the law was necessary throughout Jewish history, not just Jesus's time. A particularly clear example is Ezra and the Levites' public reading of the law to the returned exiles who no longer knew Hebrew in Neh. 8. The people needed help understanding, so Ezra and the Levites read the Hebrew text and then interpreted it. One sees here a clear example of specific literate skills being restricted to a particular class (the priestly class in this case) and not available to the population at large. Nehemiah 8:7–8 describes the situation: "The Levites helped the people to understand the law, while the people remained in their places. So they read from the book, from the law of God, with interpretation. They gave the sense, so that the people understood the reading." With its clear distinction between those who did not know Hebrew and so listened and "remained in their places" and those who did know Hebrew and thus read and taught, this passage is strikingly similar to first-century descriptions of synagogue roles, which are important to this study and will be discussed further below. Important to note at present, though, is that, in a context like Ezra's, or others such as the instance closer to Jesus's time when the young men chopped the Roman eagle off the gate of the temple after listening to two experts on "the laws of our fathers" and were subsequently burned alive for those actions,[47] those individu-

---

44. In the words of Seth Schwartz, *Imperialism and Jewish Society, 200 B.C.E. to 640 C.E.*, JCM (Princeton: Princeton University Press, 2001), 74, "Mastery of the Torah was a source of power and prestige." Consider also Overman, *Matthew's Gospel*, 69: "One source of the Pharisees' popularity and influence with the people no doubt was their reputation as the most accurate interpreters of the law." On the connection between literacy and power in ancient Judaism, see further M. D. Goodman, "Texts, Scribes and Power in Roman Judaea," in *Literacy and Power in the Ancient World*, ed. Alan K. Bowman and Greg Woolf (Cambridge: Cambridge University Press, 1994), 99–108.

45. Josephus, *Ant.* 20.12.1 §§263–65 (Feldman, LCL).

46. Snyder, *Teachers*, 11, helpfully refers to such individuals as "text-brokers."

47. Josephus, *J.W.* 1.33.2–4 §§648–55.

als giving the teaching and instruction—the scribal-literate individuals—held considerable sway.

Clarifications of Scribal Literacy

Since literacy and its social manifestations in Jesus's context were different in a variety of ways from the context of the modern industrialized world (and similar in other ways), it would perhaps be useful to pause briefly to clarify what I am *not* claiming. I am not claiming that every Pharisee, Sadducee, scribe, priest, or member of an authoritative group of interpreters was necessarily a scribal-literate person. Scribal-literate authorities in and around the temple precincts (like those portrayed in the Gospels) were likely better trained than scribal-literate authorities in more rural areas. It may have even been the case that some members of groups viewed as scribal-literate were, in reality, just beginning their training or even illiterate.[48] Furthermore, I am not claiming that every person who functioned as a text-broker in Roman Palestine was a scribal-literate text-broker. In the same way that preachers and teachers today who do not know the biblical languages nevertheless function as text-brokers, popular prophets in Jesus's time also appealed to Scripture and its precedents as their source of authority.[49] In short, not every member of a scribal-literate Jewish group was necessarily scribal-literate, and not every text-broker was a member of a scribal-literate group.

Despite these realities, it remains the case that the constituency of groups such as scribes, Pharisees, and especially priests was substantially more educated than their largely illiterate contemporaries who worked the land for a living, and were recognized as such. The second-century BCE scribe Jesus ben Sirach refers to the social divide between scribal-literate Torah experts and manual laborers in his laudatory praise of the scribe.

---

48. Thus *m. Yoma* 1.3 and 1.6 suggest the possibility of a high priest who could not read. Cf. also the *pty* ("simpleton," García Martínez and Tigchelaar) priest in 4Q266 13.6. Snyder, *Teachers*, 58–59, notes illiterate and less literate Epicureans.

49. As one example, a certain Theudas persuaded many to follow him to the Jordan River, where he would, in the style of Moses (Exod. 14:21–22), Joshua (Josh. 3:7–4:1), and Elijah and Elisha (2 Kings 2:8, 13–14), miraculously part the waters (Josephus, *Ant.* 20.5.1 §§97–99; Acts 5:36). No source describes Theudas as either a scribal-literate or scribal-illiterate person, but the point is that he would not need to be able to read the Jewish holy text in order to appeal to it and appropriate it. Under some circumstances, uneducated text-brokers may have had more popular appeal among uneducated audiences (Craig S. Keener, *The Gospel of John: A Commentary*, 2 vols. [Peabody, MA: Hendrickson, 2003], 1:712n86; John P. Meier, *A Marginal Jew: Rethinking the Historical Jesus*, 4 vols., ABRL [New York: Doubleday; New Haven: Yale University Press, 1991–2009], 1:268).

The wisdom of the scribe depends on the opportunity of leisure; only the one who has little business can become wise. How can one become wise who handles the plow, and who glories in the shaft of a goad, who drives oxen and is occupied with their work, and whose talk is about bulls? . . . So too is every artisan [*tektōn*] and master artisan [*architektōn*] who labors by night as well as by day; . . . So too is the smith, sitting by the anvil. . . . So too is the potter sitting at his work and turning the wheel with his feet; . . . All these rely on their hands, and all are skillful in their own work. . . . Yet they are not sought out for the council of the people, nor do they attain eminence in the public assembly [synagogue]. They do not sit in the judge's seat, nor do they understand the decisions of the courts; they cannot expound discipline or judgment, and they are not found among the rulers. . . . But they maintain the fabric of the world, and their concern is for the exercise of their trade. How different the one who devotes himself to the study of the law of the Most High! (Sir. 38:24–39:1)

Sirach refers specifically to the scribe, but his claim, as noted above, is generally applicable to other interpretive authorities in the scribal-literate class, such as priests, Sadducees, and Pharisees. Josephus often refers to the Pharisees as the most accurate interpreters of the law,[50] and Philo describes those who read and teach in synagogues as priests and elders.[51] The aforementioned example of Ezra provides an example of a scribal-literate person being both a priest and a scribe (Neh. 8:1–2, 9).

Various Jewish groups who distinguished themselves from each other on other bases nevertheless shared in possession of scribal literacy. Since this class, or at least the members of it whom Sirach has in mind, did not have to work with their hands for survival (38:31), they were able to devote themselves "to the study of the law" (39:1).[52] (One should note that this did not rule out the possibility that they might choose to work and acquire manual-labor skills

---

50. Josephus, *J.W.* 1.5.2 §110; 2.8.14 §162; *Life* 38 §191.

51. Philo, *Hypoth.* 7.12–13. In light of this statement, Philo's subsequent claim that all Jews know the law to the extent that they do not need to consult scribal authorities must be seen as polemical rhetoric. The role of scribal authorities in giving instruction on the law to the populace is ubiquitous in the sources. Cf. also Carr, "Literacy," 888.

52. In the prologue to the translation of Sirach, the grandson of Jesus ben Sirach also refers to the connection between education, scribal-literate skills of reading and writing, and devotion to the law:

Now, those who read the scriptures must not only themselves understand them, but must also as lovers of learning be able through the spoken and written word to help the outsiders. So my grandfather Jesus, who had devoted himself especially to the reading of the Law and the Prophets and the other books of our ancestors, and had acquired considerable proficiency in them, was himself also led to write something pertaining to instruction and wisdom.

in addition to their scribal-literate education.)[53] "The opportunity of leisure" afforded a member of this class the time that it took for one to become the type of interpretive authority who "seeks out the wisdom of all the ancients, and is concerned with prophecies; he preserves the sayings of the famous and penetrates the subtleties of parables; he seeks out the hidden meanings of proverbs and is at home with the obscurities of parables" (39:1–2). This is why Josephus, who elsewhere connects leisure to scribal-literate skills,[54] claims that Jews "give credit for wisdom to those alone who have an exact knowledge of the law and who are capable of interpreting the meaning of the Holy Scriptures."[55]

These points relate to the rest of this study in two specific ways. First, when I use the adjective "scribal" to refer to scribal authority, scribal culture, or the scribal elite, I refer to scribal-literate authorities in general, not scribes specifically. This usage of terminology may justify the accusation that I have not distinguished carefully enough between various Jewish groups. In defense, I can only note that a Jewish teacher's possession (or lack) of scribal literacy is more important for the topic at hand than the specific group to which he belonged and that first-century sources themselves often indicate overlap between these groups, which are nevertheless distinguished from the population at large as interpretive authorities.[56] For the same reasons, the final chapter of the book focuses upon the historicity of Jesus's conflict over Scripture and authority with scribal-literate authorities in general without becoming entangled with which specific scribal-literate authorities they were.

Second, as should now be clear, the real issue concerning Jesus's literacy is not whether he could read or write in any language at all. Jesus may have been able to sign a contract and read directional signs. These manifestations of literate abilities were not sources of concern for his detractors, however. Their concern centered on his scribal-literate status—whether his teachings on God, Moses, the law, purity, and so forth were undergirded with a literate education

53. Sirach's point is not that members of the scribal-literate class cannot engage in manual labor, but rather that members of the manual-labor class cannot engage in the type of study found in the scribal-literate class. Paul and other scribal-literate individuals engaged in manual labor (1 Thess. 2:9; Acts 18:3; cf. Acts 20:34; *m. 'Abot* 2.2; and Philo's descriptions of the Essenes in *Prob.* 12.81–82; *Hypoth.* 11.6–9). Manual laborers, however, according to Sirach, cannot do what scribes do. Maccoby, *Jesus*, 181, is therefore misguided to argue, specifically in reference to Jesus, that carpenters could be Pharisees on the basis that some Pharisees (Hillel and Shammai) engaged in manual labor. On Mark 6:3//Matt. 13:55, which place Jesus in the manual-labor class, see the next chapter.

54. Josephus, *Ag. Ap.* 1.9 §50.

55. Josephus, *Ant.* 20.12.1 §265 (Feldman, LCL).

56. Josephus, *Life*, 39 §197, refers to Jozar, who is a priest and a Pharisee. Mark 2:16, Luke 5:30, and Acts 23:9 refer to scribes who were part of the Pharisees. One could also note the Synoptic Gospels authors' frequent interchanging of the groups. See chap. 5.

that allowed him to speak about the law as an authority who can consult it. This study is therefore focused specifically on whether he held scribal literacy.

The Social Perception of Literacy

Sirach's association of the manual-labor class with particular activities and the scribal-literate Torah student with avoidance of those activities is important because it highlights a sixth complexity in Jewish scribal culture, and a serially underappreciated aspect of that culture: the social perception of literacy. The social perception of scribal literacy/authority is crucial to my argument about Jesus, and I will return to it in chapter 4. I offer some preliminary observations here.

First, as Sirach indicates, certain activities were indicative of having or not having scribal literacy, insofar as they indicated whether one belonged to the scribal-literate class. According to Sirach, scribes sit in the judge's seat (38:33), potters sit at the wheel (38:29); scribes are found among rulers (38:33), laborers are found among oxen and bulls (38:25); scribes are sought for the council (38:32), artisans work day and night (38:27). What one does, in Sirach's view, indicates the class to which one belongs, especially as it relates to one's ability to study Torah. Like Sirach, Matthew's Jesus explicitly refers to some of the social markers of scribal-literate authority in his condemnation of the scribes and Pharisees in Matt. 23. The scribes and Pharisees sit on Moses's seat (23:2); they expect to be watched by others (23:5); they attend banquets and, once there, receive honor (23:6); they sit in the best seats in the synagogue (23:6); and people pay their respects when they see them in the market (23:7). These activities, as much as reading in public or copying a scroll, marked them as scribal-literate authorities. Equally, and explicitly in Sirach, one's participation in manual labor marked one as outside the scribal-literate group of Torah authorities.

Second, the attachment of scribal literacy to scribal authority (and scribal authority to particular activities) in the perception of first-century Jews created an interesting social reality. Even if an individual Pharisee, priest, or the like was illiterate, an average agrarian Judean likely viewed him as a scribal-literate individual until he proved otherwise, and did so on the basis of the scribal-literate company he kept. To say it another way, since many of the social manifestations of scribal literacy/authority did not necessitate the public demonstration of scribal-literate skills, but rather resided upon (essentially correct) *assumptions* about the scribal-literate status of the group as a whole, under certain conditions one did not have to read or write in public in order for some people to assume that one could.

These six issues concerning literacy and authority—majority illiteracy, degrees of literacy, reading and writing as separate skills, multilingualism, scribal literacy, and the social perception of literacy—are collectively quite important for understanding the origins of Jesus's conflict with scribal authorities because they manifested in concrete historical contexts where Jesus came in contact with those authorities.

Scribal Literacy and Synagogue Roles

One particularly important such context was synagogue. Although archaeologists have not yet unearthed a first-century synagogue in Galilee,[57] that there were synagogues in Galilee and that Jesus taught in them are beyond a reasonable historical doubt.[58] "It seems clear that the historical Jesus made use of synagogues as strategic settings for enacting and proclaiming his message of the coming kingdom."[59]

Descriptions of synagogues in and around the time of Jesus confirm a particular set of recognizable roles in the synagogue. Scribal-literate teachers read and interpreted the text. Manual laborers, having broken from their weekly labor, listened to the Law read. As was already mentioned, these distinctive class-based roles appear already in the description of Ezra's reading of the law in Neh. 8. Similarly, Josephus says,

> He appointed the Law to be the most excellent and necessary form of instruction, ordaining, not that it should be heard once for all or twice or on several occasions, but that every week men should desert their other occupations and assemble to listen to the Law and to obtain a thorough and accurate knowledge of it.[60]

57. See, however, the caption for fig. 1.1.

58. Literary, archaeological, and epigraphic evidence exists for first-century synagogues in the land of Israel as well as the Diaspora (see Lee I. Levine, "Synagogues," *EDEJ* 1260–71; Anders Runesson, Donald D. Binder, and Birger Olsson, eds., *The Ancient Synagogue from Its Origins to 200 C.E.: A Source Book* [Leiden: Brill, 2010]). The remains of a third/fourth-century synagogue at Capernaum in Galilee, likely built upon a first-century synagogue, can be visited today (see fig. 1.1).

59. Anders Runesson, "The Historical Jesus, the Gospels, and First-Century Jewish Society: The Importance of Synagogues for Understanding the New Testament," in *City on a Hill: Essays in Honor of James F. Strange*, ed. Daniel Warner and Donald D. Binder (Mountain Home, AR: BorderStone, 2013), n.p. Runesson also discusses the two types of synagogues: public synagogues for the general populace and association synagogues like those of the Essenes (n.p.). See further his "Entering a Synagogue with Paul: Torah Observance in First-Century Jewish Institutions" (paper presented at the annual meeting of the Society of Biblical Literature, Chicago, November 18, 2012), 4–8. According to the Gospels, Jesus operated exclusively in public synagogues.

60. Josephus, *Ag. Ap.* 2.17 §175 (Thackeray, LCL); cf. *Ant.* 16.2.4 §43.

Baker Photo Archive

Figure 1.1. The remains of a synagogue in Capernaum dating from around the third or fourth century CE. This synagogue was built upon a previous structure dating to the first century CE, most likely the synagogue mentioned in Mark 1:21–29//Luke 4:31–38; 7:1–5; and John 6:59. For discussion, see Runesson, Binder, and Olsson, *Ancient Synagogue*, 29–32; as well as Craig A. Evans, *Jesus and His World: The Archaeological Evidence* (London: SPCK, 2012), 45–49.

Importantly, Josephus claims that those who break from their labor listen; they do not read themselves. Rather, as Philo (first century CE) claims,

> [The lawgiver] required them to assemble in the same place on these seventh days, and sitting together in a respectful and orderly manner hear the laws read so that none should be ignorant of them. . . . But some priest who is present or one of the elders reads the holy laws to them and expounds them point by point till about the late afternoon.[61]

Once again, one notes that those who break from their labor do not read and teach, but listen to others perform these activities. This does not mean they were inactive in discussion and debate, and the open architecture of

61. Philo, *Hypoth.* 7.12–13 (Colson, LCL). Cf. also his description of the Palestinian Essene Sabbath gathering in *Prob.* 12.81–82, which was an association synagogue rather than a public synagogue. Although not reliable for the first century CE and discussing a Diaspora synagogue rather than one in the land of Israel, later rabbinic descriptions of the Alexandrian synagogue mention that manual laborers all sat together during the Sabbath gathering (*y. Sukkah* 55a–b [5.1]; *t. Sukkah* 4.6).

synagogues would have facilitated involvement.[62] But they were not the readers and textual authorities.

Therefore, when average Palestinians went to a public synagogue gathering on the Sabbath and learned the Law or Prophets, they did so by listening to someone else read on their behalf. These roles were a product of at least two related factors. First, given the overall low literacy rates, the majority of synagogue attendees could not have read the text even if they had wanted to do so, regardless of whether the text was written in Hebrew or Greek.[63] Indeed, it is likely that already in the first century the practice of giving an interpretation of the text in Aramaic had begun.

Second, the reading of the law was serious business. The very origins of the synagogue in Judaism are traceable to the public reading of the law.[64] "By the first century C.E., the Torah had become the holiest object in Judaism outside the Temple itself and its appurtenances," so "there can be little question that scriptural readings constituted the core of [Second Temple] Jewish worship in the synagogue."[65] The Theodotus inscription, from a pre-70 CE Jerusalem synagogue, claims Theodotus's very reason for building the synagogue was "for the reading of the Law and the teaching of the commandments."[66] So important is the reading of Scripture that even the highly textual Qumran community would not allow members to read publicly unless they could do so without having to "sound it out." According to 4Q266:

> [And anyone who is not quick to under]stand, and anyone w[ho speaks weakly or staccato], [with]out separating his words to make [his voice] heard, [such men should not read in the book of] [the Torah], so that he will not lead to error in a capital matter [. . .] [. . .] his brothers, the priests, in service.[67]

62. Cf. Runesson, "Historical," n.p., who notes the significance of the open architecture; also "Entering," 4–5.

63. Hezser, "Private," 471: "Every male adult Jew was invited to serve as Torah reader in the synagogue, but only a few individuals will have had the necessary reading skills to carry out this duty."

64. Runesson, "Historical," n.p.

65. Lee I. Levine, *The Ancient Synagogue: The First Thousand Years*, 2nd ed. (New Haven: Yale University Press, 2005), 146, 150, respectively. See also Stephen K. Catto, *Reconstructing the First-Century Synagogue: A Critical Analysis of Current Research*, LNTS 363 (London: T&T Clark, 2007), 116; Levine, "Synagogues," 1263; Runesson, "Entering," 4.

66. See further Catto, *Reconstructing*, 120. For a convenient image and description online, see http://www.kchanson.com/ancdocs/greek/theodotus.html.

67. 4Q266 5.2.1–4 (García Martínez and Tigchelaar). Alternatively: "Whoever speaks too fast (or: too quietly, lit., swift or light with his tongue) or with a staccato voice and does not split his words to make [his voice] heard, no one from among these shall read the Book of [the] La[w] that he may not misguide someone in a capital matter" (Vermes).

This text refers to the difficulties of reading ancient manuscripts publicly. It also implicitly witnesses to the difficulty of being able to "search" to find a particular text in manuscripts that had no chapter-and-verse divisions, indicating what a specialized and technical ability that was. Luke's Gospel (4:17) and John's Gospel (5:39; 7:52) attribute this skill to scribal-literate authorities, and I will return to these texts in the next chapter. Combined with low literacy rates, the importance of the reading of the Torah points once more to why scribal-literate Torah authorities had so much social power: they were among the few qualified to perform a liturgical act that was at the very core of Jewish identity.

Similar to these sources, New Testament texts that refer to the public reading of the law are consistent with the idea that the synagogue was where scribal-literate individuals provide access to the text for those who cannot read it on their own (Acts 15:21; 2 Cor. 3:15). Additionally, as Millard notes, in the Synoptic Gospels Jesus addresses scribal-literate authorities with the question "Have you not read?" (for example, Matt. 12:3, 5; 21:16; Mark 12:26; Luke 10:26) but addresses "the crowds" by referencing what they "have heard that it was said" (Matt. 5:21, 27, 31, 33, 38, 43).[68]

First-century synagogues were thus locations for the display of socially scripted roles. Although all present may have participated in the discussion and debate to various degrees, scribal-literate individuals read and taught the Scriptures for the illiterate manual-labor populace. As a result of being authorities in the sacred text, they received honor and esteem in the synagogue and the marketplace. Manual laborers, having broken from their work and incapable of reading the Hebrew holy text anyway, listened to the Law read aloud.

Summary

This chapter has taken an important first step in answering the question "What kind of teacher was Jesus?" by addressing a prior question: "What kind of teachers were there?" Although there are many possible responses to that question, I have argued that a scribal-literate line divided authoritative teachers from everyone else. Furthermore, the sources sometimes portray those holding scribal authority in contradistinction to members of the manual-labor class. This point is crucial to understanding both the present chapter and those that follow because Jesus was constantly battling not just authorities but specifically scribal-literate authorities—scribes, Pharisees, Sadducees, priests, and the like. Related to this point, I observed in this chapter that scribal literacy

68. Millard, *Reading*, 158.

and scribal authority intertwined with various social activities in Jesus's time, revealing a particular "scribal culture" associated with those activities. One could have walked into a synagogue gathering and judged whether someone was a scribal-literate interpretive authority by whether he took on roles associated with such authority (reading the text, interpreting the text) or roles associated with the manual-labor audience (listening).

Of course, such boundaries between scribal-literate authorities and scribal-illiterate manual laborers were products of social roles and expectations, not physical barriers. A member of the manual-labor class could have, theoretically, participated in some activities associated with the teachers who could read Scripture for themselves, such as expounding the text. In light of the available sources, such an occurrence would certainly have been atypical, but not impossible. According to Mark's Gospel and Matthew's Gospel, that is precisely what Jesus of Nazareth, the Galilean teacher, did. Luke's Gospel, however, has a different take on what happened when Jesus taught in a synagogue. This intra-Gospel disagreement is the topic of chapter 2.

2

Jesus as Teacher in the Gospels

Questioning, Rejecting, and Affirming the Nazarene

"How does this man know letters when he has never been taught?" (John 7:15 AT)

This chapter offers perhaps the most important—and overlooked—reason why knowing which type of Second Temple Jewish teacher Jesus was is not a simple matter: first-century Christians already disagreed on the issue. These differences of opinion are particularly clear in the portrayals of Jesus's return to his hometown synagogue in Mark 6, Matt. 13, and Luke 4. Before proceeding to the intra-Gospel debate over Jesus, however, I start with John's Gospel and the only first-century text that addresses Jesus's scribal-literate status directly.

How Does This Man Know Letters When He's Never Been Taught? (John 7:15)

The conviction that there was already confusion over Jesus's scribal-literate status in the first century CE is one that I share with the author of John's Gospel. According to John 7:15, "the Jews" question Jesus's pedagogical qualifications upon hearing him teach. Translated literally, their response is, "How does this man know letters [*grammata oiden*] when he has never been taught?"

Unfortunately, modern English translations obscure the fact that Jesus's audience questions his teaching qualifications generally by questioning his literacy specifically. They translate the Jews' question about Jesus's knowledge of letters more generally in terms of "learning" and "study." Consider the following translations:

"How does this man have such learning, when he has never been taught?" (NRSV)

"How did this man get such learning without having been taught?" (NIV)

"How is it that this man has learning, when he has never studied?" (ESV)

"How did this man get such learning without having been taught?" (TNIV)

"He's never been taught! How has he mastered the Law?" (CEB)

Jesus's studies, learning, and knowledge of the law are part of the Jews' question. But the Greek phrase *grammata oiden* ("knows letters") refers more specifically to a form of study, learning, and knowledge of the law that was the product of a literate education. The previous chapter described this as scribal literacy and noted that this type of Torah study was the possession of a slim fraction of the population. These English translations thus fail to communicate the full significance of the Jews' question and its relation to class distinction. The Jews are not asking whether Jesus ever goes to synagogue and discusses Torah with others; whether he cherishes the text, contemplates it, or even knows what it says. They are asking specifically whether he is an educated, authoritative teacher of Moses who can access the text on his own. If one is to render the sense of the Greek rather than translate literally, "How can this man read Scripture, when he has never been educated?" might be a better translation.[1]

But the Jews do not ask this question because Jesus has just read in front of them and demonstrated scribal literacy. Jesus's oral teaching prompts their question. As to the question itself, scholars have cited it as evidence that Jesus was illiterate and as evidence that he was literate.[2] Both interpretations are right to a degree. They both gain traction from the confusing nature of the Jews' query. The first clause in the Jews' statement ("How does this man know letters? . . .") assumes that Jesus knows letters and is therefore a scribal-literate teacher. The second clause (". . . when he has never been taught?") assumes that Jesus is uneducated and therefore not a scribal-literate teacher. One mistake scholars make in interpreting this passage (an exceedingly easy one to make) is to base their opinions on only one of the clauses rather than both. However we interpret John 7:15, though, we must explain both clauses.

Another mistake that scholars have made in assessing this passage is to fail to note that this opinion, whatever one understands it to be, is the opinion of the Jews in the passage; that is, the opinion of characters and not the authoritative narrator. Sometimes the perspective of characters in the Gospels aligns with the perspective of the narrator, as when Simeon and Anna identify

---

1. Although the phrase *grammata oiden* can refer to reading skills or writing skills (for examples of both, see Keith, *Jesus' Literacy*, 92–100), literate education in first-century Judaism seems to have focused on reading the Torah. See chap. 1.

2. See the short history of research in Chris Keith, "The Claim of John 7.15 and the Memory of Jesus' Literacy," *NTS* 56.1 (2010): 48–50. Already in the third century CE, Origen read John 7:15 as evidence of Jesus's illiteracy (*Comm. Matt.* 10.17).

the baby Jesus as the Messiah, Savior, and promised king in Luke 2:25–40, or Philip identifies Jesus as "him about whom Moses in the law and also the prophets wrote" in John 1:45. At other times, however, a character's perspective on Jesus is incorrect or woefully insufficient from the perspective of the narrator, such as Peter's misunderstanding of Jesus's identity as Messiah in Mark 8:27–38//Matt. 16:13–28 or the Capernaum crowd's assumption that Jesus's identity as Joseph's son is antithetical to his claim to be the bread of life in John 6:41–42.[3] The perspectives of characters are not always reliable. In contrast, the perspectives of the Gospel narrators are always reliable within the story world.[4] The key for understanding the claim of John 7:15, therefore, is the narrator's perspective.

Unlike Mark, Matthew, and Luke, all of whom offer a narratorial perspective on Jesus's scribal-literate status, the narrator and author of the Fourth Gospel does not offer a direct opinion.[5] In the verse that immediately follows, Jesus asserts that his teaching is that of the Father and not his own. But there is no attempt on the part of Jesus or the narrator to answer directly the Jews' question about Jesus's educational qualifications. The *claim* of John 7:15 is simply that at least one of Jesus's audiences considered him to be the type of person whose oral teaching reflects scribal literacy even though they assume he does not possess it.[6] In short, the narrator portrays Jesus as the type of teacher who can make people confused over his scribal-literate status.

The Synoptic Debate over Jesus the Synagogue Teacher

If nothing else, the Synoptic Gospels serve to validate the claim of John 7:15— there were indeed multiple opinions about Jesus's scribal-literate status in the first century. These multiple opinions are particularly clear in a disagreement

3. On the Gospel authors' usage of characters in their presentation of Jesus's identity, see further Chris Keith and Larry W. Hurtado, eds., *Jesus among Friends and Enemies: A Historical and Literary Introduction to Jesus in the Gospels* (Grand Rapids: Baker Academic, 2011).

4. Not all narrators in literature are reliable, but the narrators in the Gospels are omniscient and reliable. See, for example, the comments on the Markan narrator in Malbon, *In the Company*, 8–9; Rhoads, Dewey, and Michie, *Mark as Story*, 39–46. More generally, see the dated but still helpful work by Seymour Chatman, *Story and Discourse: Narrative Structure in Fiction and Film* (Ithaca, NY: Cornell University Press, 1978), 148–49.

5. The narrator and implied author are not always the same entity in a narrative, as is clear in a book like *The Adventures of Huckleberry Finn*. In John's Gospel, however, there is no readily discernible distinction between the two.

6. The Jews' comparison of Jesus's teaching abilities to those of scribal-literate teachers stands in contrast to the narrators' assessments of Jesus's teaching in Mark 1:22//Matt. 7:29. See further below.

between the Synoptic authors in their respective narrations of Jesus's return to his hometown synagogue early in his ministry (Mark 6:1–6//Matt. 13:54–58// Luke 4:16–30). This disagreement occurs in the midst of substantial agreement between the authors, however—to the extent that, with the majority of scholars, I affirm that Mark, Matthew, and Luke are narrating the same account.[7] In each account, Jesus is ultimately rejected and speaks his famous line concerning a prophet not receiving honor in his hometown (Mark 6:4// Matt. 13:57//Luke 4:24; cf. John 4:43).

The significance of another aspect of these texts' portrayals of Jesus should already be obvious in light of the previous chapter: Jesus *teaches* in synagogues.[8] In fact, each author claims that, by teaching in the Nazareth synagogue, Jesus was simply doing in his hometown what he had already done elsewhere in Galilee to great applause (Mark 1:21–28, 39; cf. 3:1–6; Matt. 4:23–25; 9:35–36; 12:9–14; Luke 4:14–15). Luke further claims that teaching in a synagogue on the Sabbath was Jesus's custom (Luke 4:16; cf. Mark 10:1).

In portraying Jesus as a synagogue teacher, these texts attribute to Jesus actions reserved exclusively for the scribal-literate class in the evidence we have (see chap. 1). The portrayals are a bit more nuanced than this simple description may imply, however. Their details reveal that, although all three Synoptic Gospels agree that Jesus acted like a scribal-literate teacher in the synagogue, they do not agree about whether he did so legitimately. Agreeing with the majority scholarly opinion that Mark was the earliest of the Gospels, I begin with Mark's portrayal of Jesus as a carpenter who gets rejected as a synagogue teacher in his hometown.[9]

Jesus the Carpenter in Mark 6:3

According to Mark, when Jesus began to teach in his hometown synagogue, the audience "took offense at him" (6:3) and asked, "Is not this the carpenter,

7. Among many others, W. D. Davies and Dale C. Allison Jr., *A Critical and Exegetical Commentary on the Gospel of Matthew*, 3 vols., ICC (Edinburgh: T&T Clark, 1988–97), 2:452; I. Howard Marshall, *The Gospel of Luke: A Commentary on the Greek Text*, NIGTC (Grand Rapids: Eerdmans, 1978), 179. For a representative of the view that Mark and Luke narrate distinct visits to Nazareth, see William Lane, *The Gospel according to Mark*, NICNT (Grand Rapids: Eerdmans, 1974), 201n2.

8. Jesus teaches in synagogues in John's Gospel as well (John 6:59; 18:20).

9. Only the secondary argument of this chapter, concerning Matthew's and Luke's alterations to Mark, depends on my assumption of Markan priority (the theory that Mark wrote first). The primary argument, that there were differences of opinion concerning Jesus's scribal-literate status already in the first century, does not depend on it and would stand even if one instead assumed Matthean priority.

the son of Mary and brother of James and Joses and Judas and Simon, and are not his sisters here with us?"[10] The crowd is astonished at Jesus's wisdom and powerful deeds in 6:2. Mark 6:3 clarifies why they are astonished: they know him, know his family, and know that they are from manual-labor stock. The Greek word that English Bibles translate as "carpenter" is *tektōn*. In addition to "carpenter," it also meant "builder," "joiner," or "smith." In general, it referred to manual laborers who worked with wood, stone, or metal. Broader definitions such as "craftsman," "artisan," or "workman" are also accurate. Christians throughout the ages have attributed the specific meaning of "carpenter" to Jesus in light of early Christian and pagan traditions that Jesus and his father, Joseph, were woodworkers.[11]

Some scholars have seen the synagogue audience's identification of Jesus as a carpenter as confirmation that Jesus was part of the Galilean illiterate peasantry.[12] In Jewish tradition, however, there are examples of carpenters who display some degree of literate skills,[13] and carpenters could reside closer to the top of the social pyramid than the bottom.[14] These examples do not mean that these circumstances applied to all Jewish carpenters in Jewish history or Jesus in particular. But they do give warrant for being cautious in making automatic assumptions about the relationship between manual labor and Jewish peasantry.

More important, though, whatever limited literate abilities and social status a first-century Jewish carpenter might have mustered, his literate abilities and status would have paled in comparison to those of an educated scribal-literate Torah teacher. Indeed, Sirach includes "every carpenter and master carpenter" (*pas tektōn kai architektōn*; 38:27) in the large grouping of manual laborers whom he contrasts with the scribe who devotes himself to Torah study (38:24–39:1). As has already been discussed, Sirach's opinion is not that these are not Torah-devout people. His point is that their lives of manual

10. A few manuscripts of Mark's Gospel, including $\mathfrak{P}^{45}$ f^{13} and 33, read "son of the carpenter" at Mark 6:3 instead of "carpenter." Most likely, these readings are assimilations to Matt. 13:55, which I discuss below.

11. Justin Martyr, *Dial.* 88; *Inf. Gos. Thom.* 13.1–3; Celsus, in the work of Origen, *Cels.* 6.34; Origen, *Cels.* 6.36.

12. Especially John Dominic Crossan, *The Beginnings of Christianity: Discovering What Happened in the Years Immediately after the Execution of Jesus* (San Francisco: HarperCollins, 1999), 234–35, 350; *Jesus: A Revolutionary Biography* (New York: HarperCollins, 1994), 23–26.

13. Bezalel and Oholiab, whose work Exod. 35:32, 35 LXX identifies as "master carpentry/craftsmanship" (*architektonias*), write "Holy to the LORD" in Exod. 39:30 MT.

14. Second Kings 24:14 includes "all carpenters" (*pan tektona*) among the prominent leaders whom Nebuchadnezzar takes into exile, while "the poor of the land" remain. According to Sir. 38:32, carpenters and other manual laborers are appreciated socially to the degree that "wherever they live, they will not go hungry."

labor do not afford them the leisure time to become textual experts, whereas the scribe's life does.

Against this sociohistorical backdrop, I must underscore a fact that New Testament scholars routinely ignore or overlook: Mark 6:1–6 and its parallel in Matt. 13:54–58 constitute the lone example of a member of the manual-labor class actively teaching in a Second Temple Jewish synagogue in the historical record.[15] Although Jesus's actions in this text are inconsistent with the rest of the historical record, the Nazarenes' rejection of him is utterly consistent with it. Their rejection expresses the exact same opinion as Sirach, Philo, Josephus, and others concerning who textual authorities are and who they are not, and thus who performs what role in synagogue. The Nazarenes' claim is that Jesus, as a carpenter, does not belong in the role of a teacher; he belongs instead with his family and fellow manual laborers. Some people refer to this posture as "putting on airs" or "getting above your raising." Lane rewords their complaint as "Is he not a common worker with his hands even as the rest of us are?"[16]

Along these lines, it is important to recall a brief point from the previous chapter. Examples of members of the scribal-literate class who also engaged in manual labor, such as the apostle Paul or the famous Pharisees Hillel and Shammai, do not disprove this point about the disassociation of manual labor and the acquisition of scribal literacy.[17] Similar to the positive affirmation of participating in manual labor alongside Torah study in *m. 'Abot* 2.2 or Philo's descriptions of the Essenes as textual authorities and manual laborers,[18] these examples are people who *reside in the scribal-literate class* and whose position is therefore, strictly speaking, not comparable to Jesus's situation in Mark 6. Of course members of the scribal-elite class could engage in manual labor, just as Supreme Court justices might choose to landscape their own homes. But to claim that a member of the manual-labor class could engage in scribal-literate activity is another matter, just as it would be another matter to assert

15. Luke 4:16–30 is not an example of Jesus, as a manual laborer, teaching in a synagogue because Luke never refers to Jesus as a manual laborer. In fact, he strategically recategorizes Jesus as a member of the scribal-literate class in multiple ways. See below.

16. Lane, *Gospel according to Mark*, 202. Similarly, Casey, *Jesus*, 144: "They did not welcome him as a remarkable religious figure because he was already known to them as a normal person and they stated this normality by referring to his job as well as his family."

17. *Contra* Maccoby, *Jesus the Pharisee*, 181.

18. Philo describes some of the Essenes reading and explaining the text to others who cannot understand (*Prob.* 12.81–82), and elsewhere he describes the community as engaging in manual labor (*Hypoth.* 11.6–9). The Essenes are hardly indicative of the rest of Second Temple Jewish culture. If one is to equate them with the Qumran community, which seems likely, they are not exceptions to this rule but rather examples of a scribal community with members at different stages of scribal education. The Essene synagogue was an association synagogue, not a public synagogue like those in which Jesus taught (see chap. 1).

that professional landscapers can sit on the Supreme Court. In Mark 6 (and Matt. 13, see below), Jesus's hometown rejects him explicitly on the basis that he is a manual laborer, not because he is a member of the scribal elite who occasionally also works with his hands.

Jesus, Teaching, and Scribal Authority in Mark's Gospel

Before proceeding to Matthew's adaptation of Mark's version of the Nazareth synagogue incident, we should stop to see how this event in Mark 6 fits within Mark's fuller portrayal of Jesus as a synagogue teacher. This step is especially necessary since the identification of Jesus as a carpenter who does not belong in the role of a synagogue teacher is, like the Jews' opinion in John 7:15, the opinion of characters and not the narrator. In contrast to the Johannine narrator, however, who never comments one way or another on Jesus's scribal-literate status, Mark seems to share the opinion of the Nazareth synagogue audience.

In at least four ways, Mark's overall portrait of Jesus as a teacher coheres with the Nazareth audience's assessment that Jesus does not belong in the role of a scribal-literate teacher in a synagogue. First, explaining the Capernaum synagogue's reaction to Jesus upon his first visit to a synagogue in Mark's Gospel, Mark explicitly states that Jesus's teaching is unlike that of scribal-literate teachers (1:22).[19] Like the synagogue audience later in Nazareth, the crowd in the Capernaum synagogue is astonished at Jesus's teaching activity, with Mark even using the same Greek word (*ekplēssō*) to describe both audiences' astonishment (1:22; 6:2). Mark explains the astonishment in Capernaum: "For he taught them as one having authority, and not as the scribes" (1:22). This assessment of Jesus's pedagogical status coheres with Sirach and, more importantly, the Nazareth synagogue audience in Mark 6. When it comes to Torah teaching and authority, a carpenter is not like scribes.

Before moving on, two points of clarification concerning Mark 1:22 are necessary. The first point of clarification relates to Mark's layered portrayal of the reception of Jesus as a synagogue teacher in different Galilean locales. Despite their similarities in being astonished at Jesus's actions, the eventual responses to Jesus in Capernaum and Nazareth differ strongly. In Capernaum, the synagogue audience's astonishment will blossom into adulation and contribute to Jesus's growing popularity in Galilee (1:27–28). In his hometown, however, the synagogue audience's astonishment will deteriorate into rejection and Jesus's reciprocal astonishment at their disbelief (6:3–6). A crucial

---

19. *Pace* Larry W. Hurtado, *Mark*, UBCS (Grand Rapids: Baker Books, 1989), 26, who claims the crowds make the contrasting statement.

factor in the differing responses is the role of Jesus's performance of powerful deeds in their assessment of him. The crowd in Capernaum is astonished, but permits him to continue teaching, during which he casts out an unclean spirit (1:23–26). According to Mark 1:27–28, the combination of (1) Jesus's teachings and (2) miraculous deeds (3) in a synagogue leads to their positive reception of Jesus and the spread of his fame. Jesus's activities elsewhere in Galilee consist of the same trifecta (1:39; 3:1–6), though he also attracts attention outside the synagogue between Sabbaths (2:1–28; 3:7–12, 19b–35; 4:1–9; 5:14, 21–43). In Nazareth, the synagogue rejects Jesus as a teacher despite his miraculous deeds, which 6:2 mentions, and thus fails to incorporate those deeds into their view of him as a pedagogue. Their rejection is significant enough that it hinders Jesus's ability to perform additional miraculous deeds (6:5–6).

Collectively, these examples reveal Mark's full portrait of Jesus's contemporaries' reception of him as a synagogue teacher who compensates for status as a carpenter with healings and exorcisms. Where an audience is willing to allow Jesus's exorcisms and healings to impact their view of his identity, he is accepted as a synagogue teacher. Where the members of an audience do not allow Jesus's exorcisms and healings to influence their view of his identity (and instead rely upon what they have always known to be true about him, namely, that he is a carpenter), he is rejected as a synagogue teacher. Mark's portrayal of Jesus in this regard further reveals his conviction that Jesus's teachings and performance of miraculous deeds were so thoroughly intertwined that acceptance/rejection of one was tantamount to acceptance/rejection of the other.

The second point of clarification concerns previous interpretations of Mark 1:22. My suggestions above do not ignore or contradict the possibility that Mark may also be referencing differences of teaching style between Jesus and the scribes, or perhaps differences in content. He could be claiming that Jesus appeals to no external authority whereas the scribes recite something close to what we later see in the rabbinic material ("Rabbi X taught this, Rabbi Y taught that"). He could be claiming that Jesus is apocalyptic and scribes are not. He could be claiming that Jesus performs healings and exorcisms while scribes do not. He could also be claiming that Jesus's opinions on the law, purity, fasting, Sabbath, and similar issues differ from those of the scribes. Scholars typically interpret the distinction between Jesus and the scribes, and thus Mark's assessment of it, along these lines.[20] As the introduction to this book showed, scholars have likewise proposed all these distinctions as possible

20. As just a few examples, see Mary Ann Beavis, *Mark*, Paideia (Grand Rapids: Baker Academic, 2011), 51–52; James R. Edwards, *The Gospel according to Mark*, PNTC (Grand Rapids: Eerdmans, 2002), 55; R. T. France, *The Gospel of Mark*, NIGTC (Grand Rapids: Eerdmans, 2002), 102; Mary Healy, *The Gospel of Mark*, CCSS (Grand Rapids: Baker Academic, 2008),

causes for the conflict between Jesus and authoritative teachers. And, similar to my assessment of those proposals in the introduction, these explanations for Mark's statement are possibilities and likely correct to one extent or another. In accounting for Mark's statement in these ways, however, scholars have overlooked the crucial additional issue that, in explaining the audience's surprise that Jesus would function as a synagogue teacher—a position that is associated with scribal literacy throughout the available historical evidence— Mark states explicitly that Jesus is not like teachers who hold scribal literacy. In addition to other possible differences, Jesus's teaching is not like that of the scribes because they were recipients of a scribal-literate education.[21] Jesus is not from the class that has access to such pursuits of elite culture. Or so says the Markan Nazareth synagogue audience.

Along these lines, I briefly note the second, third, and fourth ways in which Mark's overall portrayal of Jesus as a synagogue teacher coheres with the Nazareth audience's criticism that, as a carpenter, Jesus dwells outside the class of scribal-literate synagogue teachers. Second, Mark includes no statement that the audience spoke from misunderstanding. Although technically this is an argument from (Mark's) silence, it is pertinent because Mark elsewhere comments that characters have misunderstood (6:52), as does Jesus within the narrative (8:17, 21). No such statement occurs here. Third, once exposed as a carpenter in his hometown, Jesus never sets foot in a synagogue in the rest of Mark's narrative. Fourth, and related to this lack of a return to the synagogue, Mark later claims that Jesus's custom (*hōs eiōthei*) was to teach spontaneously as crowds gathered around him (Mark 10:1). These third and fourth points of coherence between Mark's orchestration of the narrative and his characters' assessment of Jesus in Mark 6:3 may seem insignificant. They will be particularly significant, however, when I discuss Mark 6:3's reception-history, and specifically Luke's reception of it. Luke 4:16 claims the opposite in saying that Jesus's custom (*kata to eiōthos*) was to teach in synagogues on the Sabbath.

Summary of Mark's Presentation of Jesus the Rejected Synagogue Teacher

I may be giving readers the impression that I am arguing that Mark does not affirm Jesus as a teacher. That is not the case. Quite to the contrary, Mark

---

46; Puig i Tàrrech, *Jesus*, 283; Vincent Taylor, *The Gospel according to St. Mark* (London: Macmillan, 1963), 172.

21. Edwards, *Gospel*, 54, comments on the specialized nature of scribal training and knowledge in a low-literacy environment. He accounts for the difference between Jesus and the scribes in terms of authority generally (55, 56), however, and not in terms of social class.

portrays Jesus as a powerful and effective teacher. In fact, when Mark says that Jesus taught with "authority" and "not as the scribes" in 1:22, the word he uses for "authority" (*exousia*) also means "power." Mark clearly considers Jesus a powerful teacher.

The point, rather, is that Mark portrays Jesus as a powerful teacher whose contemporaries did not expect him to be a *synagogue* teacher because he was a member of the manual-labor class. Despite consistent identifications of Jesus as outside scribal-literate circles, sometimes his audiences nevertheless allow him to teach in a synagogue and thus experience the benefits of his healing and exorcistic ministries. And despite scribal-literate authorities' disapproval of Jesus (2:6–7, 16, 24; 3:6, 22) and despite, or possibly because of, his critiques of them (2:17, 25; 3:23–27), his popularity increases in Galilee. The words of Mark 1:39 describe Jesus's successful early teaching career: "He went throughout Galilee, proclaiming the message in their synagogues and casting out demons" (more fully 1:21–28; 3:1–5). As this summary statement indicates, Jesus's reputation as a synagogue teacher grows from his performance of these powerful deeds while occupying the social space of a scribal-literate teacher. Jesus's career in this regard is so successful that a synagogue leader himself, Jairus, comes to Jesus for the healing of his daughter shortly before Jesus's return to his hometown (5:22–43).

Once Jesus attempts to occupy this social space in his hometown among those who know him best, however, their expectation that he is not a synagogue teacher receives reinforcement from their knowledge that he is a carpenter. The rejection in Mark 6 is not rooted in the fact that Jesus dared to present himself as a teacher or their general dislike of him. He had, in fact, earlier attracted a large crowd in his hometown in 3:19–20. Their rejection is rooted specifically in the fact that he, as a carpenter, put himself in the position of a scribal-literate Torah authority in the synagogue.

Jesus the Son of the Carpenter in Matthew 13:55

In his version of the Nazareth synagogue incident (Matt. 13:54–58), Matthew largely follows Mark in presenting Jesus as a member of the manual-labor class whose hometown rejects him as a synagogue teacher. In the Matthean account, Jesus enters the synagogue in his hometown and begins to teach, to the crowd's astonishment (Matt. 13:54). Matthew repeats Mark's usage of *ekplēssō* to describe the astonishment. The Matthean crowd's astonishment will deteriorate into their rejection of Jesus, his statement that a prophet is not honored in his hometown, and his lack of miracles (13:57–58).[22] As in Mark's Gospel, once Jesus's hometown synagogue rejects him, he never again appears in a synagogue in Matthew's Gospel.

In the midst of these similarities, however, Matthew makes a change to Mark's version of the Nazareth synagogue incident that is highly significant for the present topic. When the crowd identifies Jesus, they refer to him as "the son of the carpenter" rather than "the carpenter."

Mark 6:3: "Is this not the carpenter?"

Matt. 13:55: "Is this not the carpenter's son?"

More fully, their question reads, "Is this not the carpenter's son [*ho tou tektonos huios*]? Is not his mother called Mary? And are not his brothers James and Joseph and Simon and Judas? And are not all his sisters with us?" (Matt. 13:55–56).

Already in the early fifth century CE, Augustine claimed, "Neither is there anything to marvel at in this, since He might quite fairly have been designated by both these names."[23] Despite Augustine's dismissal, scholars have debated the reasons for Matthew's alteration to Mark, and for good reason. If there was essentially no difference between the two, why did Matthew feel compelled to change Mark, especially when he left so many other features of Mark's account unchanged?

One possible explanation for Matthew's alteration is that he simply desired a more "Jewish style" of reference for Jesus, by which is meant a patronymic rather than a matronymic identification.[24] Alternatively, in light of the slight differences between Mark's and Matthew's respective references to Jesus's parentage—"the carpenter, the son of Mary" (Mark) versus "the son of the carpenter [whose] mother is called Mary" (Matthew)—some scholars posit that the change is attributable to early Christian concerns over Jesus's legitimacy, virgin birth, or both.[25] Another possibility, which is not mutually exclusive

22. Significantly, whereas Mark 6:5 claims that Jesus "was not able to perform" (*ouk edynato . . . poiēsai*) miracles in his hometown, Matt. 13:58 claims only that he "did not perform" (*ouk epoiēsen*) them.

23. Augustine, *Cons.* 2.42.90 (*NPNF*[1] 6:144).

24. Ulrich Luz, *Matthew 8–20*, trans. James E. Crouch, Hermeneia (Minneapolis: Fortress, 2001), 302. See also Casey, *Jesus*, 144.

25. For theories that reflect this concern over Jesus's legitimacy and/or the virgin birth, see, inter alia, Adela Yarbro Collins, *Mark*, Hermeneia (Minneapolis: Fortress, 2007), 288, 290–291; Davies and Allison, *Matthew*, 2:456–57; Frans von Segbroeck, "Jésus rejeté par sa patrie (Mt 13,54–58)," *Bib* 48 (1968): 182. Contrary to some claims (Joachim Gnilka, *Das Evangelium nach Markus [1,1–8,26]*, EKKNT 2.1 [Zurich: Benziger, 1978], 219; H. Schürmann,

to the other suggestions, is that Matthew could have been disturbed by the identification of Jesus directly as a carpenter. Luz claims it would have been disturbing because the Jesus tradition elsewhere says nothing about Jesus having a profession,[26] while others think it was Jesus's "working class origins" themselves, not the tradition's failure elsewhere to mention them, that was the problem.[27]

This last possibility, that Matthew found Jesus's identity as a carpenter to be embarrassing or otherwise problematic, is the most likely primary catalyst for his change of Jesus from "the carpenter" to "the son of the carpenter." The major objection to this theory is that Matthew would not have viewed direct identification as a carpenter to be a slur upon Jesus because manual labor was an honorable undertaking for Jewish teachers.[28] This objection suffers on two counts, however. First, it reads in the precise opposite direction from Mark 6:3 and Matt. 13:55, where the synagogue audiences cite Jesus's manual-labor status explicitly as a cause for their rejection of him as a synagogue teacher. Second, the Jewish teachers whom scholars cite to support their objection all come from *within* the scribal-literate class (see the preceding footnote). As discussed above, the question is not whether people who studied the Torah in light of their scribal-literate abilities could also engage in manual labor, or whether that was a good thing. The question is whether those who worked with their hands for their livelihoods also had the finances and leisure time available to acquire a scribal-literate education. Class distinctions did not prevent the first scenario; they did prevent the second scenario.[29]

Of course, we cannot climb inside the head of Matthew (or any other author) and decipher in detail his intentions and anxieties. One can, however, find further support for the theory that Matthew viewed Mark's direct

---

"Zur Traditionsgeschichte der Nazareth-Perikope Lk 4,16–30," in *Mélanges bibliques en homage au R. P. Béda Rigaux*, ed. Albert Descamps and André de Halleux [Gembloux: Duculot], 197), identifying a man by reference to his mother was not entirely unheard of in the ancient world (Lars Hartmann, "Mk 6,3a im Lichter einiger griechischer Texte," *ZNW* 95 [2004]: 276–79), including Judaism (Casey, *Jesus*, 144–45).

26. Luz, *Matthew 8–20*, 302.

27. Inter alia, Kim Haines-Eitzen, *The Guardians of Letters: Literacy, Power, and the Transmitters of Early Christian Literature* (New York: Oxford University Press, 2000), 117–18; Wayne C. Kannaday, *Apologetic Discourse and the Scribal Tradition: Evidence of the Influence of Apologetic Interests on the Text of the Canonical Gospels*, SBLTCS 5 (Atlanta: Society of Biblical Literature, 2004), 118–19; Douglas E. Oakman, *Jesus and the Economic Questions of His Day*, SBEC 8 (Lewiston, NY: Edwin Mellen, 1986), 176 (quotation).

28. Davies and Allison, *Matthew*, 2:457; Peter M. Head, *Christology and the Synoptic Problem: An Argument for Markan Priority*, SNTSMS 94 (Cambridge: Cambridge University Press, 1997), 70; Maccoby, *Jesus the Pharisee*, 181.

29. The exception was slaves in wealthy households who were trained in scribal-literate skills.

identification of Jesus as a carpenter as problematic in the broader reception-history of Mark 6:3 and Matthew's overall portrayal of Jesus's relationship to pedagogical authority.

Matthew and the Reception-History of Mark 6:3

The reception-history of Mark 6:3 begins in the first century with Matthew's and Luke's overwhelmingly likely use of him as a source. Neither reproduces Mark's direct identification of Jesus as "the carpenter." As we have seen, Matt. 13:55 has "the carpenter's son." Luke 4:22 instead uses "son of Joseph," eliminating any reference at all to the manual-labor class in association with Jesus's family. I am currently of the mind that John also knew Mark's Gospel. If he did, it is worth noting that John too has a synagogue audience refer to Jesus as "the son of Joseph" (John 6:42), though this synagogue is in Capernaum (6:24, 59), not Nazareth. Therefore, every instance or possible instance of the reception of Mark 6:3 in the first century moves away from Mark's direct identification of Jesus as "the carpenter."

Mark 6:3's reception-history also includes early Christian scribes' production of new handwritten manuscripts of Mark's Gospel by copying prior manuscripts. In several ancient manuscripts of Mark's Gospel, the scribe has changed "the carpenter" at Mark 6:3 to "the son of the carpenter." These copies of Mark's Gospel thus exhibit the exact same move away from direct identification of Jesus as a carpenter as we see in Matthew's retelling of the Nazareth incident. The earliest such manuscript, $\mathfrak{P}^{45}$, is our earliest extant copy of Mark's Gospel and comes from the early third century CE.[30] This "Matthean" reading of Mark 6:3 also appears in the Old Latin tradition from as early as the fifth century (MSS *e b i*) and in other ancient translations. In the sixth century, the Palestinian Syriac tradition goes several steps further than Matthew's Gospel and the copies of Mark's Gospel that preserve the Matthean reading. It omits "the carpenter" from Mark 6:3 altogether![31]

On the one hand, the manuscripts that preserve the Matthean reading "the carpenter's son" at Mark 6:3 could simply be an example of scribal desires to harmonize one Gospel text with another. It would make sense that scribes harmonized in the direction of Matthew's Gospel since Matthew's Gospel was substantially more popular than Mark's Gospel in the early church, if

30. Technically, $\mathfrak{P}^{45}$ has a missing section (*lacuna*) at this point in the text, but from the spaces and sizes of the letters, scholars can confidently reconstruct that it reads *tou tektonos ho huios* ("the son of the carpenter").

31. Bruce M. Metzger, *A Textual Commentary on the Greek New Testament*, 2nd ed. (Stuttgart: Deutsche Bibelgesellschaft, 1994), 76.

the surviving manuscripts are any indication. In fact, 𝔓⁴⁵ is the only copy of Mark's Gospel that we have from the second and third centuries, while we have twelve copies of Matthew's Gospel from the same period.[32]

On the other hand, a harmonization theory alone cannot explain why Matthew, Luke, and John *all* decided not to follow Mark in the first century.[33] More specifically, a harmonization theory cannot alone satisfactorily explain the fact that every single one of these manuscripts and traditions that alter Mark 6:3—from the first century to the sixth century—moves away from direct identification of Jesus as a carpenter.[34] Not a single reception of Matt. 13:55 in church tradition or manuscripts of Matthew's Gospel harmonizes in the other direction by replacing "the son of the carpenter" with Mark 6:3's "the carpenter." Although the harmonization theory may be correct to an extent, we also need to account for a unidirectional harmonization pattern in the early church.

Elsewhere, Mark 6:3's reception-history provides a satisfactory explanation for why Matthew and these other early Christians may have desired to soften or remove Mark's direct identification of Jesus as a carpenter. Already by the second century, Christianity had begun to make inroads with elite Greco-Roman culture, which "in general was not impressed with what it saw."[35] During this time a pagan critic named Celsus wrote a polemical attack on Christianity titled *On the True Doctrine*. His stinging criticisms of Jesus and Christians were so effective that in the third century—that is, about the same time as a Christian scribe was copying 𝔓⁴⁵—the Christian intellectual Origen still felt it necessary to offer a response. He wrote a rebuttal titled *Against Celsus*. No copies of Celsus's *On the True Doctrine* have survived, but thankfully Origen quoted long sections in *Against Celsus*. In one such section, we see that Celsus found Christians particularly worthy of ridicule because "their teacher [*didaskalos*] . . . was a carpenter [*tektōn*]."[36] He further mockingly connects their veneration of a carpenter to their veneration of a wood cross. Celsus drives the point home by asking, "Would not an old

32. Larry W. Hurtado, *The Earliest Christian Artifacts: Manuscripts and Christian Origins* (Grand Rapids: Eerdmans, 2006), 20.

33. Haines-Eitzen, *Guardians*, 117.

34. Cf. Head (*Christology*, 69–70), who thinks Jewish appreciation for manual labor makes it unlikely that Matthew would have viewed Jesus's identification as a carpenter as a problem but acknowledges that the argument that Matthew did see it as a problem "has the advantage of coherence with scribal alterations of Mark's text away from the identification of Jesus as a carpenter."

35. Michael W. Holmes, introduction to *The Apostolic Fathers: Greek Texts and English Translations*, 3rd ed. (Grand Rapids: Baker Academic, 2007), 14.

36. Origen, *Cels.* 6.34 (PG 11:1348).

woman who sings a story to lull a little child to sleep have been ashamed to whisper such tales as these?"[37]

Two things about Celsus's mockery of Jesus the carpenter and teacher are significant. First, he is clearly dependent upon Mark 6:3 since this is the only place in all of early Christian discourse where Jesus himself is called a carpenter. Second, Celsus reveals the same opinion, rooted in distinctions of social class, as Sirach and the Nazareth synagogue audience in Mark 6:3: authoritative teachers are not carpenters. Celsus thus finds it laughable that Christians' main teacher would be a carpenter, just as he finds Christianity laughable in general because it was "successful only among the uneducated because of its vulgarity and utter illiteracy."[38] For Celsus, uneducated followers had an uneducated teacher. On account of these facts, Christians should be ashamed and the rest of humanity should dismiss Christianity.[39]

In *Against Celsus*, Origen responded directly to the charge that Jesus was a carpenter, and his response is exceedingly interesting. He says, "Furthermore, he [Celsus] did not observe that Jesus himself [*autos ho Iēsous*] is not described as a carpenter [*tektōn*] anywhere in the gospels accepted in the churches."[40] Origen's response is highly interesting because Mark's Gospel, which the churches accepted, explicitly *does* refer to Jesus as a carpenter. There are a number of theories as to why Origen denied this fact, the most likely of which is that his copy of Mark's Gospel, like 𝔓[45], had the Matthean reading "son of the carpenter" at Mark 6:3.[41] Regardless of why Origen says this, the statement itself reveals just the type of Christian apologetic response

37. Origen, *Cels.* 6.34 (Chadwick).

38. Origen, *Cels.* 1.27 (Chadwick).

39. Interestingly, Origen concedes that Jesus and the disciples were not educated (*Cels.* 1.29, 62). See further below as well as the discussion of Gamble, *Books*, 1–2.

40. Origen, *Cels.* 6.36 (Chadwick; PG 11:352).

41. Origen elsewhere comments on the differences between the Markan and Matthean versions of the Nazareth synagogue incident but says nothing of this difference (*Comm. Matt.* 10.16). For further discussion of scholarly theories concerning Origen's curious statement, see Keith, *Jesus' Literacy*, 138–39. One theory worth mentioning here is that Origen, too, was embarrassed about the implications of "the carpenter" reading at Mark 6:3 (which he knew under this theory), wanted to deny it, and so "corrupted the text for apologetic purposes" (Haines-Eitzen, *Guardians*, 118). Although this theory would fit well with my current argument that Matthew and other Christians preferred this reading for such reasons, it is not the best explanation for Origen's specific usage of the Matthean reading. Elsewhere, Origen concedes that Jesus was uneducated (*Cels.* 1.29; *Comm. Matt.* 10.17) and that the apostles were uneducated as well (*Cels.* 1.62). He does not seem, therefore, to hesitate in acknowledging Jesus's lack of pedagogical qualifications. More likely is that Origen was simply interested in scoring points on Celsus, and thus pointed out an error on a technicality, or at least what he thought was an error because his copies of Mark had the Matthean reading.

that Matthew's slight alteration of Mark 6:3 (which Origen definitely knew)[42] enables. And from Mark 6:3's reception-history, it is clear that other Christians were interested in using that reading instead of the Markan reading. In this light, Origen's Greek is significant. He uses what scholars call the "intensive *autos*" in order to say precisely that the text does not identify Jesus *himself* as a carpenter; the implication being that it identifies Joseph as a carpenter. Origen's apologetic response bursts through the crack of daylight that Matthew's alteration provides, thereby showing that this alteration could defuse the charge that Jesus was unqualified to be a teacher *if that charge was based on his identity as a carpenter*, which it was for Celsus.

Therefore, Mark 6:3's reception-history reveals a consistent pattern. The text is not always altered. When it is altered, though, scribes consistently alter it away from directly identifying Jesus as a carpenter. The reception-history also indicates why this might prove advantageous to those Christians who identify Jesus as their teacher. Matthew does not entirely remove Jesus's association with the manual-labor class, since he acknowledges that he is the son of the carpenter. As Origen's response to Celsus indicates, though, even minimal distancing of Jesus from direct identification as a carpenter could be useful to those wanting to defend him as a teacher. And when it comes to early Christians who wanted to defend Jesus as a teacher, Matthew is perhaps without peer.

Jesus, Teaching, and Scribal Authority in Matthew's Gospel

In addition to cohering with Mark 6:3's reception-history, the theory that Matthew sought to distance Jesus from direct identification as a carpenter in order to affirm his status as a teacher coheres strongly with Matthew's broader portrayal of Jesus's relationship to scribal authority in his Gospel. Indeed, the alteration of "the carpenter" to "the carpenter's son" displays in nuce Matthew's image of Jesus as a teacher who resides outside scribal-literate circles but is nevertheless a serious pedagogical authority in his own right.

Similar to Mark, Matthew agrees with the Nazareth synagogue audience's estimation that Jesus does not hold the scribal-literate pedigree to function as a synagogue teacher. This conviction is perhaps clearest in Matt. 7:29's verbatim repetition of the narratorial assessment (from Mark 1:22) that Jesus's teaching was "not as their scribes."[43] The crowd whose astonishment the narrator interprets with this comment is the audience of the Sermon on the Mount

---

42. Origen, *Comm. Matt.* 10.17.
43. Matthew adds only the pronoun "their" (*autōn*).

in Matthew's Gospel, rather than the Capernaum synagogue as in Mark's Gospel. The important point, however, is that Matthew too describes Jesus's teaching in contrast to that of scribal-literate authorities. Furthermore, and as already noted, despite his earlier successes in synagogues in Galilee, Jesus never again appears in a synagogue in Matthew's Gospel after being rejected in Nazareth. Matthew therefore repeats Mark's portrayal of Jesus as someone who experienced mixed receptions as a synagogue teacher. Matthew's contrast of Jesus with scribes in 7:29 coheres with this assessment, as does his contentment to leave Jesus associated with the manual-labor class as "the carpenter's son" in 13:55.

Yet, compared to Mark, Matthew displays a considerably heightened desire to portray Jesus as a teaching authority in his own right—not a scribal-literate authority, but the scribes' serious pedagogical rival. As one example, Matthew includes a long block of Jesus's teaching at 5:1–7:29 that Mark either did not know or chose to omit. Typically referred to as the Sermon on the Mount, this text portrays Jesus as an authoritative Jewish teacher. By placing him on the mountain while giving new instructions to his audience (Matt. 5:1; 8:1), Matthew describes Jesus in terms of Moses, who brought the law to Israel from the mountain (Exod. 19–34).[44] Matthew is likely going further, though, portraying Jesus as a teacher superior to Moses and paralleling him with God the lawgiver. Only God gave the law on the mountain; Moses received the law on the mountain.[45] Within the sermon, Jesus asserts his authority over, ability to add to, and fulfillment of Moses and the Mosaic law (Matt. 5:17–48). Matthew here presents Jesus as, if not a rabbi, at least a rabbinic-style teacher who comments on the Hebrew Scriptures. He "conceives of the Sermon on the Mount itself as a sort of summing up, as Jesus' take on the law and the prophets."[46]

A second example of Matthew's enhanced portrayal of Jesus as a teacher is Jesus's prolonged attack on scribal authority in Matt. 23. Jesus debates with scribal authorities in each of the canonical Gospels, but Matt. 23 is distinct in both its presentation and intensity. In rapid-fire succession with no interruption, Jesus criticizes where scribes and Pharisees sit in the synagogue (23:2), their failure to practice what they preach (23:3), their oppression of others and laziness (23:4), and their disingenuous acts of piety that are intended for public notice (23:5)—and that is just in the first five verses of

---

44. See further Dale C. Allison Jr., *The New Moses: A Matthean Typology* (Edinburgh: T&T Clark, 1993).

45. Chris Keith, "Jesus outside and inside the New Testament," in *Jesus among Friends and Enemies*, 22–23.

46. Allison, *Studies*, 210.

the chapter! Throughout the rest of the chapter, Jesus consistently criticizes them as hypocrites (23:13, 15, 23, 25, 27, 29), refers to them as blind guides whose converts are children of hell (23:15–16), and ultimately lays at their feet responsibility for every murder of a righteous person in the entire Hebrew Bible/Old Testament (23:35–36).

Jesus's criticisms of scribal authority in Matt. 23 are not solely designed to denigrate scribes and Pharisees, however. They also highlight scribes and Pharisees' inadequacy *compared to Jesus* as a teacher and thus are designed equally to bolster Jesus's pedagogical identity and express his superiority. This observation brings us to the third—and most explicit—example of Matthew's comparatively stronger image of Jesus the teacher, which also comes from Matt. 23. Following that chapter's opening lines, Jesus further chastises scribal authorities for loving "to have people call them rabbi" (23:7). Jesus then instructs his disciples that, for this reason, they are not to be called "rabbi" and explains why: "But you are not to be called rabbi, for you have one teacher [*didaskalos*], and you are all students. And call no one your father on earth, for you have one Father—the one in heaven. Nor are you to be called instructors, for you have one instructor, the Messiah" (Matt. 23:8–10). No other Gospel author includes this statement concerning Jesus as the "one teacher," which highlights its significance for Matthew in particular. As Byrskog notes, "Jesus' statement 'for one is your teacher' in 23:8 carries a significance which goes far beyond its immediate context. The notion is an important feature in Matthew's whole narrative and an index to realities—conceptions and practices—in his community."[47]

In affirmation of Byrskog's assessment, one may recall from chapter 1 above that, in Matthew's Gospel, no one else is, in fact, referred to as "teacher" (*didaskalos*). Matthew reserves this title exclusively for Jesus. Later, Christians in the second and third centuries would also assert that Jesus is the one and only teacher for Christians.[48] This Christian claim begins here with Matthew, though. Along with the Sermon on the Mount and Jesus's denigration of scribal-literate authorities, the assertion that Jesus is the only teacher reveals clearly Matthew's comparatively more robust portrayal of Jesus as a pedagogical authority of his own—in contrast to, superior to, yet clearly in competition with scribal authority.

---

47. Samuel Byrskog, *Jesus the Only Teacher: Didactic Authority and Transmission in Ancient Israel, Ancient Judaism and the Matthean Community*, ConBNT 24 (Stockholm: Almqvist & Wiksell, 1994), 399.

48. Ignatius, *Eph.* 15.1; *Magn.* 9.1; Clement of Alexandria, *Strom.* 1.12.3; 5.98.1; 6.58.1–2. See also Clement's *Christ the Educator*.

Summary of Matthew's Presentation of Jesus as the Rejected Synagogue Teacher

Why Matthew was concerned to portray Jesus as a stronger pedagogical authority than Mark is a matter of debate. Some scholars have argued that Matthew himself was a converted rabbi.[49] If this is correct, or even close to correct, then perhaps Matthew's literary brushstrokes moved Jesus slightly closer to Matthew himself.[50] This notion would make sense of why Matthew, although stopping short of making Jesus a scribal-literate authority, portrays him as more like them than does Mark. Regardless of why Matthew pursues this authorial strategy, Matthew's softening of Jesus's direct association with the manual-labor class coheres with it.

Jesus, Son of Joseph and Synagogue Reader in Luke 4:16–30

If Matthew approached Mark 6:3's identification of Jesus as "the carpenter" with hesitation, Luke approached it with outright rejection. Similar to Mark's and Matthew's version of the Nazareth synagogue incident, Luke's version portrays Jesus as a synagogue teacher whose hometown rejects him, resulting in his statement about a prophet receiving no honor in his hometown (Luke 4:24). Unlike in Mark's Gospel and Matthew's Gospel, however, Jesus's rejection in the Lukan version has nothing to do with his manual-labor status. In fact, in Luke's Gospel, Jesus is not a member of the manual-labor class but rather a legitimate scribal-literate authority.[51] At least five differences between Luke and Mark demonstrate that Luke's changes are not "extremely slight"[52] but rather purposeful and result in moving Jesus from the manual-labor class to the scribal-literate class.

---

49. Ernst von Dobschütz, "Matthew as Rabbi and Catechist," trans. Robert Morgan in *The Interpretation of Matthew*, ed. Graham Stanton, 2nd ed., SNTI (Edinburgh: T&T Clark, 1995), 27–38; repr. from *ZNW* 27 (1928): 338–48: "Our first evangelist is plainly a Jewish Christian who has undergone rabbinic schooling. He is a converted Jewish rabbi" (32). He speculates that Matthew was a pupil of Rabbi Jochanan ben Zakkai (28, 33).

50. Allison, *Studies*, 210, rightly observes that we cannot know Matthew's rabbinical status, but that Matthew's "stylistic proclivities do put him closer to the rabbis than to any other group." Consider also Steve Moyise, *Jesus and Scripture* (London: SPCK, 2010), 57: "It is easily demonstrated that Matthew wishes to portray Jesus as an exegete of Scripture (like himself)."

51. The rest of this section is modified from Keith, *Jesus' Literacy*, 142–45 (used with permission of T&T Clark).

52. Lane, *Gospel according to Mark*, 201n2.

The first and perhaps most readily obvious difference is that the accusation that Jesus or his father is a carpenter disappears in Luke's account.[53] Luke's audience identifies Jesus simply as "Joseph's son" (Luke 4:22; cf. John 6:42).

"Is this not the carpenter?" (Mark 6:3)

"Is this not the carpenter's son?" (Matt. 13:55)

"Is this not Joseph's son?" (Luke 4:22)

Second, in addition to the difference between how the characters *within* the narratives identify Jesus, Luke's perspective as narrator differs from Mark's (and Matthew's). Like Mark 1:22//Matt. 7:29, Luke 4:32 associates Jesus's teaching abilities with his "authority" or "power" in a statement that is nearly verbatim in the Synoptic Gospels. All the authors use *ekplēssō* for the audience's astonishment and *exousia* for Jesus's power. Unlike Matthew, however, Luke fails to repeat Mark's explanation that this authority made Jesus "not as the scribes."

They were astounded [*ekplēssō*] at his teaching,
for he taught them as one having authority [*exousia*],
and not as the scribes. (Mark 1:22)

The crowds were astounded [*ekplēssō*] at his teaching,
for he taught them as one having authority [*exousia*],
and not as their scribes. (Matt. 7:28–29)

They were astounded [*ekplēssō*] at his teaching,
because he spoke with authority [*exousia*]. (Luke 4:32)

Noticeably absent in the Lukan version is the final statement that contrasts Jesus with scribes. Thus Luke's narrative of Jesus's activity in synagogues drops from Mark's accounts the crowds' identification of Jesus as a carpenter and the narrator's statement that he was unlike the scribes—rhetorical moves that corroborate one another.

53. Richard Rohrbaugh, "Legitimating Sonship—A Test of Honour: A Social-Scientific Study of Luke 4:1–30," in *Modelling Early Christianity: Social-Scientific Studies of the New Testament in Its Context*, ed. Philip F. Esler (London: Routledge, 1995), is therefore incorrect when he speaks of the Lukan Jesus as a "village carpenter" (189) and Joseph as "a lowly village artisan" (194). These identifications appear nowhere in Luke. It seems that Rohrbaugh has unwittingly imported the themes of the Markan and Matthean versions of the Nazareth synagogue incident into his reading of the Lukan version. Similarly, Bruce Chilton, *Rabbi Jesus: An Intimate Biography* (New York: Doubleday, 2000), 99, 101.

Third, and as important as it is neglected, Luke attributes directly to Jesus scribal-literate skills that status as a carpenter would preclude.[54] He claims that Jesus stood up "to read" in the synagogue and was handed a scroll of the prophet Isaiah. Upon receiving it, he "unrolled the scroll" (4:17), "found the place where it was written," and "rolled up the scroll" (4:20) before handing it back and beginning to preach (with Luke narrating the content of the reading between Jesus's rolling and unrolling of the scroll). Luke's attribution of scribal-literate skills to Jesus is clear. He claims that Jesus stood up "in order to read" (4:16) and portrays Jesus as familiar with manuscripts. Jesus unrolls the text, locates a particular reading—that is, identifies the beginning and ending in an un- or lightly demarcated script—and rolls the text back up.[55] As chapter 1 observed, the ability to read publicly, identifying words quickly in script, was not a skill that most Palestinian Jews of the first century CE possessed. Even some of the highly textual Qumranites did not possess these skills, as 4Q266 indicates.

Fourth, whereas the Markan and Matthean Jesus never again enters a synagogue after his rejection, the Lukan Jesus teaches in a synagogue immediately in the next pericope (Luke 4:31, 33). As was mentioned earlier, Luke describes synagogue teaching as Jesus's custom (*kata to eiōthos autō*) (4:16), whereas Mark claimed Jesus's custom was to teach crowds as they gathered around him (Mark 10:1). Luke's Jesus is, therefore, not a synagogue teacher who is unlike the scribes and whose hometown exposes him as an imposter to the position. He belongs in the position of a teacher in synagogues on the Sabbath and regularly occupies that position before and after his visit to Nazareth (Luke 4:15, 16–30, 31–37, 44; 6:6; 13:10).

Fifth, consistent with the aforementioned changes, Luke also alters the reasons for Jesus's rejection in his narration of the Nazareth synagogue event. Since Jesus is not a carpenter or the son of one in Luke 4, but rather a legitimate scribal-literate synagogue teacher, the audience ultimately rejects Jesus for reasons unrelated to a class distinction between Jesus and synagogue teachers.

---

54. Especially in light of this point, I confess astonishment at Casey, *Jesus*, 162, who claims that Luke 4:16–30 is simply "a longer version of Mark 6.1–6" and therefore proceeds to cite the *Lukan* Nazareth pericope as evidence "from Mark" (!) of "Jesus' detailed knowledge of the scriptures in Hebrew." He then claims that "minimalist guesses about the general rate of literacy in the Galilean countryside" are irrelevant for Jesus. Quite to the contrary, the differences between Mark and Luke reveal precisely why rates of literacy are important for understanding how the Gospel authors conceptualized Jesus as a teacher of the Scriptures.

55. Botha's argument that Luke portrays a "cultural event" or simply a public interpretation of the Scriptures—that is, does not portray Jesus as literally reading from the text—fails to account for precisely this aspect of Luke's account (Pieter F. Craffert and Pieter J. J. Botha, "Why Jesus Could Walk on the Sea but He Could Not Read or Write," *Neot* 39.1 [2005]: 30–31).

In contrast to Mark's and Matthew's accounts, Luke claims that the initial response to Jesus's teaching, which prompts their patronymic identification of him, is positive: "All spoke well of him and were amazed at the gracious words that came from his mouth. They said, 'Is not this Joseph's son?'" (4:22). The catalyst for their eventual rejection of Jesus in Luke's Gospel is Jesus's seeming preemptive attack that, despite their initial positive reception of him, anticipates rejection. After their "gracious words" (4:22), Jesus alters the tone of the situation by stating that he will not perform miracles because "no prophet is accepted in the prophet's hometown" (4:24), adding insult to injury by citing Gentiles who received Elijah's miracles (4:25–27).[56] "When they heard this, all in the synagogue were filled with rage" (4:28).

Jesus, Teaching, and Scribal Authority in Luke's Gospel

In the same manner that Mark 6:3's "the carpenter" fits with Mark's portrayal of Jesus outside the scribal-literate class and Matt. 13:55's "the carpenter's son" fits with Matthew's portrayal of Jesus as outside the scribal-literate class but nevertheless the one and only teacher, Luke 4:22's patronymic identification and omission of any reference to carpentry fit with Luke's portrayal of Jesus as a teacher who is quite firmly in the scribal-literate class. The previous discussion detailed some of the more obvious ways in which Luke portrays Jesus as a scribal-literate synagogue teacher. Here I mention three more instances that come from gospel tradition that is unique to Luke's Gospel. First, only Luke mentions that Jesus and John the Baptist are relatives (Luke 1:36, 39–41). This bit of family information is significant for the present discussion because Luke alone also tells his readers that John the Baptist's father was a priest (Luke 1:8–9). And in Luke alone John the Baptist's father demonstrates at least some literate abilities, since he writes "His name is John" on a wax tablet (Luke 1:63). It is difficult to know how much literate ability Luke considers John's father to have had based on this meager example.[57] Regardless, in Jewish tradition there is a long-standing connection between scribal literacy, teaching, and the priesthood.[58] It likely is not coincidence that the only Gospel

56. Thus, Jesus's lack of performance of miracles is due to anticipated rejection in Luke, whereas he cannot or does not perform miracles in Mark 6:6//Matt. 13:58 because of their immediate rejection. On the Elijianic typology in this passage, see John C. Poirier, "Jesus as an Elijianic Figure in Luke 4:16–30," *CBQ* 71.2 (2009): 349–63; Rafael Rodríguez, *Structuring Early Christian Memory: Jesus in Tradition, Performance and Text*, ESCO/LNTS 407 (London: T&T Clark, 2009), 162–73.

57. See further Keith, *Jesus' Literacy*, 80.

58. 2 Chron. 17:7–9; Neh. 8:1–9; Sir. 45:17; *T. Levi* 13.2//4Q213 1.1.9, 12; *Jub.* 45.15; 4Q266 14.6–8; Josephus, *Life* 1 §§1–6.

that portrays Jesus as a scribal-literate Torah teacher is also the only Gospel that connects him in familial terms to the priesthood.

Second, Luke aligns Jesus with the scribal-literate class in his account of the twelve-year-old Jesus's trip to the temple in Luke 2:41–51. After three days of searching for him, Jesus's parents find him "in the midst of the teachers [*didaskalōn*]" in the temple (2:46). Contrary to the suggestion of some scholars,[59] this location of Jesus among the teachers indicates Luke's conviction that he was their peer and not a pupil.[60] Luke further indicates that Jesus belongs in the discussion by attributing the teachers' positive reception of him to their amazement at his understanding (2:47) and his parents' negative rebuke to their lack of understanding (2:50). Therefore, whereas Mark and Matthew prepare their readers for Jesus's eventual rejection as a synagogue teacher in Nazareth by noting earlier in their narratives that he was "not like the scribes" (Mark 1:22//Matt. 7:29), Luke prepares his readers for his contradictory view of Jesus's scribal-literate status by aligning Jesus earlier in his narrative with the scribal-literate class.

Third, Luke alone narrates Jesus's postresurrection interpretation of Scripture, wherein he functions as a text-broker to the disciples. While talking with two disciples on the road to Emmaus who do not recognize him, Jesus chastises them for failing to believe the prophets (Luke 24:25–26). According to Luke, Jesus then proceeds to instruct the disciples on interpretive matters: "Then beginning with Moses and all the prophets, he interpreted to them the things about himself in all the scriptures" (24:27). After they recognize Jesus and he departs, the disciples then speak of how Jesus "was opening the scriptures" to them earlier (24:32). Subsequently, the resurrected Jesus appears to them again at the end of Luke's narrative. Once again Luke casts him as an authoritative exegete of all Jewish Scripture: "Then he said to them, 'These are my words that I spoke to you while I was still with you—that everything written about me in the law of Moses, the prophets, and the psalms must be fulfilled.' Then he opened their minds to understand the scriptures" (24:44–45). Whereas Matthew ends his Gospel with the Great Commission, Luke ends his Gospel with the Great Interpretation. This portrayal of Jesus is consistent with Luke's alignment of Jesus with the scribal-literate class. All three of these examples further indicate that Luke's omission of the reference to Jesus in association with carpentry coheres with his broader portrait of Jesus.

59. Noval Geldenhuys, *The Gospel of Luke*, NICNT (Grand Rapids: Eerdmans, 1951), 127; Marshall, *Gospel of Luke*, 127–28.

60. Correctly noted by François Bovon, *Das Evangelium nach Lukas (Lk 1,1–9,50)*, EKKNT 3.1 (Zurich: Benziger, 1989), 157; Joel B. Green, *The Gospel of Luke*, NICNT (Grand Rapids: Eerdmans, 1997), 155n10.

*Summary of Jesus the Synagogue Teacher and Reader
in Luke 4:16–30*

In summary, Luke agrees with Mark and Matthew on the following: Jesus
occupied the position of a scribal-literate teacher in his hometown synagogue;
the initial response was astonishment/amazement; this event ultimately led
to the rejection of Jesus and his statement that a prophet is not honored in
his hometown. Luke disagrees with Mark and Matthew, however, on several issues: whether Jesus was a manual laborer or scribal-literate teacher
(Luke claims the latter); whether Jesus occupied that pedagogical position
surreptitiously (Luke claims he does not, as a handler of manuscripts and
reader); whether the initial response of astonishment/amazement was positive (Luke claims it was); whether the ultimate reason for their rejection was
Jesus's class or his statements (Luke claims Jesus's statements prompted it);
and whether Jesus returned to a synagogue (Luke claims he did, and immediately). These differences between Mark 6:1–6 and Luke 4:16–30 share
a common thread by which Luke eliminates the identification of Jesus as a
member of the manual-labor class and describes him as a member of the
scribal-educated class. Already in the first century, Luke was going further
than receptions of Mark 6:3 in the first century (Matt. 13:55), third century
($\mathfrak{P}^{45}$, Origen), or even sixth century (Palestinian Syriac) in denying the ap-
plicability of "carpenter" to Jesus.

Conclusions

Portrayals of Jesus as a member of the manual-labor class and as a member
of scribal-literate culture rippled well beyond the first century CE. I have
elsewhere argued that a scribe's late second-century or third-century insertion
of the story of the adulteress (John 7:53–8:11), where Jesus demonstrates the
ability to write (John 8:6, 8) in the company of scribes (8:3), is an attempt
to resolve the Jews' questioning of Jesus's and Galileans' scribal literacy in
John 7:15–52.[61] Additionally, Origen in the third century will acknowledge
that Jesus was uneducated, whereas sarcophagus carvings of Gospel scenes
in the fourth century portray Jesus holding a scroll.[62]

This chapter has demonstrated, however, that whether Jesus was a teacher
who held scribal literacy was already a debated topic at the earliest stages of

61. Keith, *Pericope*, 119–260.
62. Origen, *Cels.* 1.29. For examples of sarcophagi carvings, see figures 4.1 and 4.2 in chapter 4
below. For further examples and discussion of the primary sources, see Keith, *Jesus' Literacy*,
156–63.

Christianity to which we have access. Already in the first century, Christians portrayed Jesus as someone whose audiences questioned him as a scribal-literate teacher (John 7:15), rejected him as a scribal-literate teacher (Mark 6:3//Matt. 13:55), and accepted him as a scribal-literate teacher (Luke 4 and throughout). This discussion leads to a very obvious question: Who was right?

3

Assessing
the Texts

*Authenticity, Memory,
and the Historical Jesus*

One suspects that secular historians would find New Testament scholars unduly credulous in some directions and unduly skeptical in others.[1]

The project of trying to separate authentic from inauthentic material in the Jesus tradition is fundamentally misconceived. The workings of memory and oral tradition simply do not allow such a neat separation.[2]

In the previous chapter, I detailed a disagreement over Jesus's scribal-literate status in early Christianity. Mark and Matthew portray Jesus as someone who assumed the role of a synagogue teacher despite being a member of the manual-labor class, whether as a carpenter or carpenter's son. Luke portrays Jesus as someone who legitimately took the role of a synagogue teacher since he was a member of the class of scribal-literate interpreters of the law, capable of handling manuscripts and finding passages in script. These texts constitute one of those situations where, much like the differing portrayals of the day of Jesus's death or the thieves on the crosses, the Gospels present readers with mutually exclusive historical options.[3] Jesus was either a scribal-illiterate

---

1. R. S. Barbour, *Traditio-Historical Criticism of the Gospels*, SCC 4 (London: SPCK, 1972), 27.
2. Eric Eve, *Behind the Gospels: Understanding the Oral Tradition* (London: SCM, 2013), 181.
3. The Synoptic Gospels collectively identify the day of Jesus's death as Passover day proper, with Jesus and his disciples having eaten the Passover meal the preceding evening before his arrest (Mark 14:12–31//Matt. 26:17–35//Luke 22:7–38). According to John's Gospel, Jesus was crucified on the Day of Preparation prior to Passover (19:14, 31, 42), with the meal not yet having been eaten (18:28; 19:31). With regard to the co-crucified bandits/criminals, according to Mark's and Matthew's Gospels, the two bandits both chastised him (Mark 15:27, 32//Matt. 27:38, 44). According to Luke's Gospel, one of the criminals defended Jesus against the chastisements of the other, for which he received Jesus's promise that he would enter paradise (Luke 23:32, 39–43). In John's Gospel, neither of the co-crucifieds speaks (John 19:18).

No shortage of ink has been spilled in attempts to reconcile these disagreements. These attempts often force the texts to say something other than what they seem to say on the surface. I appreciate the words of the late New Testament scholar and churchman F. F. Bruce on this topic: "The question 'how does that square with inspiration' is perhaps asked most insistently when one part of Scripture seems to conflict in sense with another. I suppose much

teacher who did not belong in the position of a teacher in a synagogue or a scribal-literate teacher who did belong in the position of a teacher in a synagogue. He cannot have been both. Our first-century Gospel evidence thus prompts the question "Who was right?"

The next chapter will argue that Mark was right—Jesus most likely was not a scribal-literate teacher. That conclusion, in and of itself, is not new, as we will see. What is new, however, is my further argument that Mark's *and* Luke's images of Jesus were anchored in Jesus's life. I will arrive at this conclusion via a historical method that has come to be known as the "memory approach" since its goal is to account for how early Christians came to remember Jesus in the various ways they did. The memory approach leads a significant recent trend in Jesus studies that consists of scholars abandoning the century-old "criteria approach" to the historical Jesus. These issues directly affect how one postulates the actual past of the historical Jesus, and thus my solution to the issue of Jesus's scribal-literate status in chapter 4. A short overview of the current state of historical Jesus studies is thus necessary before returning to Jesus's scribal-literate status.

A Brief Introduction to Historical Jesus Studies

The subfield of New Testament scholarship dedicated to assessing the historical claims of the Gospels (and other sources for Jesus's life) is known as historical Jesus studies. Its object of pursuit is the "historical Jesus," a phrase that means different things for different scholars. For some scholars, "historical Jesus" refers to the man Jesus as he "really was." In this stream of historical Jesus research, there is an explicit or implicit attempt to reconstruct "what really happened" over and against the claims of the Gospels. Scholarly proposals for the historical Jesus have been diverse and even contradictory, though. In light of this lack of consensus, other scholars use "historical Jesus" to refer

---

depends on the cast of one's mind, but I have never been greatly concerned to harmonize them. My faith can accommodate such 'discrepancies' much more easily than it could swallow harmonizations that place an unnatural sense on the text or give an impression of special pleading" (*In Retrospect: Remembrance of Things Past* [Glasgow: Pickering & Inglis, 1980], 311–12). More important for present purposes, instances like these in the Gospels give scholars opportunities to speculate about the past because one can theorize what nexus of historical reality and commemoration could have produced both interpretations (similarly, Le Donne, *Historiographical*, 13). In this light, if the texts said the same thing, our historical inquiry would be hindered; the narrative of our representations of the past would be the poorer for the congruity. Differing images of Jesus in the Gospels enhance our capacity to ask historical questions and should thus be embraced as opportunities for those who care about the Jesus of history to approach his past.

to scholarly reconstructions of Jesus, which can necessarily only ever be approximations of Jesus as he "really was."[4] Postmodern historiography further buttresses this perspective with its focus on the inherently subjective nature of both the sources and writing of history.[5] It has shown conclusively the erroneous nature of historical positivism, which assumes that we can attain an objective reconstruction of the past. In the most recent developments of this stream of historical Jesus research, the attempt is not to *reconstruct* the past over against the Gospels, but to *represent* the past in light of the Gospels.[6] This may seem like an insignificant shift of focus. It is not. This shift redefines not only the historian's task as it relates to the historical Jesus but also the role of the Gospels as historical sources in that task. I will return to this matter shortly, as the present study falls into this most recent stream of historical Jesus research. First, however, it will be useful to consider why scholars quest after the historical Jesus in the first place.

To a great extent, the modern quest for the historical Jesus is a product of the Enlightenment's antisupernaturalism. As scholars became skeptical of the historical veracity of the Gospels' accounts of supernatural events, they inevitably asked what, after all, *did* happen. They thus offered theories,

---

4. A third stream of Jesus research concerns the "real Jesus." Luke Timothy Johnson coined this term in response to the historical Jesus of the Jesus Seminar, a minority (but vocal) group of skeptical Jesus scholars in the 1980s and 1990s (*The Real Jesus: The Misguided Quest of the Historical Jesus and the Truth of the Traditional Gospels* [San Francisco: HarperSanFrancisco, 1996], 142). The "real Jesus" refers to the Jesus whom Christians affirm as a historical figure but whose significance and identity transcend history—"not a figure of the past but of the present, not an object of scholarly research but the subject of obedient faith" (Luke Timothy Johnson, "Learning the Human Jesus: Historical Criticism and Literary Criticism," in *The Historical Jesus: Five Views*, ed. James K. Beilby and Paul Rhodes Eddy [Downers Grove, IL: IVP Academic, 2009], 155). In this sense, some scholars insist that the "historical Jesus" can never equate to the "real Jesus."

5. See especially Anthony Le Donne, *Historical Jesus: What Can We Know and How Can We Know It?* (Grand Rapids: Eerdmans, 2011).

6. Jens Schröter, "Von der Historizität der Evangelien: Ein Beitrag zur gegenwärtigen Diskussion um den historischen Jesus," in *Der historische Jesus: Tendenzen und Perspektiven der gegenwärtigen Forschung*, ed. Jens Schröter and Ralph Brucker, BZNW 114 (Berlin: de Gruyter, 2002), 205; repr. in his *Von Jesus zum Neuen Testament: Studien zur urchristlichen Theologiegeschichte und zur Entstehung des neutestamentlichen Kanons*, WUNT 204 (Tübingen: Mohr Siebeck, 2007), 105–46. On the methodological issues, see further Chris Keith, "Memory and Authenticity: Jesus Tradition and What Really Happened," *ZNW* 102.2 (2011): 155–77, expanded in *Jesus' Literacy*, 27–70; "Indebtedness of the Criteria Approach to Form Criticism and Recent Attempts to Rehabilitate the Search for an Authentic Jesus," in *Jesus, Criteria, and the Demise of Authenticity*, ed. Chris Keith and Anthony Le Donne (London: T&T Clark, 2012), 25–48. According to this perspective, then, "Historical portrayals of Jesus . . . are also hypotheses about how things could have been" (Jens Schröter, "Jesus of Galilee: The Role of Location in Understanding Jesus," in *Jesus Research: An International Perspective*, ed. James H. Charlesworth and Petr Pokorný [Grand Rapids: Eerdmans, 2009], 38; emphasis removed).

such as Paulus's ideas that Jesus did not really walk on the water or rise from the grave; rather, he walked along the seashore, and he merely slipped into a coma only to resuscitate later.[7] Their assumptions about the naïveté of the prescientific ancient worldview loomed large in their efforts to get behind the Gospels.[8]

Antisupernaturalism is not the only catalyst for historical Jesus work, however. Those of a more confessional stripe might say that the Christian doctrine of the incarnation, the conviction that God revealed himself in the form of the human being Jesus of Nazareth in a particular place and time in world history, not only supports but outright requires asking questions about Jesus the man in history.[9] From this perspective, historical Jesus research is simply an effort to take this doctrine seriously. For such scholars, the Gospels as historical sources aid in attempts to ask and answer such questions, even if they do not provide objective access to the past. Of course, there remain those who would insist that the Gospels are direct reflections of the past, if not in the realm of published scholarship at least in the realm of real life. I have had several of them, including former colleagues, knock on my office door and shout this claim in my general direction. But this position is untenable on the Gospels' own accounts and amounts to failure to take the Gospels seriously. This brings us to the next catalyst for historical Jesus work.

More strongly related to the current topic, sometimes the Gospel texts themselves raise the questions. Jesus did not both have and not have scribal literacy just like he did not die on two different days. In these cases, asking which text most likely reflects the actual past is a natural outworking of careful exegesis. Careful exegesis also reveals that the Gospel authors are, at times, explicit about the facts that (1) what those around Jesus thought about him during his life was different from what they later came to believe about him and (2) the Gospels are written from the later perspective. John 2:22 states that the disciples did not understand that Jesus's claims about the destruction

7. See discussion in Albert Schweitzer, *The Quest of the Historical Jesus: A Critical Study of Its Progress from Reimarus to Wrede*, trans. F. C. Burkitt (Baltimore: Johns Hopkins University Press, 1968), 52–53. Schweitzer sums up Paulus: "He had an unconquerable distrust of anything that went outside the boundaries of logical thought" (48).

8. In a later period, Rudolf Bultmann, "New Testament and Mythology," in *Kerygma and Myth*, ed. Hans Werner Bartsch, trans. Reginald H. Fuller, rev. ed. (New York: Harper Torchbooks, 1961), 5, would reflect this sentiment: "It is impossible to use electric light and the wireless and to avail ourselves of modern medical and surgical discoveries, and at the same time to believe in the New Testament world of spirits and miracles."

9. C. Stephen Evans, *The Historical Christ and the Jesus of Faith: The Incarnational Narrative as History* (New York: Oxford University Press, 1996).

and rebuilding of the temple referred to his death and resurrection until after those events. John 12:16 says they did not understand Jesus's procession into Jerusalem until later.[10] According to Mark 8:27–33//Matt. 16:13–23, Peter did not understand Jesus's identity as "Christ" during his ministry. Mark 3:21 claims that at one point Jesus's family thought he was crazy. In these texts, the authors point to a distinction between the lived experience of Jesus and a fuller understanding of his identity and significance that they acquired only later. In doing so, they also give the lie to the notion that the Gospels are historiographically unsophisticated.

Therefore, there are many impetuses for historical Jesus work, just as there are scholars of many differing perspectives, with differing motives, involved in the discussion.[11] Although this topic is interesting in its own right, I will not prolong this general introduction to historical Jesus studies any further. Instead, one matter in particular requires substantial attention because of the debate it has generated in the last ten or fifteen years: the criteria of authenticity. The debate over criteria of authenticity has been a microcosm of the larger shifts in Jesus scholarship that I mentioned earlier.

The Criteria Approach to the Historical Jesus

For roughly one hundred years, the predominant way that scholars have determined whether any given event or saying from the Gospels went back to the historical Jesus was through criteria of authenticity.[12] These criteria come in a variety of shapes and sizes, but all function like filters through which one pours the gospel tradition. The traditions that emerge separated from the rest are considered "authentic," that is, historically reliable, and therefore are christened for usage in reconstructions of the historical Jesus. A particularly

10. Ian H. Henderson, "Memory, Text and Performance in Early Christian Formation," in *Religion und Bildung: Medien und Funktionen religiösen Wissens in der Kaiserzeit*, ed. Christa Frateantonio and Helmut Krasser, PAWB 30 (Stuttgart: Franz Steiner, 2010), 167, describes John's Gospel as "shockingly self-conscious" in this regard. Further on this topic, see Larry W. Hurtado, "Remembering and Revelation: The Historic and Glorified Jesus in the Gospel of John," in *Israel's God and Rebecca's Children: Christology and Community in Early Judaism and Christianity*, ed. David B. Capes et al. (Waco: Baylor University Press, 2007), 195–226.

11. For a succinct introduction, see the various views in Beilby and Eddy, *Historical Jesus*, especially the contributions of Robert M. Price, "Jesus at the Vanishing Point," 55–83, and Darrell L. Bock, "The Historical Jesus: An Evangelical View," 249–81.

12. As demonstrated by Anthony Le Donne ("The Rise of the Quest for an Authentic Jesus: An Introduction to the Crumbling Foundations of Jesus Research," in *Jesus*, 3–17) and Dagmar Winter ("Saving the Quest for Authenticity from the Criterion of Dissimilarity: History and Plausibility," in *Jesus*, 115–24), aspects of the criteria of authenticity stretch back even further than one hundred years.

popular criterion of authenticity has been the criterion of dissimilarity.[13] It states that anything in the Gospels that is dissimilar from Second Temple Judaism on the one hand and dissimilar from early Christianity on the other hand is likely authentic to the historical Jesus. In other words, if it did not come from before Jesus (Judaism) or after Jesus (the church), it must have come from Jesus. The logic of "dissimilarity" functions as the filter. Another popular criterion is the criterion of multiple attestation. It states that the more independent sources there are for a given tradition, the more likely it is to be authentic to the historical Jesus. In this case, "multiple independent witnesses" serves as a filter. Once a given criterion has been applied, the body of separated gospel traditions should enable a scholar to reconstruct a coherent image of the historical Jesus. So goes the thinking.

Form-Critical Roots

Although certain aspects of the criteria approach's internal logic go back to well before the nineteenth century, the criteria approach as a formal methodology is a direct outgrowth of the twentieth century. More specifically, it is an outgrowth of form criticism, the dominant methodology in New Testament criticism at that time (especially in Germany).[14] Form critics attempted to recover the early oral tradition behind the written Gospels. They believed that later Christians had—like a potter who molds raw materials into an artistic finished product—reshaped the oral tradition in processes that culminated with the written Gospel narratives. The shape of this finished product occurred in the hands of later Hellenistic Christians. The raw materials they used in the process came from an earlier Palestinian strand of Christianity, which was responsible for the oral tradition. The divide between early oral tradition and later written tradition thus paralleled the divide between early Palestinian Christianity and later Hellenistic Christianity.[15] Although the form critics were interested in the early tradition, the first order of business in recovering it became identifying the work of the

13. Ernst Käsemann, "The Problem of the Historical Jesus," in *Essays on New Testament Themes*, trans. W. J. Montague, SBT 41 (London: SCM, 1964), 37, famously regarded the criterion of dissimilarity as the "one case . . . [where] we have more or less safe ground under our feet."

14. Keith, "Memory," 155–77; repr. in *Jesus' Literacy*, 27–70; idem, "Indebtedness," 30–37; Jens Schröter, "The Criteria of Authenticity in Jesus Research and Historiographical Method," in *Jesus*, 50.

15. The form critics believed earliest (Palestinian) Christianity was simply too illiterate to be capable of producing the Gospels as literary works (esp. Martin Dibelius, *From Tradition to Gospel*, trans. Bertram Lee Woolf, SL 124 [New York: Charles Scribner's Sons, 1934], 5, 9, 37, 39, 61, 234).

later Christians.[16] In this sense, in practice adherents of form criticism were as interested in the work of the later Christians reshaping the tradition as they were in the work of the earlier Christians with the oral tradition.

The form critics remained interested in recovering the earlier oral tradition, however, and believed that, unlike a potter's work, they could strain the raw materials (oral tradition) from the finished product (written Gospels). Their path to the earlier oral state of the tradition began with stripping away the tradition of the interpretation of later Hellenistic authors. Theoretically, then, removing isolated traditions from the narrative frameworks of the written Gospels would leave disparate pieces of the oral tradition. Having "ripped [those traditions] from their context"[17] and thus stripped them of later Christian theology, the form critics then used them to reconstruct the oral tradition according to their hypotheses about how the oral tradition was transmitted. They would group together accounts of Jesus with similarities and forward theories about how those groups were transmitted together. Particularly prominent "forms" in this theory were parables, controversy stories, miracle stories, pronouncement stories, and so on. The two principal form critics, Martin Dibelius and Rudolf Bultmann, even structured the chapters of their books according to these forms.[18]

For readers who lack familiarity with form criticism or advanced theological studies, the previous paragraph may have just read like utter gibberish. Here is what you really need to know: As *the* dominant method in New Testament scholarship at the time, form criticism was obsessed with reconstructing something "behind" the written Gospels. That something was the oral tradition, which had started as pristine in the early church but through constant preaching in different circumstances had, like a snowball going downhill, rolled along through the years and picked up layers of ecclesiastical theology. The end product of this process was the written Gospels, which enshrined both the pristine oral tradition and the later theology in which it was now embedded. Form critics wanted to get past, through, or around that later theology and to the earlier state of the tradition. They thus reconstructed the oral tradition by first and foremost trying to eliminate from the Jesus tradition the influence of the Gospel authors. This is the crucially important point. For the form critics,

16. Rudolf Bultmann, *The History of the Synoptic Tradition*, trans. John Marsh, rev. ed. (Oxford: Basil Blackwell, 1972 [1963]), 11: "I do not think it is possible to have a scientific discussion as to whether the stories about Jesus or the tradition of his sayings first attained a fixed form. The needs of the Church giving rise to both traditions would have made themselves felt at the same time. In any case, the important and compassable problem is to get to those needs."

17. Eve, *Behind*, 28.

18. Dibelius, *From Tradition*; Bultmann, *History*.

the path to the past behind the text began with isolating individual units of the Gospels from the interpretive narratives of the Gospels.[19]

At its core, therefore, form criticism believed the written Jesus tradition in the Gospels was essentially bifurcated—some arose from the past behind the texts and could be recovered; some arose from the present circumstances of the Gospel authors and had to be bypassed. Implicit is the important assumption that scholars can identify which traditions belong in which pile and separate them accordingly. Needless to say, this casting of the New Testament critic as a scientist in pursuit of objective historical data, with both the historian-turned-scientist and the resultant data theoretically detached from the hindrance of theological commitments, reflects the historical positivism of the modern era. This point is crucial for why Jesus studies not only did change in light of postmodern historiography but had to change.

From Form Criticism to the Criteria Approach

As part of his form-critical methodology, Bultmann advocated a version of (what would soon become) the criterion of dissimilarity in his *History of the Synoptic Tradition*, first published in German in 1921.[20] Bultmann's student Ernst Käsemann went further and put form-critical principles to service in search of the historical figure of Jesus, thereby substituting the historical Jesus for the oral tradition as the past reality behind the text that scholars were attempting to reconstruct.[21] He formally inaugurated the criteria approach to the historical Jesus in a famous 1953 lecture when he said, "With the work of the Form-Critics as a basis, our questioning has sharpened and widened until the obligation now laid upon us is to investigate and make credible not the possible unauthenticity of the individual unit of material but, on the contrary, its genuineness."[22] Käsemann proposed that scholars should turn their attention to the possibly authentic pile now instead of focusing upon the inauthentic pile that arose from later Christians. Significantly, though, the means for getting "behind" the text remained unchanged—separation of the gospel tradition from early Christian theological interpretation. His comment "with the work of the Form-Critics as a basis" indicates that form criticism still serves the role of rendering inauthentic any tradition that is attributable to the early church,

19. For the emphasis on "individual units of the tradition" in form criticism, see Bultmann, *History*, 3–4.

20. Ibid., 205.

21. Käsemann, "Problem," 37. On the substitution of the historical Jesus for the oral tradition, see further Keith, "Memory," 163–65; repr. in *Jesus' Literacy*, 38–40; idem, "Indebtedness," 34–35.

22. Käsemann, "Problem," 34.

as does his further explanation about how the search for authentic tradition assumes the conclusions of form criticism and then moves beyond them:

> It is Form Criticism which has rendered us the best service here. But even Form Criticism leaves us in the lurch when we come to ask what are the formal characteristics of the authentic Jesus material. It cannot be otherwise, for Form Criticism is concerned with the *Sitz-im-Leben* [life-situation] of narrative forms and not with what we may call historical individuality. The only help it can give us here is that it can eliminate as unauthentic anything which must be ruled out of court because of its *Sitz-im-Leben*.[23]

Similarly remaining from form criticism is the focus upon the "individual unit of material" detached from the interpretative frameworks of the Gospel authors. With this foundation in place, scholars in search of the authentic Jesus eventually developed other criteria to isolate traditions from the narrative and test their authenticity.[24] We now have the criterion of coherence, criterion of Semitic influence, criterion of embarrassment, criterion of multiple attestation, and others.[25] Each works with different foci, but all operate under the general method of using a criterion to "authenticate" particular sayings or actions of Jesus. The criteria approach therefore also remains firmly entrenched in form criticism's historical-positivist program of attaining objective historical data detached from interpretation/theology.

The Criteria Approach's Survival beyond Form Criticism

New Testament scholarship eventually abandoned the form criticism of Bultmann and others.[26] But the criteria approach managed to outlive its parent,

---

23. Ibid.

24. Reginald H. Fuller, "The Criterion of Dissimilarity: The Wrong Tool?" in *Christological Perspectives: Essays in Honor of Harvey K. McArthur*, ed. Robert F. Berkey and Sarah A. Edwards (New York: Pilgrim, 1982), 42; Norman Perrin, *Rediscovering the Teachings of Jesus* (New York: Harper & Row, 1967), 39; *What Is Redaction Criticism?*, GBS (Philadelphia: Fortress, 1969), 71.

25. Dennis Polkow, "Method and Criteria for Historical Jesus Research," in *Society of Biblical Literature 1987 Seminar Papers*, ed. Kent Harold Richards, SBLSP 26 (Atlanta: Scholars Press, 1987), 338, counted twenty-five criteria in 1987. In 2000, Stanley E. Porter, *The Criteria for Authenticity in Historical Jesus Research: Previous Discussion and New Proposals*, JSNTSup 191 (Sheffield: Sheffield Academic Press, 2000), 126–237, proposed three new criteria: Greek language and its context, Greek textual variance, and discourse features. In 2009, Robert L. Webb, "The Historical Enterprise and Historical Jesus Research," in *Key Events in the Life of the Historical Jesus: A Collaborative Exploration of Context and Coherence*, ed. Darrell L. Bock and Robert L. Webb (Grand Rapids: Eerdmans, 2009), 71–72, proposed another new criterion: the criterion of inherent ambiguity.

26. Christopher Tuckett, "Form Criticism," in *Jesus in Memory: Traditions in Oral and Scribal Perspectives*, ed. Werner H. Kelber and Samuel Byrskog (Waco: Baylor University Press,

surviving—indeed thriving—into the so-called Third Quest for the historical
Jesus in the 1980s–2000s, where it figured prominently in the work of scholars
as diverse as those of the Jesus Seminar and John P. Meier.[27] The criteria approach has also found affirmations in the 2010s.[28] In some cases, the criteria
approach even managed to detach itself from form criticism in the conscious-
ness of scholars.[29] This is not to suggest that there were no detractors in the
intervening period. Hooker famously objected to the criterion of dissimilarity
as a historical tool in the early 1970s.[30] Others, too, mounted objections.[31] But
these were exceptions. Most New Testament scholarship continued to employ
the criteria approach to the historical Jesus.[32]

The Demise of the Criteria Approach

Despite the criteria approach's historic roots and longevity, historical Jesus
scholarship in the last ten to fifteen years has witnessed an emphatic turn away
from it in some quarters.[33] Growing dissatisfaction with the criteria approach

2009), 37: "The various challenges and criticism which have been directed against the model of
form criticism as developed by Dibelius and Bultmann are serious. That model, in precisely that
form, is probably no longer sustainable."

27. Robert W. Funk and the Jesus Seminar, *The Acts of Jesus: The Search for the Authentic
Deeds of Jesus* (New York: HarperCollins, 1998), 24–36; Meier, *Marginal*, 1:167–95, 4:13–17,
respectively. See also Craig L. Blomberg, "The Authenticity and Significance of Jesus' Table
Fellowship with Sinners," in *Key Events*, 217–19, 243; Webb, "Historical," 60–75.

28. Warren Carter, "The Disciples," in *Jesus*, 82; Casey, *Jesus*, 108–20 (combines the criterion
of Semitic influence [Aramaic] with criterion of plausibility); Le Donne, *Historical Jesus*, 42–52,
140n5 (and *Historiographical Jesus*, 87–91, published 2009); Moyise, *Jesus*, 31–32, 37, 62, 77,
82, 93; cf. 41, 44, 47, 48, 68, 72, 78, 94, 118.

29. See examples in Keith, "Indebtedness," 27–29.

30. Morna D. Hooker, "Christology and Methodology," *NTS* 17 (1970): 480–87; idem, "In
His Own Image?," in *What about the New Testament? Essays in Honour of Christopher Evans*,
ed. Morna Hooker and Colin Hickling (London: SCM, 1975), 28–44; idem, "On Using the
Wrong Tool," *Theology* 75 (1972): 570–78.

31. Barbour, *Traditio-Historical Criticism*, esp. 25–27; Sanders, *Jesus and Judaism*, 15–18
(cf., however, 252).

32. Consider Dale C. Allison Jr., "How to Marginalize the Traditional Criteria of Authenticity," in *Handbook for the Study of the Historical Jesus*, ed. Tom Holmén and Stanley E. Porter,
4 vols. (Leiden: Brill, 2010), 1:5: "My own judgment is that Morna Hooker some time ago persuasively exposed the flaws of the criterion of dissimilarity, and it is a blight on our field that,
upon publication of her conclusions, most of us continued to call upon dissimilarity whenever
we pleased instead of letting the thing fall into its deserved oblivion." He had earlier also stated,
"The objection of Morna Hooker, first raised three decades ago, has never been successfully
answered" (*Jesus of Nazareth: Millenarian Prophet* [Minneapolis: Fortress, 1998], 5).

33. Important publications in this period include Allison, *Constructing*, x, 9–10, 153–54, 231;
idem, *The Historical Christ and the Theological Jesus* (Grand Rapids: Eerdmans, 2009), 22–23,
54–60; idem, "How to Marginalize," 3–30; idem, *Jesus of Nazareth*, 1–7; David S. du Toit, "Der
unähnliche Jesus: Eine kritische Evaluierung der Entstehung des Differenzkriteriums und seiner

reached its apex with the 2012 publication of *Jesus, Criteria, and the Demise of Authenticity*, which I and Anthony Le Donne edited. This volume's contributors reveal the wide variety of reasons why scholars are abandoning (or should abandon) this long-standing methodology in historical Jesus research.

Some scholars find particular criteria of authenticity no longer tenable. Building on her earlier work with Theissen,[34] D. Winter demonstrates that the criterion of dissimilarity's severing of Jesus from Second Temple Judaism and early Christianity "results in a historical Jesus who is not intelligible in a historical sense, devoid of human relations, context and background."[35] Further, the criterion harbors an "anti-Judaist, if not anti-Semitic, view of Jewish religion."[36] Le Donne addresses the criterion of coherence, which scholars have often coupled with the criterion of dissimilarity. He finds it salvageable to an extent, but argues in general that the criterion, in all its various applications, fails to represent the complex relationship between Jesus's public career and early Christian communities.[37] Stuckenbruck addresses the criterion of Semitic influence, which assumes that the Jesus tradition developed unidirectionally from Aramaic or Hebrew to Greek and therefore posits that traditions in the Gospels showing Semitic flavor (such as Jesus's usage of *abba* for God) are more likely to be authentic. Stuckenbruck shows that the base assumptions of this criterion crumble in the face of the realities of the linguistic environments of Jesus and the transmitters of the tradition, which were dominated by multilingualism but also multidirectional linguistic developments.[38] Equally problematic is the criterion of embarrassment. Rodríguez exposes it as a subjective tool that does not reveal traditions that were embarrassing to early Christians so much as render traditions embarrassing against the background of particular scholarly theories of early Christianity.[39] Goodacre addresses

---

geschichts- und erkenntnistheoretischen Voraussetzungen," in *Der historische Jesus*, 88–129; Eric Eve, "Meier, Miracle, and Multiple Attestation," *JSHJ* 3 (2005): 23–45; Keith, "Indebtedness," 25–48; idem, "Memory," 155–77 (expanded in *Jesus' Literacy*, 27–70); Chris Keith with Larry W. Hurtado, "Seeking the Historical Jesus among Friends and Enemies," 269–88; Rafael Rodríguez, "Authenticating Criteria: The Use and Misuse of a Critical Method," *JSHJ* 7 (2009): 152–67; Thatcher, *Jesus the Riddler*, xvii–xxiii; Gerd Theissen and Dagmar Winter, *The Quest for the Plausible Jesus: The Question of Criteria*, trans. M. Eugene Boring (Louisville: Westminster John Knox, 2002).

34. Theissen and Winter, *Quest*.

35. D. Winter, "Saving," 124.

36. Ibid.

37. Anthony Le Donne, "The Criterion of Coherence: Its Development, Inevitability, and Historiographical Limitations," in *Jesus*, 95–114.

38. Loren T. Stuckenbruck, "'Semitic Influence on Greek': An Authenticating Criterion in Jesus Research?," in *Jesus*, 73–94. Further on this point, see S.-I. Lee, *Jesus*.

39. Rafael Rodríguez, "The Embarrassing Truth about Jesus: The Criterion of Embarrassment and the Failure of Historical Authenticity," in *Jesus, Criteria, and the Demise of Authenticity*, 132–51.

the criterion of multiple attestation, a mainstay of historical Jesus studies for centuries. He shows that the attempt to identify "independent" witnesses has failed to take sufficient account of the complex relationships between the Synoptic Gospels and the *Gospel of Thomas*.[40]

In the same volume, Dale Allison, Jens Schröter, and I take a broader perspective on the issues and argue that the criteria approach as a whole represents ill-conceived historiographical method that is essentially stuck in historical positivism. The central problem along these lines is the authentic/inauthentic dichotomy that lies at the base of the criteria approach, as well as the concomitant assumptions that scholars can identify and separate the Jesus tradition along these lines. This approach to the Jesus tradition treats the Gospels as a mix of uninterpreted Jesus traditions that reflect the actual past of the historical Jesus and interpreted Jesus traditions that have grown to reflect the perspectives of the early Christians transmitting them.[41] Hooker long ago questioned this very treatment of the Jesus tradition: "It is probable that any rigid division of material into 'authentic' and 'non-authentic' distorts the picture. All the material comes to us at the hands of the believing community, and probably it all bears its mark to a lesser or greater extent."[42] Elsewhere I have argued in depth what I summarized briefly above; namely, that the criteria approach has uncritically inherited all these assumptions—(1) that the Gospels include "authentic" and "inauthentic" tradition, which scholars can (2) identify and (3) separate—directly from form criticism.[43] I build upon these arguments in my contribution to *Jesus, Criteria, and the Demise of Authenticity*, arguing further that more recent attempts to rehabilitate the criteria approach have not yet dealt with this fundamental problem.[44] Likewise, and among other points, Allison claims, "Running units through the gauntlet of the traditional criteria presupposes that there is a clear distinction between what is authentic and what is not, which is a very misleading proposition."[45] On the basis of theories of history, Jens Schröter argues similarly. He shows that the criteria approach's bifurcation of the Jesus tradition ignores that "the inextricable connection of past and present is . . . an important characteristic of the Jesus

40. Mark Goodacre, "Criticizing the Criterion of Multiple Attestation: The Historical Jesus and the Question of Sources," in *Jesus*, 152–69.

41. Consider Udo Schnelle, *Theology of the New Testament*, trans. M. Eugene Boring (Grand Rapids: Baker Academic, 2009), 68, who presents the criteria of authenticity as capable of "filter[ing] out historically authentic sayings of Jesus from the broad stream of tradition, separating them from later interpretations and contemporizing accretions."

42. Hooker, "Christology," 486. More recently, Eve, *Behind*, 181–83.

43. Keith, "Memory," 155–77; idem, *Jesus' Literacy*, 27–70.

44. Keith, "Indebtedness," 25–40.

45. Dale C. Allison Jr., "It Don't Come Easy: A History of Disillusionment," in *Jesus*, 196.

stories of the Gospels,"[46] not an obstacle for scholars to overcome. Although some recent scholars have continued to defend the criteria approach,[47] for these reasons and others I consider it irreparably broken and invalid as a historical method. The issue for the scholarly agenda now is to define a post-criteria quest for the historical Jesus.

The Memory Approach and the Return to the Text

No formal method has replaced the criteria approach. Recent post-criteria Jesus research has, however, exhibited a shared set of assumptions that I and others have referred to as the "Jesus-memory approach" or simply "memory approach" in light of the prominent role of social memory theory.[48] The quotation of Schröter above indicates one of the central features of this emerging Jesus research—taking seriously the connection of the past and the present. Of the criteria approach's many deficiencies, its severing of the past and the present is perhaps its most historiographically irresponsible feature. By separating the tradition into authentic tradition from the historical Jesus and inauthentic tradition from early Christians, the criteria approach assumes that there are Jesus traditions in the Gospels that one can strip of interpretation and reduce to raw historicity, something like an objective reflection of the actual past.

The precise problem with this assumption is that no aspect of past reality survives into the present in an uninterpreted form. The past, when it survives at all, survives only in the interpretations that render it memorable to those who recall it. Hermeneutical refashioning of words, actions, and events occurs right from the very beginning, from the point in time at which a person or group of people perceives those words, actions, and events. Far from being a detriment to the modern historian, then, the interpretations of the remembering person or community are the past's only means of survival, the only means by which the historian even has something with which to work. If, therefore, "authentic" tradition refers to tradition detached from interpretation—and

---

46. Schröter, "Criteria," 68.
47. Gerd Häfner, "Das Ende der Kriterien? Jesusforschung angesichts der geschichtstheoretischen Diskussion," in Knut Backhaus and Gerd Häfner, *Historiographie und fiktionales Erzählen: Zur Konstruktivität in Geschichtstheorie und Exegese*, BThSt 86 (Neukirchen-Vluyn: Neukirchener Verlag, 2007), 97–130. Consider also Puig i Tàrrech, *Jesus*, 58: "A criterion . . . is not infallible but neither is it superfluous."
48. Keith, "Memory," 165–77; repr. in *Jesus' Literacy*, 50–70; Schröter, "Criteria," 50–51. For a succinct introduction to social memory theory, see Alan Kirk, "Social and Cultural Memory," in *Memory, Tradition and Text: Uses of the Past in Early Christianity*, ed. Alan Kirk and Tom Thatcher, SemeiaSt 52 (Atlanta: Society of Biblical Literature, 2005), 1–24.

in the criteria approach, it does—then this is particularly problematic. No such tradition exists or ever did exist. The recent onslaught of applications of social memory theory in New Testament and Gospels studies, to which I have contributed, has therefore exposed this outdated approach to tradition that the criteria approach inherited from form criticism.[49] Any serious modern scholarly approach to the Gospels as historical sources must recognize the (in the words of Schröter) "inexplicable connection of past and present" in the Gospels that makes modern scholarly assessment of them possible and renders that assessment, as re-presentation of the past, part of that ever-evolving process.[50] The historian's task in this sense is not *reconstruction* of the past with leftover parts but *representation* of the past, an informed hypothesis about what it could have looked like in light of the sources that remain from it and what we can know about the historical contexts in which those sources took the shapes they did.

I must strongly underscore an important related point. Taking the connection between the past and the present in the Gospels seriously does not mean approaching the Gospels uncritically.[51] The "past" in this sense refers to the inertia of previous interpretation, of which the actual past is one of any number of possible contributors. Thus, affirming that all portrayals of the past are related to the actual past in one form or another does not determine at the outset *how* they are related. It may be the case that some portrayals of the past are fabrications, and it is the historian's job to make these decisions.

49. This is not to claim that all scholars applying social memory theory to the Gospels agree with my particular argument that the criteria are an outgrowth of form criticism. For a fuller bibliography of applications of social memory theory to New Testament studies, see Keith, "Memory," 166n46; repr. in *Jesus' Literacy*, 52n109. Specifically related to the untenable dichotomy of authentic/inauthentic, and inter alia, see Allison, *Constructing*, 1–30; du Toit, "Unähnliche," 118–22; Eve, *Behind*, n.p.; Keith, "Claim," 55–57; idem, "Indebtedness," 38–40; idem, "Memory," 170–73; repr. in *Jesus' Literacy*, 61–65; Alan Kirk, "Memory Theory and Jesus Research," in *Handbook*, 1:809–42; "The Tradition-Memory Nexus: Finding the Origins of the Gospel Tradition," in *Keys and Frames: Memory and Identity in Ancient Judaism and Early Christianity*, ed. Tom Thatcher, SemeiaSt (Atlanta: Society of Biblical Literature, forthcoming 2013), n.p.; Alan Kirk and Tom Thatcher, "Jesus Tradition as Social Memory," in *Memory*, 31–34, 38–39; Rodríguez, "Authenticating," 152–67, esp. 156n15; idem, *Structuring*, 219, 224–25; Jens Schröter, "Criteria," 49–65, 69–70; idem, "The Historical Jesus and the Sayings Tradition: Comments on Current Research," *Neot* 30.1 (1996): 151–68; idem, "Jesus of Galilee," 36–38. See also Le Donne, *Historiographical*, 41–92; idem, *Historical Jesus*; idem, "Theological Distortion in the Jesus Tradition: A Study in Social Memory Theory," in *Memory in the Bible and Antiquity*, ed. Loren T. Stuckenbruck, Stephen C. Barton, and Benjamin G. Wold, WUNT 212 (Tübingen: Mohr Siebeck, 2007), 163–77, though I have elsewhere argued that his continued employment of the criteria of authenticity in the first two of these publications is at odds with his sophisticated historiography (Keith, "Indebtedness," 44–47).

50. Schröter, "Criteria," 68; also 64. Cf. also Jens Schröter, *Jesus von Nazaret: Jude aus Galiläa—Retter der Welt*, 3rd ed., BG 15 (Leipzig: Evangelische Verlagsanstalt, 2006), 24–25.

51. Similarly, Rodríguez, *Structuring*, 224–25.

The point, however, is that those fabrications did not magically appear out of thin air. They were reactions to concrete social and historical circumstances. If a historian believes a tradition to be unhistorical or "inauthentic," the proper historical task is to explain (as far as we are able) how a nexus of event and commemoration could have led to that portrayal of the past.[52] In contrast, the criteria approach casts to the side traditions that fail to pass the criteria of authenticity.

Stated otherwise, this approach to the historical Jesus via the Gospels does not dictate the decisions a scholar must make.[53] It is not the business of theory to do the work of the theorist. This approach simply asserts that representations of the past must "be guided and controlled by the historical material" insofar as it must explain their existence.[54] "Sources protect us from misapprehensions, but they do not tell us what we should say."[55] Some texts will be more historically likely than others, and some representations of the past will be easier for scholars to argue than others. But those decisions must be made on a case-by-case basis in light of the mnemonic evidence and what can be known about the sociohistorical contexts in which Christians came to accept that mnemonic evidence. "This eventually means that the sources on which our representations of the past are based do not permit every interpretation, but they also do not lead to one specific image of the past."[56] Explicit or implicit accusations that those using memory theory have some sort of apologetic purpose are therefore simply misplaced in terms of the larger field, even if accurately addressing a handful of scholars.[57] Equally misplaced are suggestions that social memory theory, in and of itself, suggests the reliability of the tradition. Arguments determine scholarly decisions about reliability; the memory approach merely sets historiographical ground rules for the discussion.

The memory approach thus joins other critical approaches to the Gospels in reflecting what I have elsewhere referred to as an advance of the critical discussion through a "return to the text."[58] This return to the text insists on

52. Rodríguez, *Structuring*, 213, puts this point succinctly: "Even if we agree that 'miracles' do not—because they *cannot*—happen, questions persist regarding why people perceived miraculous events . . . and how they talked about their perceptions."

53. Schröter, "Criteria," 64.

54. Ibid., 61. Similarly, Allison, *Constructing*, 15–22.

55. Schröter, "Criteria," 64.

56. Ibid., 63.

57. Zeba A. Crook, "Collective Memory Distortion and the Quest for the Historical Jesus," *JSHJ* 11.1 (2013): 53–76; Paul Foster, "Memory, Orality, and the Fourth Gospel: Three Dead-Ends in Historical Jesus Research," *JSHJ* 10 (2012): 191–202. Foster's description of social memory theorists and New Testament scholars who use them is woefully misrepresentative of the full scholarly discussion.

58. Keith with Hurtado, "Seeking," 281–88.

the Gospels' status as historical sources that must be explained rather than explained away. Rather than commencing the quest for the historical Jesus behind the text, it commences it with the claims of the text.

Summary

This brief chapter has been a bit more jargon- and footnote-laden than other sections of the study thus far. The more technical tone has been necessary because the manner in which scholars go about asking historical questions of the Gospels is a complex matter with a long history and a present that is currently breaking from that history. Even amid the detail offered here, however, I have made no attempt to be comprehensive. Instead, I have focused specifically on how one should treat historical sources when they conflict, as do the portrayals of Jesus's scribal-literate status in Mark (and Matthew) and Luke. According to the criteria approach, one would test each portrayal with a battery of criteria to see if it was authentic. Scholars would then proceed to discuss the historical Jesus in light of the image determined to be authentic, leaving aside the image determined to be inauthentic. The entire procedure would ignore the stark reality that, already in the first century CE, Christians believed both things about Jesus.[59] This fact needs a historical explanation regardless of which portrayal proves closer to historical reality. I have therefore introduced the memory approach to the historical Jesus as a more viable historical method. It may be true that Mark and Luke cannot both be accurate, but the decision as to who is accurate should include a proposal for how Christians came to believe both already in the first century CE. With this general methodology asserted, the next chapter will offer just such a proposal.

---

59. Barry Schwartz, "Christian Origins: Historical Truth and Social Memory," in *Memory*, 49: "Bultmann's and Halbwachs's common failure is their refusal even to ask how pericopae, texts, and physical sites reflected what ordinary people of the first century believed."

4

Jesus and
Scribal Literacy

Possession and Perception

> Nothing entitles us to assume that Jesus, from a given moment onward
> . . . took off the scholar's gown to become a prophet.[1]

> Jesus deliberately cut across the gap between the scribal theologian and
> the ignorant עמי הארץ ("people of the earth"), a gap which was a distin-
> guishing mark of Palestinian Judaism in his day.[2]

This chapter will argue that Mark's image of a scribal-illiterate Jesus is more historically likely than Luke's image of a scribal-literate Jesus. My full argument is that Jesus was not a scribal-literate teacher, but that many of his contemporaries thought he was, and they did so as a result of his pedagogical activities. The discussion will break into three sections: a consideration of prior suggestions about the contradictory images of Jesus as a teacher; a proposal for Jesus as a scribal-illiterate teacher; and a further proposal for how Jesus's pedagogical activities likely yielded mixed perceptions of his status as a teacher. Overall, I suggest that the variety of opinions that we see in our first-century sources was present among Jesus's contemporaries during his ministry, as suggests John 7:15.

Previous Suggestions: Kelber and Crossan

Although many scholars have forwarded arguments for Jesus as literate or illiterate,[3] very few have offered an explanation for the presence of both images of Jesus in the Gospels. Two scholars who have offered such theories are Werner Kelber and John Dominic Crossan. Although differing in nuances,

---

1. Bornkamm, *Jesus*, 96.
2. Hengel, *Charismatic*, 50. Although he offers no full argument, in line with this chapter and chap. 2, Hengel cites John 7:15 and Mark 6:3 as evidence against the notion that Jesus attended a rabbinic school.
3. See the history of research in Keith, *Jesus' Literacy*, 8–23.

both advocate the view that Christians originally remembered Jesus as an illiterate person because he was, in fact, an illiterate person. Later Christians then fabricated the literate Jesus in light of their present circumstances.

Werner Kelber claims that the four canonical Gospels portray Jesus as an uneducated oral teacher and not "as a reader, writer, or head of a school tradition."[4] He acknowledges, however, that John 8:6, 8 and John 7:15 both attribute to Jesus some degree of literacy. He dismisses John 8:6, 8 as a "parody of formal, literary writing," a common dismissal that I have elsewhere argued is unwarranted in light of the verbs used to describe Jesus's writing (*katagraphō* in 8:6 and *graphō* in 8:8).[5] Regardless, Kelber understands John 7:15 to portray Jesus as a "man of literacy."[6] How did an oral illiterate historical Jesus become a "man of literacy" in John's Gospel? Kelber identifies Matthew as the responsible party: "The specifically scribal, Rabbinic model of Jesus the authoritative interpreter of the Torah was clearly shaped by the theological interests of Matthew."[7] Chapter 2 demonstrated that Matthew does, indeed, have a heightened image of Jesus as a teacher, although Kelber overlooks the ways in which Matthew also identifies Jesus in contrast to the scribal class (Matt. 7:29; 13:55). Nevertheless, for Kelber, the historical Jesus was unlettered, and the scribal Jesus was a creation of Matthean theology. Four pages prior to these comments, he assesses Luke's image of Jesus similarly: "The notion of Jesus as expounder of Scripture (Luke 4:16–22; cf. 24:27) reflects this evangelist's literary, visualist proclivities more than the linguistic realities of the life of Jesus."[8] Sixteen years after *The Oral and the Written Gospel*, Kelber again affirmed, "Jesus was a speaker, not a scribe, and not even a rhetorical composer by way of dictation."[9]

John Dominic Crossan also insists that Jesus was illiterate. He says, "Jesus was a peasant from a peasant village. Therefore, for me, Jesus was illiterate until the opposite is proven."[10] He reiterates on the same page: "Jesus did

4. Werner H. Kelber, *The Oral and the Written Gospel: The Hermeneutics of Speaking and Writing in the Synoptic Tradition, Mark, Paul, and Q*, VPT (Bloomington: Indiana University Press, 1983), 18.

5. That is, regardless of its implications for the historical Jesus, John 8:6, 8 is a claim that Jesus was capable of alphabetized writing. See Keith, *Pericope*, 27–52.

6. Kelber, *Oral*, 18.

7. Ibid.

8. Ibid., 14.

9. Werner H. Kelber, "The Quest for the Historical Jesus from the Perspective of Medieval, Modern, and Post-Enlightenment Readings, and in View of Ancient, Oral Aesthetics," in *The Jesus Controversy: Perspectives in Conflict*, by John Dominic Crossan, Luke Timothy Johnson, and Werner H. Kelber, RLS (Harrisburg, PA: Trinity, 1999), 75.

10. Crossan, *Birth*, 235. See also his *The Essential Jesus: What Jesus Really Taught* (New York: HarperCollins, 1994), 21; idem, *Jesus*, 25.

not—and, in my opinion, could not—write." Crossan notes, however, that Luke "presume[s]" a literate Jesus in Luke 4:16–20.[11] How did early Christians get from an illiterate historical Jesus to Luke 4's presumption of Jesus's literacy? Crossan proposes that Christianity went through a larger shift from an orality-based religion to a text-based religion: "Jesus' kingdom-of-God movement began as a movement of peasant resistance but broke out from localism and regionalism under scribal leadership."[12] The implication is that, as Christianity became more scribal, so did its image of its founder.

Ignoring differences in detail, Kelber's and Crossan's theories for Jesus's literacy have important similarities. Both argue that the historical Jesus was illiterate and that Christian portrayals of Jesus in literate terms are later developments. Both also suggest that the shift in images of Jesus was part of a larger shift of Christianity away from its oral origins and toward scribal culture.[13]

As a first point of criticism, contrary to the Kelber/Crossan theory, it is more helpful to focus on Jesus's scribal literacy specifically rather than his literacy generally. The Gospels show no concern for the latter issue while, as chapter 2 demonstrated, they show considerable concern for the former issue. In addition to this slight but significant distinction, my proposal for the scribal-literate status of Jesus consists of both agreement and further disagreement with the general contours of the Kelber/Crossan theory. I agree that Jesus most likely was a scribal-illiterate teacher. I also agree that early Christian portrayals of Jesus exhibit a demonstrable progression toward a more scribal Jesus. I disagree, however, that these later images of a scribal-literate Jesus are creations of the later church, rooted primarily in their theological proclivities. I begin with agreements.

The Scribal-Illiterate Jesus

Jesus most likely was not a scribal-literate teacher, as Mark 1:22//Matt. 7:29, Mark 6:3//Matt. 13:55, and the second clause of the Jews' question in John 7:15 suggest. In the final analysis there are really only two options: Jesus was a scribal-literate teacher, or he was not. Since the early church came to remember him in both categories, then, the question is whether they came to remember a historically scribal-illiterate Jesus as a scribal-literate Jesus or

11. Crossan, *Birth*, 235. See also Crossan, *Jesus*, 26. Similarly, Chilton, *Rabbi*, 99.
12. Crossan, *Birth*, 235.
13. Cf. also Meier's reference to the "partial transformation of a Galilean rabbi into a Gentile guru" (*Marginal*, 4:652).

came to remember a historically scribal-literate Jesus as a scribal-illiterate Jesus; and why they would have done one or the other. The former of these possibilities is most likely for three reasons: Jesus's sociohistorical context; a clear progression toward scribal literacy in early Christian images of Jesus; and the sociohistorical context of early Christianity.

Jesus's Sociohistorical Context

The first reason why Jesus most likely was not a scribal-literate teacher is that the overwhelming majority of first-century Jews were illiterate (ca. 90–97 percent). This fact, as well as the lack of any clear evidence of a widespread system for first-century Jewish literate education (see chap. 1), favors the likelihood of the Markan image of the scribal-illiterate Jesus over the Lukan scribal-literate Jesus. I must underscore that Jesus's sociohistorical context *favors* the Markan image of Jesus. It does not by itself prove it. Background information is *informative* for the historian attempting to account for the evidence, not *determinative* for the historian's decision.

This point reveals a slight difference between why I favor a scribal-illiterate historical Jesus and why Kelber and Crossan do. They see the oral or peasant nature of Jesus's sociohistorical context as determinative for Jesus's scribal-literate status. This logic is clearest in Crossan's statement "Jesus was a peasant from a peasant village. *Therefore* . . . Jesus was illiterate until the opposite is proven."[14] I have reservations about the usefulness of the term "peasant" for Jesus, but the bigger problem with this line of thinking is that history is littered with exceptions to generalities. Most women in antiquity were illiterate, but some were literate, even highly literate.[15] Most American slaves were illiterate, but Frederick Douglass was literate.[16] Most people at the time of Jesus were illiterate, but that does not tell us directly whether he was. History is messier than historians' attempts to represent it. In this specific instance, the historian's choice is not whether Jesus was like everyone else at his time. One can have that discussion, but it leads necessarily into a cul-de-sac of endless debate about what an "average" person was like and how "average" Jesus may (or may not) have been. The historian's choice is whether Mark's Jesus or Luke's Jesus is more historically likely for a first-century Nazarene. What we know of this world suggests that Mark's image of Jesus is substantially more likely than Luke's.

---

14. Crossan, *Birth*, 235 (emphasis added).
15. Origen employed female calligraphers (Eusebius, *Hist. eccl.* 6.23.1–2).
16. Frederick Douglass, *Narrative of the Life of Frederick Douglass, An American Slave*, 6th ed. (London: H. G. Collins, 1851).

The Development of Early Christian Images of Jesus toward Scribal Literacy

The second reason that a scribal-illiterate historical Jesus is more likely is the development of early Christian images of Jesus. Kelber and Crossan posit a trend in early Christianity toward a more scribal Jesus. Neither offers sustained argumentation, but chapter 2 of this book reinforces their suggestions. There I detailed the transition from Mark's image of Jesus the carpenter (Mark 6:3) to Matthew's image of Jesus as the son of the carpenter and supreme teacher (Matt. 13:55; 23:8), from Mark's image of a scribal-illiterate Jesus (Mark 6:1–6) to Luke's image of a scribal-literate Jesus (Luke 4:16–30), and from Mark's claim that Jesus taught "not like the scribes" (Mark 1:22//Matt. 7:29) to John's claim that the Jews thought Jesus taught like those with scribal literacy (John 7:15). Clearly, the later sources distance Jesus from scribal illiteracy and move him, in varying degrees, closer to scribal literacy, with Luke outright attributing scribal literacy to him.

The scribal-illiterate images of Jesus never disappeared in early Christianity, of course. Manuscripts of Mark's Gospel and Matthew's Gospel, which preserved the claims that Jesus was "not like the scribes" (Mark 1:22//Matt. 7:29) and was rejected in his hometown as a synagogue teacher (Mark 6:3//Matt. 13:55), circulated inside and outside the churches. They circulated so successfully that in the third century CE Origen was still responding to accusations of Jesus's scribal illiteracy based on Mark 6:3.[17] Similarly, in the late second century, the *Infancy Gospel of Thomas* portrays Jesus as an illiterate son of a carpenter.[18] Other Christians too continued to identify Jesus as a carpenter either with lack of comment or praise.[19]

The scribal-literate image of Jesus carried the day, however. In addition to the transitions away from scribal illiteracy and toward scribal literacy in the first-century Gospels, other Christian texts show a clear interest in locating Jesus in the scribal-educated class. Toward the end of the first century and beginning of the second century, Revelation portrays Jesus dictating letters.[20]

17. Origen, *Cels.* 6.34–36.

18. *Inf. Gos. Thom.* 13.1; 14.1 (following the versification of Ronald F. Hock, trans., "The Infancy Gospel of Thomas," in *The Complete Gospels*, ed. Robert J. Miller [Santa Rosa, CA: Polebridge, 1994]).

19. Justin Martyr, *Dial.* 88; Ephraim Syrus, *Hymns on the Nativity* 6; Augustine, *Cons.* 2.42.90; cf. *Inf. Gos. Thom.* 13.1–4; *Ps.-Mt.* 37. Several writers also note Joseph's status as a carpenter: *Prot. Jas.* 9.1; *History of Joseph the Carpenter* 2, 15; Origen, *Cels.* 1.28.

20. Rev. 1:11, 19; 2:1, 8, 12, 18; 3:1, 7, 14; 14:13. Dictation did not, of course, require literate skills. But the type of people who were wealthy enough to afford scribes tended to dwell in the educated elite class. There was thus an intrinsic connection between the means to acquire

Around the middle of the second century, the incipit (opening words) of the *Gospel of Thomas* similarly portrays Jesus dictating a text.[21] In the late second century CE, the *Infancy Gospel of Thomas* portrays Jesus as illiterate, as mentioned above, but also as beyond the need for literate education, appearing in a classroom and able to recite the alphabet.[22] In the third/fourth century, the *Narrative of Joseph of Arimathea* portrays Jesus reading and writing (to my knowledge the only text that attributes both skills to Jesus).[23] I have also elsewhere argued that the insertion of the *Pericope Adulterae*'s grapho-literate Jesus (John 8:6, 8) into the Gospel of John is roughly datable to the third century CE and a response to the Jews' questioning of his, as well as Nazarenes', scribal literacy in John 7:15–52.[24] The Abgar legend's date is difficult to determine, but it appears in Eusebius's *Ecclesiastical History* by around 325 CE. In this story, Jesus writes a letter to Abgar the toparch of Edessa.[25] The Coptic version of this story has Jesus claim that he wrote the letter in his own hand[26] while the Syriac versions portray him using an amanuensis named Hanan.[27] Fourth-century Christian sarcophagi portray scenes from the Gospels but add a scroll in Jesus's hand.[28] Carvings of Gospel scenes from the fourth to sixth century similarly portray Jesus holding a scroll or codex.[29] Fourth- and fifth-century Christians (some of whom are identified as heretical by their contemporaries) attribute to Jesus authorship of gospel tradition or epistles.[30]

---

literate skills and the means to avoid using them if desired. See Roger Bagnall, *Reading Papyri, Writing Ancient History*, AAW (New York: Routledge, 1995), 25.

21. On the dating of the *Gospel of Thomas* to ca. 140 CE, see recently Mark Goodacre, Thomas *and the Gospels: The Case for* Thomas*'s Familiarity with the Synoptics* (Grand Rapids: Eerdmans, 2012), 154–71.

22. *Inf. Gos. Thom.* 15.3; 6.18, respectively.

23. *Narrative of Joseph* 3.4; 4.3.

24. Keith, *Pericope*, 203–56.

25. Eusebius, *Hist. eccl.* 1.13.10. *Decretum Gelasianum* 8.5.1–2 identifies the letter from Jesus to Abgar and the letter from Abgar to Jesus as apocryphal.

26. Kevin P. Sullivan and T. G. Wilfong, "The Reply of Jesus to King Abgar: A Coptic New Testament Apocryphon Reconsidered (P.Mich. Inv. 6213)," *BASP* 42 (2005): 113–14.

27. *Codex Add.* 14,639, folio 15b (W. Cureton, ed. and trans., *Ancient Syriac Documents Relative to the Earliest Establishment of Christianity in Edessa and the Neighboring Countries, from the Year after Our Lord's Ascension to the Beginning of the Fourth Century* [London: Williams & Norgate, 1864], 3, 140); *Doctrina Addai*, 9–10, 43 (following versification in George Howard, trans., *The Teaching of Addai*, SBLTT 16/ECLS 4 [Chico, CA: Scholars Press, 1981]).

28. See images on next page; more in Robin M. Jensen, "The Economy of the Trinity at the Creation of Adam and Eve," *JECS* 7.4 (1999): 527–46.

29. Joseph Natanson, *Early Christian Ivories* (London: Alec Tiranti, 1953), 2, 10, 12, 28, 50.

30. Adamantius, *Dialogue* 1.8; 2.13; cf. 2.14; Aphrahat, *Demonstrations* 21.1; Augustine, *Faust.* 28.4; cf. also *Cons.* 1.7.11; Jerome, *Comm. Ezech.* 44.29 (PL 25.443).

Robin Jensen

Figures 4.1 and 4.2. These carvings from fourth-century sarcophagi, or stone burial boxes, portray Jesus's healing of the man born blind (Vatican Museum inv. no. 191) and turning water into wine (Vatican Museum inv. no. 193). In both instances, a scroll has been added to Jesus's left hand.

Therefore, it is unquestionable that early Christians increasingly came to view Jesus consistently in scribal-literate terms. It is also unquestionable that this trend represents a departure from the earliest traditions in Mark's Gospel and Matthew's Gospel that describe Jesus in contrast to scribal-literate teachers.

Since I am citing evidence from substantially later than the time of Jesus, it may be worth stating clearly that I am not suggesting that images of Jesus in the second through fifth centuries directly give us fodder to postulate the historical realities of the first century. I am also not suggesting that the Markan and Matthean images of Jesus are more historically likely because they are earlier. "Earlier" does not mean "uninterpreted" and so does not necessarily mean "more reliable." The present research question emerges not from chronology directly but from the fact that early Christians came to view Jesus as both a scribal-illiterate teacher and a scribal-literate teacher: Were early Christians more likely to attribute scribal literacy to Jesus although he did not possess it, or to remove scribal literacy from him although he did possess it? The clear trend toward a scribal-literate Jesus demonstrates an overall (although not universal) early Christian preference for a scribal-literate Jesus. This trend suggests that Christians were more likely to attribute scribal literacy to Jesus than to take it away. This trend therefore favors, along with Jesus's sociohistorical context, the theory that Jesus was a scribal-illiterate teacher.

Early Christianity's Sociohistorical Context

Why might this trend have developed? The most plausible solution is that it was a reaction against criticisms of Christians as illiterate and unlearned. Chapter 2 described this sociohistorical context, briefly focusing upon the second-century pagan critic Celsus. Celsus chastised Jesus for being uneducated,[31] the disciples for being illiterate,[32] Christians for following a teacher (*didaskalos*) who was a carpenter (*tektōn*),[33] and Christians for being illiterate also.[34] Although Origen denied that the Gospels identify Jesus as a carpenter,[35] he conceded the accusations of illiteracy.[36]

Celsus was far from alone in drawing attention to these issues. Prior to Celsus, and already in the first century CE, Luke claims that the Jerusalem Jewish leadership in Acts 4:13 identified Peter and John as illiterate (*agrammatoi*) and untrained (*idiōtai*) men.[37] In the second century CE, the Christian apologist Justin Martyr acknowledges similarly that there are "those among us who do not even know the letters of the alphabet, who are uncultured and rude in speech."[38] Clement of Alexandria similarly addresses Christian illiteracy in the second century.[39] Christians' illiteracy was thus a common topic for Christians and their pagan observers, who often stressed Christians' simplemindedness as well.[40]

As Christians from Matthew onward continued to stress Jesus's pedagogical superiority in the face of attacks on Jesus's (and their) credentials, one can readily understand how some of them came to cast a historically scribal-illiterate Jesus increasingly as a scribal-literate teacher. In addition to Jesus's sociohistorical context and the progression of Christian images of Jesus away from scribal illiteracy, this background too favors the theory that the early

31. Origen, *Cels.* 1.28.
32. Origen, *Cels.* 1.62.
33. Origen, *Cels.* 6.34.
34. Origen, *Cels.* 1.27; 6.13–14.
35. Origen, *Cels.* 6.36.
36. Origen, *Cels.* 1.29, 62; cf. idem, *Comm. Matt.* 10.17.
37. Acts 4:13 presents a curiosity for the present study. As detailed in chap. 2 above, Luke consistently stresses Jesus's status as a scribal-literate teacher in his Gospel. In Acts, however, he makes no attempt to align Jesus's disciples with scribal literacy and, in fact, has the Jewish leadership recognize the disciples as Jesus's companions on the basis of their illiterate status.
38. Justin Martyr, *1 Apol.* 60 (Falls, FC).
39. Clement of Alexandria, *Paed.* 3.11.78.
40. Lucian, *Peregr.* 11; Richard Walzer, *Galen on Jews and Christians*, OCPM (London: Oxford University Press, 1949), 15; Minucius Felix, *Oct.* 5.2–4. See further Stephen Benko, "Pagan Criticisms of Christianity in the First Two Centuries AD," *ANRW* 23.2:1055–118; Allen Hilton, "The Dumb Speak: Early Christian Illiteracy and Pagan Criticism" (PhD diss., Yale University, 1997).

church came to view a historically scribal-illiterate Jesus as a scribal-literate person. This same background makes the possibility that Christians would desire to portray a scribal-literate Jesus as a scribal-illiterate teacher unlikely. What did Christians stand to gain by asserting that their "one teacher" (Matt. 23:8) was unqualified to hold that position?

The Alternative?

Against this theory, however, one could argue that what Christians stood to gain from portraying Jesus as a scribal-illiterate teacher was a higher Christology. In 1835, Strauss forwarded an argument along these lines: "The consideration that it must have been the interest of the Christian legend to represent Jesus as independent of human teachers, may induce a doubt with respect to these statements in the New Testament, and a conjecture that Jesus may not have been so entirely a stranger to the learned culture of his nation."[41] In other words, perhaps identifications of Jesus outside the scribal class (Mark 6:3//Matt. 13:55; cf. John 7:15) were cover-ups for the fact that he was actually formally educated, a fact that early Christians did not want to acknowledge because they believed Jesus's teachings came from God and not a classroom. Although Strauss offered these thoughts with much hesitation,[42] to a certain degree this proposal makes christological sense. Christians did view Jesus as (a source of) divine wisdom (for example, 1 Cor. 1:24; Eph. 1:8). Furthermore, several early Christian texts explicitly connect the issues of Jesus's scribal-literate status with his inspired or divine teaching. In John 7, Jesus follows the Jews' questioning of his scribal literacy in 7:15 with the assertion, "My teaching is not mine but his who sent me" (7:16). The *Infancy Gospel of Thomas* insists that, in taking a book, Jesus "did not read the letters in it [but] rather, he opened his mouth and spoke by the holy spirit and taught the law."[43] Origen's third-century response to Celsus's second-century attacks on Jesus's and the disciples' illiteracy was to acknowledge this fact and cite it as proof that they were divinely inspired.[44] And from a comparative perspective, one may note that illiteracy plays a prominent role in other religious traditions' veneration of their founding figure. For example, Mormons revere Joseph Smith's translation of the Book of Mormon as a divine work in light of his rudimentary

41. David Friedrich Strauss, *The Life of Jesus Critically Examined*, ed. Peter C. Hodgson, trans. George Eliot, Lives of Jesus Series (London: SCM, 1972), 202.

42. Strauss continues, "But from the absence of authentic information we can arrive at no decision on this point" (*Life*, 202).

43. *Inf. Gos. Thom.* 15.3 (Hock).

44. Origen, *Cels.* 1.29, 62.

education.[45] Similarly, Muslims revere Muhammad's reception of the Qur'an as divine work in light of his illiteracy.[46] Illiteracy here functions apologetically by guaranteeing that these religious figures could not themselves have produced the texts. In light of these factors, perhaps the historical Jesus was a scribal-literate teacher whom early Christians came to portray as scribal-illiterate in order to enhance his status as a divine pedagogue.

Assessment of the Alternative

This alternative theory makes sense from one perspective. Its downfall, however, is that the perspective from which it makes sense has at its foundation two assumptions that the evidence does not clearly support; namely, (1) that early Christians preferred a scribal-literate Jesus and (2) that christological convictions necessarily led them to this preference.

The biggest problem for the first assumption is that it runs contrary to the clear trend of Christians portraying Jesus as more, not less, literate. Here one must distinguish between early Christians' acceptance of Jesus traditions and their alterations to Jesus traditions. As the previous chapter demonstrated, Christians accepted both a scribal-literate and a scribal-illiterate Jesus as part of their overall acceptance of the Gospels that became canonical. Their modifications of those traditions, however, tell a one-sided tale. There is much evidence of Christians modifying traditions to distance Jesus from scribal illiteracy, such as Matthew's and Luke's receptions of the Markan Nazareth synagogue pericope, 𝔓[45] and other manuscripts' reception of Mark 6:3, the addition of a scroll in Jesus's hand in iconographic representations of Gospel scenes, and the Palestinian Syriac tradition's deletion of the reference to Jesus as a carpenter at Mark 6:3. There is not, however, a single example of the opposite modification. No early Christian text demonstrably modifies Jesus's image toward scribal illiteracy.

Of course, Mark's initial identification of Jesus as a scribal-illiterate teacher *could* be a christological cover-up of Jesus's otherwise scribally educated status, but this theory cannot leave the realm of speculation, as Strauss acknowledged.[47] It could just as well be an accurate representation of the historical Jesus. We have no way to determine which is more likely because we have no access to the tradition that Mark inherited and (re)shaped. One could assume the

45. The front matter of the Book of Mormon (London: West European Mission, 1959), asserts that Joseph Smith translated the book "by the gift and power of God."

46. Thomas W. Lippman, *Understanding Islam: An Introduction to the Muslim World*, 2nd rev. ed. (New York: Meridian, 1995), 37, discusses the centrality of Muhammad's illiteracy to Islam.

47. Strauss, *Life of Jesus*, 202.

Griesbach hypothesis to the Synoptic Problem, which asserts that Mark was last among the Synoptics to write and used Matthew's and Luke's Gospels as sources. The vast majority of scholars reject the Griesbach hypothesis, but even under this solution, only one text moves Jesus toward scribal illiteracy (Mark 6:3's reception of the Nazareth synagogue pericope). All the other texts that distance Jesus from scribal illiteracy would still need explanation. The only other possible instance of a Christian moving Jesus toward scribal illiteracy would be if the author of John's Gospel was dependent upon Luke, and thereby turned Luke's unquestioned scribal-literate Jesus into a Jesus who made audiences question his scribal literacy. The relationship between the Third and Fourth Gospels is far from clear, however. Scholarly proposals include complete independence of the two, Lukan dependence on John, Johannine dependence on Luke, and more complex theories of one's dependence upon an earlier or oral stage of the other. As with these other options, this one does not have enough certainty to leave the realm of possibility and enter the realm of plausibility. There thus remains no certain example of an early Christian author preferring a scribal-illiterate Jesus over a scribal-literate Jesus.

Furthermore, even those texts that clearly connect the issue of Jesus's scribal-literate status with his status as a divine or inspired teacher do not constitute clear evidence of their preference for a scribal-literate teacher. The Johannine narrator remains silent on Jesus's scribal-literate status. The *Infancy Gospel of Thomas* represents an interesting affirmation of both Mark's scribal-illiterate carpenter Jesus and Luke's scribal-literate Jesus capable of handling texts since this Jesus is simultaneously illiterate and beyond literate education, shaming his teachers. The *Infancy Gospel of Thomas* therefore receives both images of Jesus rather than demonstrating a preference for one over the other. Origen, too, seems to be an example of accepting a scribal-illiterate Jesus and making the best of it rather than preferring a scribal-illiterate Jesus. At least his need to defend Jesus against the attacks of Celsus, as well as his denial that Jesus was a carpenter (contrary to Mark 6:3), speak to why other Christians preferred a scribal-literate Jesus who did not need a defense against such charges.

As these examples indicate, the second assumption, that christological convictions that Jesus was a divine or inspired teacher necessarily led to portrayals of him as a scribal-illiterate teacher, is equally problematic. None of the Gospel authors who portray Jesus as outside scribal culture (Mark and Matthew), or of questionable scribal status (John), makes clear christological use of that fact. John 7:15–16 is the closest to doing this, but this text also provides the strongest evidence for why scholars should not assume that a high Christology necessarily led Christians to affirm Jesus as scribal-illiterate. As was just mentioned, although the narrator affirms that Jesus's teaching is the

Father's, he leaves the question of Jesus's scribal-literate status unresolved. Furthermore, in my view, all four of the canonical Gospels assert a divine Christology for Jesus, despite differences of opinion on his scribal-literate status and other matters.[48] Luke actually inverts the logic of this alternative proposal. He combines the conviction that Jesus was a spirit-inspired teacher with an affirmation of scribal literacy, not scribal illiteracy. Luke introduces the Nazareth synagogue incident by claiming, "Jesus, filled with the power of the Spirit, returned to Galilee" (4:14). It does not appear that christological convictions necessarily led to a preference for a scribal-illiterate Jesus.

Furthermore, the examples of Joseph Smith and Muhammad are not truly comparable to the example of Jesus. For both of these religious figures, their illiteracy is crucial because it relates to their direct role in the production of the religion's sacred text. In contrast, the earliest Christians did not view Jesus as having a role in the production of their texts in this sense and never discuss his (lack of) scribal literacy in these terms.[49]

Summary

The evidence therefore does not support the assumptions that Christians preferred, much less promoted, a scribal-illiterate Jesus as a result of their Christology, even if these assumptions make sense from one perspective. In light of these factors, it is overwhelmingly more likely that Christians came to view a historically scribal-illiterate teacher as a scribal-literate teacher than the opposite. The most likely historical scenario is therefore that Jesus did not hold scribal literacy. The transition away from scribal illiteracy began as early as Matthew and was completed as early as Luke. Contributions to the debate continued for centuries thereafter in the form of new traditions and modifications to literary and iconographic representations of Jesus.

The Perception of Jesus the Teacher

As should be clear, then, I agree with the general contours of the Kelber/Crossan theory that the historical Jesus did not hold scribal literacy and that early Christian portrayals of a scribal-literate Jesus are departures from historical reality. In the remainder of this chapter, however, I will concentrate on

48. Keith, "Jesus Outside," 17–30.
49. Later Christians of the fourth and fifth centuries, deemed heretical by those who represented orthodox Christianity, claimed to possess writings of Jesus. See Augustine, *Faust.* 28.4; *Cons.* 1.7.11; Jerome, *Comm. Ezech.* 44.29; *Decretum Gelasianum* 8.5.1–2.

disagreements with them concerning when and why the scribal-literate image of Jesus emerged. Although it is not impossible that a later Christian such as Luke invented the scribal-literate Jesus, it is simply more likely that the image emerged during Jesus's life, and as a result of Jesus himself.

Crucial to my argument is the role that perception played in ancient conceptions of scribal literacy. Ultimately, the actual ability or inability to read or write lay at the base of one's scribal-literate status. But a person's abilities and his or her contemporaries' assumptions about those abilities are not the same thing. The context of the person perceived, as well as the context of the perceiver, impacted the shape of the opinions that emerged in any given set of circumstances.

Perception and the Perceived

As the end of chapter 1 noted, texts such as Sir. 38–39 and Matt. 23 indicate that Second Temple Jewish scribal authorities were recognizable as much for the life they lived and social roles they occupied as their demonstration of scribal-literate skills. This means that a scribe, Pharisee, or priest did not have to pull out a copy of Isaiah and read it in the market in order for the general populace to assume that he could have done so, and therefore acknowledge him as a scribal authority. "Local judges, teachers, scribes, and so on . . . were as far as most Judeans were concerned the representatives of Torah, whether or not they were learned men who had studied the Pentateuch and learned how to interpret it."[50] Such attributions of scribal authority were based on the correct assumption that the constituency of the group was substantially more educated than everyone else, but would have led to the misperception of some individuals who were not scribal-literate but kept scribal-literate company, such as beginners in scribal training or those who had inherited authoritative positions without going through scribal training. Manual laborers, too, would have been recognized by the company they kept, as Sir. 38 claims. The context of the perceived individual would have affected others' perception of him or her.

Perception and the Perceiver

In addition to the context of the perceived individual, the context of the perceiver also would have affected his or her perception. An ancient person's perception of literate skills, including the connection between those skills and

---

50. Schwartz, *Imperialism*, 68.

the person's status, would inherently reflect his or her own scribal-literate status. There are numerous examples from the ancient world. I will here mention Petaus the slow writer, Josephus's village scribes, and Libanius's shorthand writers.

The second-century CE Egyptian village scribe (*kōmogrammateus*) Petaus was a "slow writer" whose literate abilities were limited to copying letters mechanically.[51] Evidence of his restricted skill set is a surviving papyrus (P.Petaus 121 [P.Köln inv. 328]) that he used to practice the formula "I, Petaus, village scribe, have submitted."[52] At the fifth line of text, he makes a spelling error (omission of an initial *epsilon*), which he then repeats in the next seven lines. Petaus was literate enough to copy letters mechanically, but could not read sufficiently to catch his mistake.[53]

This very specific literate skill is significant because it led Petaus to defend a colleague against a charge of illiteracy. Ischyrion, a village scribe in Tamais, had been charged with being unfit for his post, which included the accusation that he was illiterate (*agrammatos*). Petaus was consulted on the charge. He affirmed that Ischyrion, contrary to the accusation, was literate since he had signed his papers with the appropriate formula. "He was in effect offering a defence not only of Ischyrion, against whom the accusation had been directed, but also of himself and his own procedure."[54] Interestingly, then, although Ischyrion's limited abilities had been sufficient to justify the accusation of "illiterate" from a detractor, they had also been sufficient to justify the defense of "literate" from Petaus. Petaus's own limited literate abilities impacted his perception of Ischyrion.

Two other examples similarly indicate the role of perception in assessment of scribal-literate skills. One comes from the first-century Jewish historian Josephus and also concerns village scribes. According to Josephus, Alexander, son of Herod the Great and Mariamne (first century BCE), had threatened to make his brothers "village scribes (*kōmōn grammateis*), sarcastically referring to the careful education they had received."[55] Josephus reports this incident with no further comment, reflecting that mockery of the education level of village scribes among the social elite was nothing out of the ordinary and thus how some individuals could come to the conclusion that Ischyrion was

---

51. Hebert C. Youtie, "Βραδέως γράφων: Between Literacy and Illiteracy," *GRBS* 12.2 (1971): 239–61; repr. in his *Scriptiunculae II* (Amsterdam: Hakkert, 1973), 629–51.

52. Translation modified slightly from Youtie, "Βραδέως γράφων," 240.

53. Ibid., 240–41. The early Christian author of the *Shepherd of Hermas* reveals that he too was a slow writer: "I copied it [a little book] all, letter by letter, for I could not make out the syllables" (*Vis.* 2.1.4; Holmes).

54. Youtie, "Βραδέως γράφων," 240.

55. Josephus, *J.W.* 1.24.3 §479 (Thackeray, LCL).

illiterate. These examples of the social esteem for village scribes point directly to the significance of the position from which literate skills were judged. A completely illiterate farmer or blacksmith who needed to register a wedding contract, tax receipt, or land deed with a village scribe would have viewed that scribe as a literate figure and pointed to his ability to sign documents as evidence. As these examples indicate, though, members of educated elite society viewed village scribes as illiterate or at least certainly the bottom-feeders of literate society.

A third example of the role of the perceiver's context in their assessment of scribal-literate abilities comes from Libanius (fourth century CE). After Julian the Apostate removed some provincial governors from office, Libanius mocked them as having no knowledge despite the fact that they could write shorthand.[56] Shorthand writing was a rare skill in terms of the population of the ancient world at large. Even some scribes were not capable of this skill.[57] It was the product of a literate education that went beyond initial stages and thus a mark of location among the minority educated class (whether as a free person or a slave who had been trained in a wealthy household). Truly illiterate people, as well as semiliterate village scribes, would have esteemed the skill. Even some members of the educated elite privileged it, such as Quintilian.[58] And yet a high-ranking member of elite culture can also mock such individuals as lacking knowledge.

Summary

As these examples indicate, the contexts of the perceived and the perceiver impacted the conception and significance of phrases such as "literate," "semiliterate," or "illiterate." These words referred to demonstrable skills but ultimately were not static realities in the public domain. They were attributions based on others' perceptions, which were in turn based on a number of factors. Demonstration of literacy was only one factor, and a factor that did not need to be present for someone to arrive at a conclusion. Most of the ancient world was illiterate and would have viewed Petaus as literate, as he viewed himself. But not everyone held that opinion, as Ischyrion's accuser demonstrates. Most of the ancient world similarly would have seen shorthand writing as a mark of extended literate training and its possessor

---

56. Libanius, *Or.* 18.158. Norman translates: "for all their skill in shorthand, had not a scrap of sense" (LCL).

57. Cicero, *Att.* 13.25, discusses scribes (*librarii*) Spintharo and Tiro, the former of whom must take dictation syllable by syllable while the latter can follow whole sentences.

58. Quintilian, *Inst.* 1.1.28–29.

as a knowledgeable person. But not everyone held that opinion, as Libanius's mockery demonstrates. Like beauty, literacy, and the status it indicated, was in the eye of the beholder.

If one is to use the Gospels as historical sources, then, one must consider not just who Jesus was but also who he was perceived to be by those around him.[59] The origin of the Jesus tradition is an extremely complex issue, but this much can be said for certain: Despite whatever later developments of the tradition occurred at the hands of the tradents, the origins of the tradition reside in Jesus's interactions with his contemporaries and his contemporaries' interactions with each other.[60] In that vein, there are two foundational reasons that some of Jesus's audiences conceptualized him as a scribal-literate teacher while others conceptualized him as a scribal-illiterate teacher: (1) his actions invited assessment of him vis-à-vis scribal authority, and (2) he was assessed by people of varying scribal-literate statuses. In this context, I will also briefly mention the role of Scripture in his debates with scribal-literate authorities before addressing it more fully in the next chapter.

Jesus's Teaching Invited Assessment

Although the point may seem commonsensical, it is important to observe that Jesus's actions as a teacher invited assessment of his qualifications. Reading and interpreting Torah in a synagogue were recognizably scribal-literate roles.[61] When Jesus took it upon himself to teach in a synagogue rather than listen to others teach, and so occupied the position of a scribal-literate teacher instead of a manual-labor member of the audience, he placed himself in the social role of a scribal-literate authority. This very action invited assessment of his scribal-literate status, especially if other aspects of his life were perceived to be at variance with it. Similarly, if Jesus ever challenged or addressed the teaching of the scribes,[62] if he ever debated known scribal-literate authorities[63]

59. For this reason, James D. G. Dunn, *Jesus Remembered*, CM 1 (Grand Rapids: Eerdmans, 2003), 128–32, stresses the "impact" of Jesus. Consider also Allison, *Historical Christ*, 24–25: "The Nazarene never lived solely to himself, never resided exclusively within his own skin. He was always interacting with others, and their perceptions of him must constitute part of his identity, as must his post-Easter influence and significance."

60. Dunn, *Jesus Remembered*, 128–30, 239–45. For introductions to the study of the oral tradition, see Eve, *Behind*; Rafael Rodríguez, *Oral Tradition and the New Testament: A Guide for the Perplexed*, TTGP (London: T&T Clark, 2013). More comprehensively, see Tom Thatcher et al., eds., *Dictionary of the Bible and Ancient Media* (London: T&T Clark, forthcoming).

61. This paragraph and the subsequent two are slightly modified from Keith, *Jesus' Literacy*, 177–79.

62. Mark 9:11; 12:35; Matt. 23:1–12.

63. Matt. 16:1–4.

over the interpretation of Jewish Scriptures[64] or proper interpretive authority,[65] if he ever cited Scripture during such a debate[66] or accused his opponents of not knowing Scripture in such a debate,[67] if he ever offered interpretations of Torah to crowds,[68] if he ever taught in the shadow of the temple hierarchy[69]—if he ever did any of these things, then his scribal literacy and authority for such actions would inevitably have come under scrutiny.

I here take it as a safe assumption that Jesus did at least some of these things in addition to teaching in synagogues. There is, therefore, no reason to doubt the shared claim of Mark 1:22//Matt. 7:29, Mark 6:3//Matt. 13:55, and John 7:15 that Jesus's various audiences compared and contrasted him with known scribal-literate Torah authorities. There is likewise no reason to doubt that, as part of that assessment, Jesus's opponents and/or audiences questioned his authority (Mark 11:28//Matt. 21:23//Luke 20:2; cf. Mark 6:3// Matt. 13:55). These points are crucial for understanding the origins of the conflict between Jesus and the scribal elite, and I return to them in chapter 6. For now I note that these individual episodes do not have to be historical in order to acknowledge that, if Jesus ever did anything of the sort, it would inevitably have led to assessments of his scribal-literate status.

Stated otherwise, as soon as Jesus presented himself as a teacher, he would have met particular social expectations among his audiences. As Theissen observes,

> Everyone becomes part of a society with predetermined patterns of behavior. Everyone is faced with role expectations that are attached to certain positions and which cannot be avoided. It was the same for Jesus. Being perceived in the role of teacher and prophet, he had to deal with the accompanying role expectations.[70]

Similarly, Snyder notes, "Jesus and Christian teachers . . . would have encountered in their audiences the expectation that their teacher was skilled in the literature of his or her tradition."[71] This point brings the current discussion to factors that affected whether Jesus's audiences judged him to have met their expectations.

64. Mark 12:18–40; John 7:53–8:11.
65. Matt. 21:23–27; Luke 20:2–8; John 5:39–47.
66. Mark 2:25//Matt. 12:3//Luke 6:3; Mark 12:10//Matt. 21:42; Mark 12:26//Matt. 22:31; Matt. 12:5; 19:4–5; Luke 10:26; cf. Mark 12:24; Luke 20:17.
67. Mark 12:24//Matt. 22:29.
68. Matt. 5:17–48.
69. Matt. 21:23; Luke 19:47; 21:37–38; John 8:2–3, 20.
70. Gerd Theissen, "Jesus as an Itinerant Preacher: Reflections from Social History on Jesus' Roles," in *Jesus Research*, 98.
71. Snyder, *Teachers*, 190.

Mixed Audiences and Mixed Perceptions

The second foundational reason that Jesus was most likely perceived as both a scribal-illiterate teacher and a scribal-literate teacher is that his audiences consisted of individuals with differing scribal-literate statuses. The people assessing Jesus as a teacher included both scribal-literate authorities and everyday folk who had no literate education. Any given audience in any given instance may have consisted of more members of one group than the other. If Jesus engaged in teaching in or near villages[72] or by the Sea of Galilee,[73] his audience may have consisted predominantly of agrarian villagers. If Jesus was ever in the house of a Pharisee,[74] his audience may have been predominantly scribal-literate individuals. His audiences would have often included both classes as well,[75] since certain contexts would have guaranteed this mix, such as synagogues,[76] festivals,[77] and the temple.[78] When texts like Luke 15:1–2; Matt. 9:10–12//Mark 2:15–17//Luke 5:29–32; and John 7 claim that Jesus gave his teachings before tax collectors and sinners as well as scribes and Pharisees, before "the crowd" as well as the authorities, there is no good reason to doubt it. (Jesus also likely gave some teachings only in the context of his disciples.)[79] If Jesus carried out his ministry in Galilee and taught and died in Jerusalem, these two locales alone guarantee this precise variety of demographics in Jesus's audiences.

The significance of this point derives from the earlier observation that an individual's scribal-literate status impacted how he or she judged another person, in terms of the assumptions he or she might make about that person's abilities as well as a qualitative assessment of those abilities (or lack thereof). Since Jesus engaged in pedagogical activities that invited assessment of his scribal-literate status and did so before audiences of varying scribal-literate statuses, it is likely that multiple opinions about Jesus's scribal-literate status emerged early in his ministry. Even among eyewitnesses there would have been

72. Mark 6:6b; Luke 8:1; Matt. 5:1–2//Luke 6:17.

73. Mark 3:7; Matt. 13:1–3//Mark 4:1–2; Matt. 14:13–14//Mark 6:32–34//John 6:1–3.

74. Luke 7:36–50; 11:37–54; 14:1–24.

75. For example, Matt. 9:10–13//Mark 2:15–17//Luke 5:29–32; Matt. 19:2–3//Mark 10:1–2; Luke 15:1–2; John 7; 8:2, 3.

76. Matt. 4:23//Mark 1:39//Luke 4:44; Matt. 9:35–38; Matt. 12:9//Mark 3:1//Luke 6:6; Matt. 13:54//Mark 6:2//Luke 4:16; John 6:59.

77. Matt. 26:17//Mark 14:12//Luke 22:7; John 2:13; 6:4; 7:2; 10:22; 11:55.

78. Matt. 21:12–13//Mark 11:15–18//Luke 19:45–48//John 2:13–22; Matt. 24:1//Mark 13:1// Luke 21:5; John 8:2.

79. Mark 10:10–12; Matt. 13:36–43; cf. Mark 6:30–31//Luke 9:10. On this topic, see further Dale C. Allison Jr., *Resurrecting Jesus: The Earliest Christian Tradition and Its Interpreters* (London: T&T Clark, 2005), 27–55.

a variety of opinions, just as there undoubtedly were a variety of opinions about his messianic or prophetic status.[80]

For these reasons, I consider the following scenario so overwhelmingly likely that I have trouble imagining how this could not have been the case. A completely illiterate farmer and a scribe from the temple could have witnessed the exact same event in Jesus's life and come to precise opposite conclusions about his scribal-literate status. Let us say they witnessed Jesus in a debate with Pharisees in Jerusalem. The farmer, in town for a festival, ignorant of the intricacies of scribal-literate education, and unfamiliar with Jesus, could have witnessed Jesus arguing with recognizable scribal-literate Pharisees and concluded, based on the fact that Jesus was arguing Torah with them, that he too must have been a scribal-literate authority. A temple scribe, responsible for weekly Torah instruction and copying the holy texts, and thus steeped in scribal-literate education, could have witnessed the exact same argument and concluded, based on the content and style of Jesus's argumentation and the fact that he was otherwise unknown among scribal-literate society, that, although making the most of his limited abilities, he certainly was not a scribal-literate authority. This scenario of mixed audiences and mixed perceptions would not necessarily have been the case for every event in Jesus's life. It would have been the case for events where Jesus engaged in activities typically associated with scribal-literate authorities, however, especially his teaching in synagogues (see further chap. 6 below). Jesus lived, ministered, taught, healed, and died in a context where he too did not have to pull out a scroll of Isaiah and read from it in order for some of his audience members to conclude that he was capable of such a feat and others to conclude that he was incapable of such a feat.

The Shema Illustration

Such phenomena are not unknown within the cultures of scribal literacy in our own world of studying the Hebrew and Christian Scriptures. An anachronistic but thoroughly applicable illustration may clarify my point. Deuteronomy 6:4 is a core text for Jewish monotheism. It is known as the Shema since the first word in Hebrew is *šĕmaʿ* ("hear"). Here is the Hebrew with a fairly literal English translation of my own.

---

80. For example, John 7:25–31, 40–42; 9:16–17. Cf. Paula Fredriksen, *From Jesus to Christ: The Origins of the New Testament Images of Jesus* (New Haven: Yale University Press, 1988), who reflects on the fact that Jesus's actions were sufficient to convince some that he was not a messianic claimant (242–43) and others that he was (245).

שְׁמַע יִשְׂרָאֵל יְהוָה אֱלֹהֵינוּ יְהוָה אֶחָד
Hear Israel: The Lord (is) our God, the Lord (is) one.

If I walk into a classroom of freshmen and write the Hebrew of Deut. 6:4 onto the board from memory, then turn around and recite it in Hebrew, the vast majority of the students will conclude that I am an expert in Biblical Hebrew with the ability to read at sight any section of the Hebrew Bible. If, however, I recite the same text to other Bible scholars, or even a graduate student with one year of Hebrew, they will know that the Shema is one of the very first things that you learn in Hebrew. To them, my recitation of Deut. 6:4 will indicate absolutely nothing about how advanced my Hebrew abilities are. Quite to the contrary, my decision to recite a text that everyone who has ever taken even a little Hebrew could probably recite may reveal that I am not an expert but a novice, or even worse, a novice attempting to pass off my meager accomplishments as evidence of expertise.

Apart from what might happen in a classroom, even the Hebrew words on the page of this book will engender different responses from different groups of readers based on their respective familiarities with Hebrew and Bible translation. Those of you who are primarily versed in English translations may be wondering why I translated "Hear Israel" instead of "Hear, O Israel." Some of you may be wondering why the reference to God is "Lord" instead of "Lord," and others of you may know why.[81] Some of you may be wondering why the word "is" is in parentheses, and others of you may know why.[82] Those of you who have some familiarity with Hebrew may be wondering why I translated the last phrase as "the Lord (is) one" instead of "the Lord alone."[83] And the real Hebrew junkies reading this page will have already spotted a mistake in the Hebrew of the Shema above.[84] The rest of you will be oblivious, having assumed that I got it right.

If you are in this duped category who did not notice my mistake, you have just perfectly illustrated my point. My guess is that your assumption that I relayed the Hebrew correctly was based on some combination of factors involving your lack of (or limited) knowledge of Hebrew and your expectation that someone like me (a Bible scholar with advanced degrees, holding an academic

---

81. Translators use "Lord" to translate the unpronounceable divine name (*yhwh*) and "Lord" to translate the Hebrew word for "master, lord" (*'dn*). This practice has its roots in the Jewish practice of speaking the latter word in place of the former word when reading the Hebrew text aloud.

82. There is no verb of being in the Hebrew; it is inferred.

83. Either is possible. See further the discussion in chap. 5 of Jesus's citation of the Shema in John 10:30.

84. The second-to-last letter (remember, Hebrew reads right-to-left) should be ח instead of ה.

post, and writing a book about Jesus for a recognized publisher) does know Hebrew. In other words, like those in the time of Sirach, Jesus, and Matthew, you formed your opinion based on certain social cues associated with textual authority rather than having seen me read or translate Hebrew in real life. Yet, and also now as then, your assessment would differ radically from that of a person with expertise in reading Hebrew, who would have noticed my mistake and likely concluded that I, like Petaus, know enough of a language to copy it but not enough to copy correctly. I reiterate: The exact same interpretive event can be perceived differently by those with differing levels of expertise.

Additional Factors

Although I will not deal with them in depth here, at least two further conditions of Jesus's ministry strengthen my argument that mixed audiences came to mixed conclusions about Jesus's scribal-literate status. Each relates specifically to the public nature of much of his pedagogical activity. First, some of Jesus's contemporaries likely perceived him as a scribal-literate teacher if they ever concluded that Jesus had won a public debate with scribal-literate authorities. Reflecting the biases of their authors, Jesus is the winner of every single conflict story in the Gospels, to the extent that each of the Synoptic Gospels contains statements about his enemies eventually ceasing that particular tactic:

> After that no one dared to ask him any question. . . . And the large crowd was listening to him with delight. (Mark 12:34, 37)

> When they heard this, they were amazed; and they left him and went away. (Matt. 22:22)

> No one was able to give him an answer, nor from that day did anyone dare to ask him any more questions. (Matt. 22:46)

> When he said this, all his opponents were put to shame; and the entire crowd was rejoicing at all the wonderful things that he was doing. (Luke 13:17)

> And they could not reply to this. (Luke 14:6)

> For they no longer dared to ask him another question. (Luke 20:40)

One does not have to accept uncritically that Jesus won every single debate with scribal-literate authorities in order to acknowledge that, if Jesus was ever perceived to have won even once in front of the mixed audiences whom the Gospels describe, some members of that audience likely concluded that he was a scribal authority and would have cited his victory over scribal authorities as their evidence.

In line with this suggestion, and as the second condition, some of Jesus's audiences likely perceived him as a scribal-literate authority if he *cited Scripture* authoritatively in public debate with known scribal-literate authorities. These issues bring us directly to the content, historicity, and nature of the conflict between the teacher from Galilee and other teachers, and thus to the final two chapters of this book.

Conclusion

In conclusion, I suggest that mutually exclusive perceptions of Jesus as a scribal-literate teacher and a scribal-illiterate teacher emerged in Jesus's own lifetime and were largely the result of Jesus engaging in public events that invited assessment of his scribal-literate status in front of audiences of mixed scribal-literate status. The image of the scribal-literate Jesus was not, in the first instance, a creation of a later Christology or wishful Christian thinking amid pagan mockery. Later Christians may have appropriated and promoted the scribal-literate image of Jesus under such conditions, but the genesis of that image was a scribal-illiterate carpenter who at times occupied the social space of a scribal-literate teacher.[85] Luke and others were the inheritors, not the forgers, of the scribal-literate Jesus.

---

85. This conclusion raises an obvious question: Would not Jesus's disciples have known better and used their influence in the early church to correct the scribal-literate image of Jesus? Even if some Christians in authority knew better, and even if they sought to correct that image of Jesus, the scribal-literate image of Jesus would still have had room to persist until it reached Luke and others. The group of individuals who formed opinions on Jesus as a teacher was much greater than the disciples' influence. This is particularly the case for those Jews who would have seen Jesus interact with scribal-literate authorities in Jerusalem and then returned to their homes in the Diaspora. Thus, Gerd Theissen, *The Gospels in Context: Social and Political History in the Synoptic Tradition*, trans. Linda M. Maloney (Minneapolis: Fortress, 1991), 97, asks, "Would there not also have been stories among the Jesus traditions that had traveled outside the circle of his closest associates?" Furthermore, if the sociohistorical context of criticism of Jesus's and Christians' illiteracy is at all accurate, it is not necessarily clear that every Christian leader in a position of influence would have desired to correct that image. As noted above, the author of the Gospel of John is in a position to clarify whether Jesus "knew letters" or "had not been educated" (7:15 AT) but chooses not to insert an authorial opinion. In a related but different move, Matthew allows the identification of Jesus as outside the scribal-literate class to stand but edges Jesus slightly closer to scribal literacy. Some authoritative early Christians may have been happy to allow the misperceptions of Jesus's scribal-literate status to continue while others (such as Mark or Luke) were interested in asserting an opinion.

5

The Content
of the Conflict

Scripture and Authority

Have you never read in the Scriptures? (Matt. 21:42)

By what authority are you doing these things? (Mark 11:28)

The controversy narratives (or "conflict stories") consist of the accounts in the Gospels where Jesus and the scribal elite interact in a hostile manner. Some scholars distinguish between instances where Jesus and the authorities carry on a dialogue and instances where Jesus attacks them or their teachings in their absence.[1] For the purposes of this study, I will take a wide definition and include any traditions that reflect enmity between Jesus and scribal authorities. Occasionally, a positive story is mixed in among the debates, such as Jesus's commendation of the scribe as "not far from the kingdom of God" (Mark 12:34); the scribe who tells Jesus, "Teacher, I will follow you wherever you go" (Matt. 8:19; cf. Luke 9:57, "someone"); or the scribes who tell him, "Teacher, you have spoken well" (Luke 20:39). The vast majority of interactions between Jesus and the scribal elite are tension-filled, however. Furthermore, although the term "controversy narratives" typically refers to these stories as they appear in the Synoptic Gospels, things are no different in the Gospel of John. Although some of "the Jews" believe in Jesus (for example, John 11:45),[2] and the Pharisee Nicodemus even comes to him to receive teaching (3:1–21; cf. 7:50–51), in general Jesus and the authorities are not friends. He calls them children of the devil (8:44); they call him a demon-possessed sinner (8:48; 9:16, 24; 10:20).

The historicity of each of these accounts is not important for my argument. Neither this chapter nor the next will take such an approach. My concern is with the general claim of all four Gospels that the conflict between Jesus and

1. This division is a legacy of form criticism's assessment of traditions-in-kind. See especially Bultmann, *History*, 11–69.
2. The precise identity of "the Jews" in John's Gospel is a complex issue and beyond the scope of this study. For present purposes, it will suffice to observe that "the Jews" who appear as Jesus's enemies are authority figures in matters of the law.

the scribal elite centered predominantly on two issues: Scripture and authority. The next chapter will argue that this general claim has a high degree of historical plausibility. In anticipation of that argument, I will briefly survey a selection of texts that foreground each source of conflict. My artificial division of the narratives into controversies over Scripture and controversies over authority should not obscure how thoroughly intertwined these two sources of conflict are in the narratives. Furthermore, I do not intend to indicate that there were no other important aspects to the rising hostilities, such as Jesus's miracles, exorcisms, status as prophet, or status as Messiah. These, too, are significant factors in the narratives and relate to Jesus's authority. But Scripture or scriptural categories serve as the gravitational center of these controversies as the scribal elite attempt to assess Jesus's actions and authority for doing them, and thus his identity, in light of the sacred texts.

Conflict over Scripture

In most of the controversy narratives, the turning point of the debate, or at least the weapon that both parties brandish, is Scripture. Jesus and the scribal elite argue over all three of the major divisions of the Jewish Scriptures: Torah, the Prophets, and the Writings.[3] What follows will feature a sample of such debates from all four Gospels that in no way aims for comprehensiveness. The important point at present is simply to observe how prominent a role Scripture plays in the controversy narratives.

Torah

"Torah," which means "instruction" in Hebrew, refers to the first five books of the Hebrew Scriptures and Christian Old Testament: Genesis; Exodus; Leviticus; Numbers; and Deuteronomy. It is also known as the Law, Law of Moses, or Pentateuch. Torah served as the foundation of Jewish life and was so crucial to Jewish conceptions of Scripture that the phrase "the law" could function as shorthand for the rest of Scripture as well (cf. John 10:34). "The sanctity and supreme importance of Torah . . . can hardly be exaggerated."[4]

3. The Jewish canon had not closed by the time of Jesus, but it had stabilized, and Jews viewed these texts as authoritative Scripture (cf. the tripartite division in Luke 24:44). See further Lee Martin McDonald, *The Biblical Canon: Its Origin, Transmission, and Authority*, 3rd ed. (Peabody, MA: Hendrickson, 2007), 168–69; Moyise, *Jesus*, 1–2; Christopher D. Stanley, *The Hebrew Bible: A Comparative Approach* (Minneapolis: Fortress, 2010), 27–31.

4. N. T. Wright, *The New Testament and the People of God*, COQG 1 (Minneapolis: Fortress, 1992), 228.

Jews traditionally regarded Moses as the author of Torah as a whole based on claims that he wrote the law for Israel (Deut. 31:9). By the first century, the person of Moses and the Law of Moses were so thoroughly conflated that Paul could speak of "Moses" being read aloud in synagogues (2 Cor. 3:15).[5]

In light of Torah's significance for first-century Judaism, it can hardly be a surprise that Jesus and the scribal elite often argue over Moses and the law in the Gospels.[6] For example, in Mark 10:2, the Pharisees ask Jesus if divorce is legal. Jesus asks in response, "What did Moses command you?" He then exploits a discrepancy from within the law. According to Deut. 24:1–4, divorce is legal, but according to Gen. 1:27 and 2:24, which Jesus cites in Mark 10:6–8, man and woman are joined in such a fashion that divorce is prohibited (10:9).[7] In the Matthean parallel of this text (Matt. 19:3–10), Jesus answers straight from Gen. 1:27 and 2:24, with the Pharisees asking about the Mosaic exceptions in Deut. 24:1–4 (Matt. 19:7). In both texts, however, the playing field for this battle of wits between the Pharisees and Jesus is the law.

Similarly concerned with Moses and issues of marriage, Sadducees attempt to trap Jesus concerning resurrection and levirate marriage in Mark 12:18–27// Matt. 22:23–33//Luke 20:27–40. According to Deut. 25:5–10, if a man dies, his brother has the responsibility to marry his widow and have children who will legally continue the line of the deceased man. The Sadducees ask Jesus to apply these instructions to the afterlife by creating a hypothetical scenario whereby a wife goes through seven brothers and then dies herself. They end by asking Jesus, "In the resurrection whose wife will she be?" (Mark 12:23; cf. Matt. 22:28//Luke 20:33). Readers know the question is a setup because the narrator has introduced the Sadducees by noting that they do not believe in the resurrection (Mark 12:18//Matt. 22:23//Luke 20:27).[8] Furthermore, the Sadducees' failure to affirm the resurrection was related to the fact that they accepted only the Law, Torah proper, as binding Scripture.[9] Developed Jewish belief in the resurrection, as was present in the first century CE, stemmed from texts outside the Law, such as that of the valley of the dry bones in Ezek. 37:1–14. Their challenge is dually barbed, then: Jesus must apply the teach-

---

5. On the conflation of the Law of Moses and person of Moses, see further T. Francis Glasson, *Moses in the Fourth Gospel*, SBT 40 (London: SCM, 1963), 26, 86; Richard B. Hays, *Echoes of Scripture in the Letters of Paul* (New Haven: Yale University Press, 1989), 144–45; Francis Watson, *Paul and the Hermeneutics of Faith* (London: T&T Clark, 2004), 281.

6. Powell, "Do and Keep What Moses Says," 428, even claims, "Matthew's Gospel presents disputes over interpretation of Mosaic law as the most serious of all Jesus' conflicts with the religious leaders."

7. Cf. also the Qumran community's citation of Gen. 1:27 in rejecting polygamy (CD 4.21).

8. Also Acts 23:8; Josephus, *Ant.* 18.4 §16.

9. Josephus, *Ant.* 18.4 §16.

ing of Moses not merely to an absurd hypothetical situation but to an absurd hypothetical situation that, in the minds of the Sadducees, the Law does not even support. Mark and Matthew add a third barb. In these texts, Jesus has just finished debating the Pharisees (Mark 12:13–17//Matt. 22:15–22),[10] who affirm the resurrection.[11] In these accounts, the Sadducees are also putting Jesus in a position where he has to choose a side in the ongoing debate between the Pharisees and Sadducees.

Jesus's immediate response to the Sadducees is to undermine their own status as authoritative interpreters of Moses: "Is not this the reason you are wrong, that you know neither the scriptures nor the power of God?" (Mark 12:24; cf. Matt. 22:29; Luke 20:34–36). Not only does he challenge the Sadducees' rejection of resurrection by affirming it (Mark 12:25//Matt. 22:30//Luke 20:35), thus siding with the Pharisees on this issue, but he also challenges the scriptural basis for their rejection of it: "And as for the dead being raised, have you not read in the book of Moses, in the story about the bush, how God said to him, 'I am the God of Abraham, the God of Isaac, and the God of Jacob'? He is God not of the dead, but of the living; you are quite wrong" (Mark 12:26–27; cf. Matt. 22:31–32). Luke's version of the story has Jesus make the point even more emphatically: "And the fact that the dead are raised *Moses himself* showed. . . ." (Luke 20:37; emphasis added). Jesus is guilty of some eisegesis here, but one should not miss the significance of this interpretive move. If the Sadducees are going to stand on the law in order to deny the resurrection, Jesus is going to undermine them with precisely that text. Matthew and Luke both claim that Jesus's response counted as a public victory for him (Matt. 22:33//Luke 20:40; Mark makes no comment to that effect). In Mark and Matthew, interpretive authorities (a scribe in Mark 12:28; a Pharisaic lawyer in Matt. 22:34–36) approach Jesus about the greatest commandment immediately after his showdown with the Sadducees. Jesus's successful debate over Scripture leads to another discussion of Scripture.

As strong as the battle over Moses and the law is in the Synoptic Gospels, it perhaps rages more strongly in the Gospel of John. John 1:17 asserts Jesus's superiority to Moses, and the rest of the Gospel puts that statement into narrative form.[12] John 5:39–47 is a particularly instructive example of this narrative agenda, since Jesus, as in his Synoptic battles with the Sadducees, explicitly accuses the scribal-literate authorities (the Jews of 5:10, 16) of not knowing the law. According to Jesus, despite the fact that they are part of

10. The "they" of Luke 20:20 are chief priests, scribes, and elders (20:1).
11. Acts 23:8; Josephus, *Ant.* 18.3 §14.
12. See further Keith, *Pericope*, 147–50.

the privileged few who can "search the scriptures" themselves (5:39; cf. 7:52), they cannot claim Moses as an ally: "Your accuser is Moses, on whom you have set your hope. If you believed Moses, you would believe me, for he wrote about me. But if you do not believe what he wrote, how will you believe what I say?" (John 5:45–47).

Elsewhere in John's Gospel, the Jews appeal to Moses as their source of authority (9:28), and the Pharisees claim that the difference between themselves and the gullible crowd is knowledge of the law (7:48–49), specifically referencing their ability to search it themselves (7:52). It is clear, then, that Jesus is attacking their very source of authority and identity. He claims that their rejection of him reveals that they are not quite the interpreters of Moses that they think they are. One may note in this context also the late addition to the Gospel of John, the *Pericope Adulterae*, typically found in John 7:53–8:11. Although this text most likely was not in the original version of John's Gospel, it too contains a conflict story between Jesus and scribal-literate authorities ["scribes and Pharisees," 8:3] over the interpretation of Moses (8:5).[13]

The Prophets

The Prophets section of the Hebrew Scriptures contains two divisions: the Former Prophets and the Latter Prophets. The Former Prophets include the books of Joshua, Judges, Samuel, and Kings. These books narrate Israel's past from the conquest of the land to the Davidic monarchy. The Latter Prophets include Isaiah, Jeremiah, Ezekiel, and the Book of the Twelve (Hosea, Joel, Amos, Obadiah, Jonah, Micah, Nahum, Habakkuk, Zephaniah, Haggai, Zechariah, and Malachi). These books are presented as the teachings of a series of prophetic individuals who functioned as God's spokesmen, and thus as a counterbalance to the power of the kings of Israel and Judah. Often taking the form of commentary on the law, the writings of the Former and Latter Prophets too were regarded as sacred texts and authoritative. Here we consider two examples where Jesus cites the prophet Isaiah against the scribal authorities.

In the controversy over hand washing that appears in Mark's and Matthew's Gospels, Jesus cites the prophet Isaiah against Pharisees and scribes who come from Jerusalem to observe him (Mark 7:1–13//Matt. 15:1–9). The scribal authorities challenge Jesus when they notice that his disciples do not wash their hands before eating (Mark 7:2//Matt. 15:2). Modern readers may

---

13. If John 8:6, 8, where Jesus twice writes on the ground, is an allusion to God's authorship of the Decalogue in Exod. 32:16 LXX, as I have argued elsewhere (Keith, *Pericope*, 175–202), this passage also reflects the Johannine theme of Jesus's superiority to Moses.

think of this practice primarily in terms of hygiene, but for the Pharisees and scribes it was a matter of purity. Technically, the law required only priests to wash their hands, and only before their priestly duties (Exod. 30:18–21; 40:30–32). But the Pharisees had extended this need for a pure state beyond the priesthood and its activities and into everyday life. Mark explains: "The Pharisees, and all the Jews, do not eat unless they thoroughly wash their hands, thus observing the tradition of the elders" (7:3). The narrator's explanation serves to underscore that the authorities accuse Jesus's disciples of breaking "the tradition of the elders" (Mark 7:5//Matt. 15:2), a nonscriptural practice that grew around the law, not the law itself.

In response, Jesus comes nowhere close to answering their question about breaking the tradition of the elders. Instead, he undermines that tradition and simultaneously ups the ante in this challenge over legal authority. He accuses them of breaking the law itself and reinforces his point with Isaiah the prophet: "Isaiah prophesied rightly about you hypocrites, as it is written, 'This people honors me with their lips, but their hearts are far from me; in vain do they worship me, teaching human precepts as doctrines' [Isa. 29:13]. You abandon the commandment of God and hold to human tradition" (Mark 7:6–8). In Mark's account, Jesus then refers to their practice of corban, whereby one could avoid having to use earthly possessions in order to support one's parents financially by offering these possessions as gifts to God. France observes, "Just how this convenient device [corban] worked is not entirely clear."[14] What is clear in the narrative, however, is that Jesus considers the practice a blatant trespass upon the fifth commandment, which commands Israelites to "Honor your father and your mother" (Exod. 20:12//Deut. 5:16).[15] Jesus thus buttresses his citation of the prophet Isaiah with citations of Moses: "You have a fine way of rejecting the commandment of God in order to keep your tradition! For Moses said, 'Honor your father and your mother' [Exod. 20:12//Deut. 5:16]; and, 'Whoever speaks evil of father or mother must surely die' [Exod. 21:17]" (Mark 7:9–10). The Matthean version of the account places the citation of Isaiah after the reference to their failure to adhere to the fifth commandment, but it contains the same main elements of debate (Matt. 15:1–9).

There are many interesting aspects of this particular account of conflict between Jesus and the scribal elite, not the least of which is that Jesus else-where instructs a would-be follower to ignore the fifth commandment when he dismisses the man's request to bury his father first (Matt. 8:22//Luke 9:60). Most important for present purposes, however, is the manner in which Jesus

---

14. France, *Gospel of Mark*, 286.
15. The Qumran community was also critical of the practice of corban (CD 6.15).

escalates the interaction by citing Scripture. They accuse him of breaking authoritative interpretive tradition; he accuses them of breaking the law itself, thus rendering illegitimate the authority of the tradition with which they were so concerned. For good measure, he also employs Isaiah to cast his opponents as unrighteous Israelites.

Jesus cites Isaiah against his enemies similarly in John's Gospel. In John 6:41, the Jews complain about Jesus's claim to be the bread of life. In response, Jesus claims that God has determined those who come to him and cites Isa. 54:13 in support. He says, "Stop grumbling among yourselves. . . . No one can come to me unless the Father who sent me draws him, and I will raise him up at the last day. It is written in the Prophets: 'They will all be taught by God' [Isa. 54:13]. Everyone who listens to the Father and learns from him comes to me" (John 6:43–45 NIV [1984 ed.]). Isaiah 54:13 describes the children of those who will experience God's blessings when he gathers Israel to himself once more (see 54:7). By identifying those who follow Jesus with those who receive God's blessings, Jesus identifies those who grumble against him with those who do not receive God's blessings. His reference to "grumbling" also aligns them with the unrighteous Israelites who grumbled against Moses and God in the wilderness (for example, Exod. 15:24; 16:2, 8). Once again, Jesus cites the prophet Isaiah to speak to a state of affairs in his own day and divide his listening audience into those who are on the side of God and Jesus and those who are against them. In the hand-washing episode, Jesus claims Isaiah spoke of Jesus's enemies. In John 6:45, Jesus claims that Isaiah spoke of Jesus's followers, making the accusation against his enemies implicit. In both cases, Jesus employs Isaiah against the scribal elite.

The Writings

Jesus's and the scribal-literate authorities' scriptural conflicts extend also to the Writings, a diverse group of texts that includes Psalms, Proverbs, Job, Song of Songs, Ruth, Lamentations, Ecclesiastes, Esther, Daniel, Ezra-Nehemiah, and Chronicles. The status of some of these texts was debated more than others, but first-century Jews revered the Writings as authoritative as well.

In a particularly interesting tradition occurring in each of the Synoptic Gospels, Jesus challenges the teaching of the scribal elite by citing Ps. 110 (109 LXX) against them. According to Mark, Jesus challenges the teaching of the scribes, but before the crowd and in the temple (Mark 12:35–37). Matthew has Jesus instead challenge the Pharisees (Matt. 22:41), while Luke has Jesus address a group that seems to include Sadducees (Luke 20:27) and scribes (20:39). Each of these groups consisted of scribal-literate authorities.

Furthermore, each of these texts situates this account shortly after the challenge to Jesus concerning levirate marriage, and thus as part of a larger series of controversies over Scripture (see "Torah" above).

According to Mark 12:35, Jesus continues the ongoing debate over Scripture with the following provocation: "How can the scribes say that the Messiah is the son of David? David himself, by the Holy Spirit, declared, 'The Lord said to my Lord, "Sit at my right hand, until I put your enemies under your feet."' David himself calls him Lord; so how can he be his son?" (Mark 12:35–37). Jesus's citation of Ps. 110:1 in this verse can be confusing in English. The Hebrew of Ps. 110:1 uses the divine name for God (*yhwh*) for the first "Lord"; thus the psalmist's words in the Hebrew text are "YHWH said to my lord." The LXX, the Greek translation of the Hebrew Scriptures (ca. 250 BCE), consistently substitutes the Greek word for "lord" (*kyrios*) when translating the Hebrew divine name (*yhwh*). This results in the Greek word for "lord" appearing in the LXX for both the divine name and the Hebrew word for "lord" (*'dn*), both of which occur in the first verses of Ps. 110:1. Thus we have the potentially confusing Greek phrase "The lord [*kyrios*] said to my lord [*kyriō*]" (Ps. 109:1 LXX). Jesus's citation of Ps. 110:1 in Mark 12:35 and its parallel passages reflects this Greek.

In many of the controversy narratives over Scripture that involve an interpretive dilemma, the scribal elite initiate the conflict. On this occasion, Jesus proactively offers critique. He seizes upon the fact that David recognizes a lord over himself who was not the Lord Almighty and refers to this figure as the Davidic Messiah. Second Samuel 7 and 1 Chron. 17 had promised a kingly deliverer would come from David's line and thus be his son. Jewish tradition before, during, and after the first century CE took this expectation seriously.[16] Jesus's challenge undermines the scribal-literate authorities' teaching by pitting biblical texts against each other in the form of an interpretive conundrum: How can the authorities be right that the Messiah is David's son when David himself recognizes the Messiah's superiority? Jesus preemptively negates a response that would simply cite 2 Sam. 7//1 Chron. 17 by underscoring that Ps. 110, too, is inspired Scripture ("David himself, *by the Holy Spirit . . .*"). What the scribal authorities' response to Jesus's interpretation of Ps. 110:1 may have been we cannot know. I, for one, would love to have heard it. But the Gospel authors record no response. Luke says nothing else about this event, and Mark tells us only that "the large crowd was listening to him with delight" (Mark 12:37). Matthew claims that the authorities did not respond because

16. Chilton et al., *Comparative Handbook*, 387–89. No messianic interpretations of Ps. 110 are known outside the New Testament, however (390).

they realized they were beaten: "No one was able to give him an answer, nor from that day did anyone dare to ask him any more questions" (Matt. 22:46).[17] The significant point, however, is that here Jesus challenges the scribal-literate authorities at their own game—interpretation of the authoritative texts.

In John 10:34, Jesus again uses the Psalms to establish his preeminence, this time Ps. 82 (81 LXX). On this occasion, however, in addition to his superiority to David, he asserts equivalence with God. The preceding context is key to understanding his usage of Ps. 82. In John 10:30, Jesus takes it upon himself to modify the central affirmation of Jewish monotheism. The previous chapter used this text as an illustration—the Shema, Deut. 6:4. The NIV translation reads: "Hear, O Israel: The LORD our God, the LORD is one." As this translation shows, one can translate the Hebrew of the Shema as a claim for the singularity of Israel's God; that is, Israel's deity is not a pantheon of gods but "one" God. One could also translate the word for "one" (*'ḥd*) as "alone." In this sense, the Shema would emphasize the exclusive nature of Israel's God; that is, Israel's deity is God, and other gods are not. Thus the NRSV reads: "Hear, O Israel: The LORD is our God, the LORD alone." The respective translations have a slight shift of nuance, but the firm message of the Shema is that there are no other gods for the faithful Jew.

Jesus augments the Shema in a manner that makes sense in terms of the Gospel of John's high Christology, but to his contemporaries in the narrative, it looks shockingly like a failure to affirm it. At the Feast of Dedication in Jerusalem in John 10, the Jews are becoming upset that Jesus will not answer directly whether he is the Messiah: "If you are the Messiah, tell us plainly" (10:24). As in other texts we have discussed, rather than responding to the question they ask, Jesus uses Scripture in order to escalate the tension. He speaks about being the true shepherd and then asserts in John 10:30, "The Father and I are one." By stating that God is "one," Jesus evokes the Shema in Deut. 6:4. But he sneaks himself into it. He modifies the very foundation of Jewish monotheism to include himself—"The Father *and I* are one."[18] For the Jews in Jesus's audience, his claim violates the very text he modifies. They do not fail to catch the significance of what he does or to respond. After the author tells us that they picked up stones in order to stone Jesus (10:31), the

17. Mark places this statement prior to Jesus's teaching on Ps. 110:1 and after the commendation Jesus receives from the scribe concerning the greatest commandment (Mark 12:34). Luke follows Mark in putting the statement prior to the teaching on Ps. 110:1, but places it after Jesus's teaching on resurrection and Abraham (Luke 20:40).

18. Also affirming that the Shema lies behind John 10:30 is Richard Bauckham, "Monotheism and Christology in the Gospel of John," in *The Testimony of the Beloved Disciple* (Grand Rapids: Baker Academic, 2007), 250; repr. from *Contours of Christology in the New Testament*, ed. R. N. Longenecker (Grand Rapids: Eerdmans, 2005), 148–66.

Jews explain, "It is not for a good work that we are going to stone you, but for blasphemy, because you, though only a human being, are making yourself God" (10:33).

Since the Jews have rejected that Jesus's identity is (in some way) parallel to God and rejected that Jesus is faithful to Scripture, Jesus proceeds to assert the truth of both matters and uses Ps. 82 to do it. He says, "Is it not written in your law, 'I said, you are gods' [Ps. 82:6]? If those to whom the word of God came were called 'gods'—and the scripture cannot be annulled—can you say that the one whom the Father has sanctified and sent into the world is blaspheming because I said, 'I am God's Son'?" (10:34–36). As in his citation of Ps. 110 in the Synoptic Gospels, Jesus reinforces his citation of Ps. 82:6 by stating its inspired status—"and the scripture cannot be annulled." Combined with his implicit acknowledgment of the Jews' authoritative status as scribal-literate gateways to the holy texts ("*your* law"),[19] this text once more portrays Jesus as defeating his enemies on *their* turf. He out-interprets them by exposing tensions in the Scripture. Deuteronomy 6:4 asserts God's singular or exclusive nature as the only God. Nevertheless, Ps. 82:6 paints a more complex portrait of divine identity, and it is this more complex portrait that Jesus cites as scriptural support for his claims about himself vis-à-vis God. Although Jesus's enemies can claim that Scripture is on their side in rejecting his claims, Jesus can claim that Scripture is on his side in making them.

In addition to the Psalms among the Writings, Jesus also refers to historical narratives in some controversy narratives. At the beginning of Jesus's ministry in the Synoptic Gospels, some Pharisees question Jesus and his disciples for picking grain on the Sabbath (Mark 2:23–28//Matt. 12:1–8//Luke 6:1–5). Jesus responds by referring to a scriptural precedent. According to levitical law, only the priests may eat the bread of the presence (Lev. 24:5–9). Once again, Jesus pits texts against each other. For, in 1 Sam. 21:1–6, David and his men—none of whom were priests—eat the bread of the presence. In Mark 2:25, Jesus defends himself against his opponents by citing this text in a manner that mocks their status as scribal-literate interpreters: "Have you never read what David did when he and his companions were hungry and in need of food?" (cf. Matt. 12:3//Luke 6:3). In Matthew's account, for emphasis, Jesus appeals further to the law: "Or have you not read in the law that on the sabbath the priests in the temple break the sabbath and yet are guiltless?" (Matt. 12:5).

As these examples demonstrate, Scripture itself plays a crucial role—if not *the* crucial role—in the conflict between Jesus and the scribal-literate authorities that the controversy narratives portray. Most frequently the scribal-literate

19. Jesus similarly distances himself from Scripture in John 8:17; 15:25.

authorities initiate the conflict, but occasionally Jesus does as well. For both parties, the interpretive traps they set for their opposition involve conundrums that are particularly acute in light of a shared affirmation of the texts as inspired.

Conflict over Authority

Although they are fewer and will receive less attention than conflicts over Scripture, some controversy narratives focus more directly upon the issue of Jesus's authority. Once more, I emphasize that this is not to claim that one could or should separate Scripture and authority in the narratives (or the historical context of Jesus). But the rope upon which both sides tug in these narratives is Jesus's social status or position, not explicitly Scripture. Stated otherwise, the tone of the debate is "Who do you think you are?" instead of "What does this or that text say?"

Conflicts over Authority in the Synoptic Gospels

Perhaps the clearest challenge to Jesus's authority in the controversy narratives comes after Jesus's demonstration in the temple in each of the Synoptic Gospels (Mark 11:15–17//Matt. 21:12–13//Luke 19:45–46). In response to Jesus's criticisms of the temple and those responsible for its functions, the ruling elite confront him explicitly about his authority: "Again they came to Jerusalem. As he was walking in the temple, the chief priests, the scribes, and the elders came to him and said, 'By what authority are you doing these things? Who gave you this authority to do them?'" (Mark 11:27–28; cf. Matt. 21:23// Luke 20:1–2). Jesus responds with a riddle about John the Baptist that exploits John's popularity among the crowd: "I will ask you one question; answer me, and I will tell you by what authority I do these things. Did the baptism of John come from heaven, or was it of human origin? Answer me" (Mark 11:29–30; Matt. 21:24–25; Luke 20:3–4).[20] Not wanting to affirm the Baptist, but also not wanting to enrage the crowd, who "regarded John as truly a prophet" (11:32), the scribal elite respond neutrally: "We do not know" (Mark 11:33//Matt. 21:27; cf. Luke 20:7). Since they cannot give him an answer, Jesus refuses to answer their question about his authority (11:33). In this text, Jesus is able to defend his authority and honor by turning the tables on those questioning it. All the while, Jesus never actually answers their question, which is a rhetorical

---

20. On this text, and others in the controversy narratives, as a riddle, see Thatcher, *Jesus the Riddler*, 57.

skill he evinces in numerous controversy narratives as we have already seen. Furthermore, Jesus is able to get his opponents to confess ignorance publicly. Public confession of ignorance in an honor/shame culture like Second Temple Judaism was no small matter (see further chap. 6).

Another controversy narrative where the scribal elite explicitly question Jesus's authority appears in Mark 2:1–12//Matt. 9:2–8//Luke 5:17–26. Mark places the story in Capernaum, Jesus's base of operations in the early narrative of Mark. Some men lower a paralytic through the roof of a house where Jesus is teaching (Mark 2:4). Due to the faith of his friends, Jesus tells the man, "Son, your sins are forgiven" (2:5). Scribes who are present (and Pharisees in Luke 5:21) question "in their hearts" (Mark 2:6) how Jesus can claim to do such a thing: "Why does this fellow speak in this way? It is blasphemy! Who can forgive sins but God alone?" (2:7).[21] Their rhetorical question implies that Jesus does not have the authority to forgive sins; neither does anyone else for that matter. Jesus proceeds to heal the man in order to answer directly their questioning of his authority, thereby intertwining his authority to forgive with his ability to heal. "'But so that you may know that the Son of Man has authority on earth to forgive sins'—he said to the paralytic—'I say to you, stand up, take your mat and go to your home.' And he stood up, and immediately took the mat and went out before all of them" (2:10–12). In the Matthean parallel to this story, where Jesus's conflict is also with the scribes (Matt. 9:3), the narrator ends by noting the crowd's acknowledgment of Jesus's authority: "When the crowds saw it, they were filled with awe, and they glorified God, who had given such authority to human beings" (9:8).

As we will shortly see, Jesus's participation in God's distinct authority is an important theological theme in John's Gospel as well. Before moving to that discussion, however, it is worth once more noting Jesus's strong words for the scribes and the Pharisees in Matt. 23:1–12, an example where Jesus initiates the hostile language. Although there is no explicit reference to authority in this text, there can be little doubt that Jesus seeks to undermine the authority of the scribal elite by instructing his disciples not to refer to the scribes and Pharisees as rabbis or teachers. He chastises the scribal authorities' public showmanship: they "sit on Moses' seat" (23:2), "do all their deeds to be seen by others" (23:5), "make their phylacteries broad and their fringes long" (23:5), and "love to have the place of honor at banquets and the best

---

21. Those dining at the house of Simon the Pharisee ask a similar question when Jesus forgives the sins of the woman who washes his feet in Luke 7:36–50: "But those who were at the table with him began to say among themselves, 'Who is this who even forgives sins?'" (7:49).

seats in the synagogues" (23:6) and "to have people call them rabbi" (23:7). Jesus accuses them of not practicing what they preach (23:3) and predicts a day of a reversal of the social dichotomy: "The greatest among you will be your servant. All who exalt themselves will be humbled, and all who humble themselves will be exalted" (23:11–12).

Conflicts over Authority in the Gospel of John

Conflict between Jesus and the scribal elite over Jesus's authority arises in John's Gospel as well. As has already been observed, one of the core sources of conflict between Jesus and the scribal-elite Jews in the Gospel of John is that Jesus aligns himself too closely with God, as is clear in their reaction to Jesus's modification of the Shema in John 10:30. Jesus's sharing of the authority of God contributes to this conflict and is, in fact, a sustained theme throughout the narrative, even playing a prominent role in a unique element in John's account of Jesus's Roman trial. When Pilate claims he has authority over Jesus (19:10), Jesus tells him, "You would have no authority over me unless it had been given you from above" (19:11; modified from NRSV). Jesus's acknowledgment that the Father has given someone else authority in John 19:11 is another unique element in John's Gospel. The narrator claims that children of God receive their authority (*exousia*, which one could also translate "power") from Jesus in 1:12, but otherwise the only explicit conversations regarding authority (*exousia*) in this Gospel involve Jesus alone sharing in God's authority. Those occurrences are John 5:27, 10:18, and 17:2, the first two of which are part of his debates with scribal elites.

In John 5, the Jews are upset over Jesus's healing of a lame man on the Sabbath at the Pool of Bethsaida. According to the narrator, when the healed man informed the Jews that Jesus had healed him, "the Jews started persecuting Jesus" (5:16). Jesus tells them that he must be working on the Sabbath because "my Father"—not "our Father"—is working. As a result, "the Jews were seeking all the more to kill him, because he was not only breaking the Sabbath, but was also calling God his own Father, thereby making himself equal to God" (5:18). As elsewhere in John's Gospel, Jesus's further attempts to explain his relationship with the Father do nothing to allay the fears of the Jews that Jesus is putting himself in God's categories. In this case, Jesus's explanation includes his claim to judge with the judgment of God in John 5:22: "The Father judges no one but has given all judgment to the Son." Jesus casts this role in terms of his authority only five verses later when he claims, "He [the Father] has given him [the Son] authority to execute judgment, because he is the Son of Man" (5:27).

There are at least three important aspects of this claim. First, the judgment in view here is eschatological judgment, as other passages make clear (for example, 5:24; 17:2–3). "Jesus' power to judge . . . is simply another way of speaking of his power to grant eternal life."[22] Second, the Old Testament frequently associates this type of judgment with God himself: Abraham refers to God as "Judge of all the earth" (Gen. 18:25); the Psalms praise God in his capacity as judge (Pss. 9:4 [9:5 LXX]; 96:13 [95:13 LXX]) and declare that "God himself is judge" (Ps. 50:6 [49:6 LXX]); the Teacher of Ecclesiastes portrays God as the judge of one's life (Eccles. 3:17; 11:9); Isaiah asserts that "the LORD is our judge; . . . he will save us" (Isa. 33:22). Third, although God is judge in Jewish tradition, occasionally others share in the execution of his judgment. Particularly significant in this regard is Dan. 7, where Daniel envisions a Son of Man (7:13) who participates as king in the eschatological judgment of God, the Ancient One (7:9–10). In John 5:27, John has Jesus identify himself as this Son of Man who participates in this judgment of God.[23] Thus, when the Jews reject Jesus's authority to heal on the Sabbath as well as the notion that he would be "equal to God" (5:18), Jesus affirms both matters more strongly by asserting that God has given him authority to execute God's own judgment. If the Jews of John 5 had asked the question of the scribes and the Pharisees in Mark 11:27–28—"By what authority are you doing these things? Who gave you this authority to do them?"—Jesus's answer in John 5:27 would have been "God's, . . . and he did."

Jesus addresses his authority explicitly again when the Jews of John 10 challenge him. John 10 follows upon Jesus's chastisements of the Pharisees' (spiritual) blindness after the healing of the man born blind in John 9:40–41. As in previously discussed examples, they are upset that Jesus has healed on the Sabbath (9:14). Some of the Pharisees state, "This man is not from God, for he does not observe the sabbath" (9:16). Later they charge Jesus with being born in sin (9:34), possibly a reference to the fact that Joseph was not his real father and rumors of illegitimacy. During Jesus's response, in which he again affirms his unique relationship with the Father (". . . just as the Father knows me and I know the Father," 10:15), he addresses his authority specifically as it relates to his laying down his life as the good shepherd who will die for his sheep (10:11). He says, "No one takes it from me, but I lay it down of my own accord. I have authority to lay it down, and I have authority to take it up again. I have received this command from my Father" (10:18; modified from NRSV).

---

22. Marianne Meye Thompson, *The God of the Gospel of John* (Grand Rapids: Eerdmans, 2001), 118.

23. Benjamin Reynolds, *The Apocalyptic Son of Man in the Gospel of John*, WUNT 2.249 (Tübingen: Mohr Siebeck, 2008), 137–46, esp. 139–40.

In the Johannine narrative, this serves to underscore Jesus's full control over the events that are about to unfold and lead Jesus to the cross. It thus also foreshadows Jesus's later conversation with Pilate regarding who truly has authority over his life and death (John 19:10–11).

In John's Gospel, therefore, Jesus argues with the authorities over his own authority on multiple occasions. Jesus's affirmations of his own authority address christological matters beyond his status as a scribal-literate interpreter, which is otherwise a theme in John's Gospel as well (John 7:15–52; cf. 8:6, 8). Jesus judges with authority that is from God and is the authority of God. Likewise, he controls his life and death with authority that is from God. Ultimately, these narratives contribute to the christological perspective of the Gospel that Jesus has control over not just his physical life but also the eternal life of all. These issues coalesce in the other instance of Jesus's discussion of his authority in John's Gospel. In John 17, he prays to the Father, "Father, the hour has come; glorify your Son so that the Son may glorify you, since you have given him authority over all people, to give eternal life to all whom you have given him" (17:1–2). For the readers of John's Gospel, this authority is clear from the beginning to the end. Equally clear for those readers is the author's opinion that this authority was far from clear for Jesus's contemporaries and was, to the contrary, quite disputed.

Summary of Controversies of Scripture and Authority

These are not the only controversy stories over Scripture or authority. One could easily add more texts to these examples. For example, I have mentioned some texts where Jesus mocks his interlocutors' status as scribal-literate authorities with a variant of the phrase "Have you never read . . . ?" (Mark 2:25//Matt. 12:3//Luke 6:3; Mark 12:26//Matt. 22:31; Matt. 12:5), but there are others.[24] These few demonstrate, however, that when Jesus and scribal-literate authorities such as scribes, Pharisees, Sadducees, and priests engage in public battles

24. Mark 12:10//Matt. 21:42; Matt. 19:4–5; Luke 10:26; cf. Mark 12:24; Luke 20:17. Although some scholars take this question to mean that Jesus himself had read the texts to which he refers (Casey, *Jesus*, 161–62; Dunn, *Jesus*, 314; Craig A. Evans, "Jewish Scripture and the Literacy of Jesus," in *From Biblical Criticism to Biblical Faith: Essays in Honor of Lee Martin McDonald*, ed. William H. Brackney and Craig A. Evans [Macon, GA: Mercer University Press, 2007], 50; repr. in *Jesus and His World: The Archaeological Evidence* [London: SPCK, 2012], 86; Puig i Tàrrech, *Jesus*, 191), the rhetorical point of the question assumes only that his opponents were able to read the texts. As a reminder from chap. 1, knowledge of the contents of texts (textuality) does not equate with ability to access them for oneself (literacy). See further comments on these passages in chap. 6.

of wits and egos in the Gospels, the field upon which they fight is usually the Jewish Scriptures and the authority of the opposite party to interpret those Scriptures. As many of these accounts make clear, controversies over Scripture and controversies over authority are really two sides of the same coin in the Gospels. To claim one is to claim the other; to deny one to an opponent is to deny the other.

Once more, I assert that, by focusing upon Scripture and authority in the controversy narratives, I do not intend to suggest that there were no other factors contributing to the rising hostilities. This would not be correct, since the narratives are clear that issues such as Jesus's healings and exorcisms, as well as his identity as Messiah or his identity as Son of God, were also factors. All of these issues are intertwined in the narratives, as the above discussion has occasionally noted. Only a fool would attempt to exegete the Gospels by separating them. Yet it remains that Scripture and authority serve as loci in these debates in ways that other factors do not. In the debates over who Jesus is and what authority he has to be, or to claim to be, that person, the debaters almost inevitably turn to Scripture and scriptural precedents. The scribal-literate authorities attack Jesus by questioning his authority as a teacher and challenging him regarding Scripture. Jesus reciprocates by attacking their authority as teachers and challenging them regarding Scripture.

6

The Emergence of the Conflict

Its Origins and Nature

When he said this, all his opponents were put to shame. (Luke 13:17)

I do not share the view of some form critics that almost any scriptural citation in the mouth of Jesus is by definition a later insertion by the early church. Jesus would have been a very strange Jewish teacher in 1st-century Palestine if he had never quoted, commented on, or argued about the meaning of the Jewish Scriptures.[1]

This chapter will trace the origins of the conflict between Jesus and the scribal elite to the context of the historical Jesus.[2] It will do so in light of my previous argument that Jesus's scribal-literate status was a matter of debate and mixed perceptions. The question of whether the conflict that the controversy narratives portray occurred is often intertwined with questions concerning the nature of the conflict they portray. By "nature" I refer to the tone of the debate; the attitude of the participants toward one another and the goals of each party in engaging the other, as best we can understand such matters through historical research. I will argue here that the controversy narratives do not reflect debates between two parties who stand on equal footing. They reflect an attempt on the part of the scribal elite to expose Jesus as an imposter to the role of authoritative teacher, and an attempt on the part of Jesus to shame his opponents in kind. After a brief overview of previous scholarship, the first half of the chapter will address the historicity and origins of the controversy, and the second half of the chapter will address its nature.

1. Meier, *Marginal Jew*, 2:140–41. Meier rightly continues, "On the other hand, a number of points give one pause" (2:141).
2. Once more I reiterate that my concern is not with the historicity of any individual conflict story, but rather the general claim that Jesus and scribal-literate teachers had conflict over Scripture and authority.

The Historicity and Nature of the Controversy in Previous Scholarship

Previous scholarship on the historicity and nature of the conflict between Jesus and the scribal elite displays just how interrelated the two issues can be. Consideration of prior suggestions will also make clear how the matter of Jesus's scribal-literate status contributes new insights to this discussion.

The Historicity of the Controversy in Previous Scholarship

In the history of New Testament scholarship, a steady stream of scholars from different generations has viewed the controversy narratives with a skeptical historical eye. Indeed, some scholars have been quite adamant about the historical unreliability of these traditions. Consider, for example, the verdict of Paul Winter in 1961:

> All the Marcan "controversy stories," without exception, reflect disputes between the "Apostolic Church" and its social environment, and are devoid of roots in the circumstances of the life of Jesus. Some of the controversy stories have simply been constructed by the Second Evangelist himself who presented certain traditional items by framing them as a disputation.[3]

According to Winter, the texts are "devoid" of history and amount to retrojections of later Christianity's enemies onto the Gospel narratives as Jesus's enemies. "The actual opponents of Christianity, coeval with a particular evangelist, are cited as adversaries of Jesus."[4]

Paul Winter's opinion betrays the time period in which he wrote and the dominance of Bultmann's form criticism. Chapter 3 above showed that, as part of this method's attempt to excavate early oral tradition from the Gospel narratives, it assumed that these narratives primarily reflected the present circumstances of the early church rather than the past of Jesus. In this sense,

---

3. Paul Winter, *On the Trial of Jesus*, rev. and ed. T. A. Burkill and Geza Vermes, 2nd ed., SJ 1 (Berlin: de Gruyter, 1974 [1961]), 175 (emphasis removed). Elsewhere, Winter is not so emphatic. On the same page, he limits his skepticism to the Pharisaic controversy narratives: "There is some historical foundation in references to the hostility of the priests towards Jesus; there is none in citations of Pharisaic antagonism." Similarly, he earlier admits the theoretical possibility that the Markan controversy narratives are historically accurate, while simultaneously disallowing this admission any practical effect: "There are cases in which the reference to some argument or other could go back to an actual occurrence in the life of Jesus, yet the Marcan form of presentation does not allow of any historical deduction as to the cause, or setting, of the dispute concerned" (160).

4. Ibid., 170 (emphasis removed).

form criticism was predisposed against affirmations of the historicity of the gospel traditions, and the controversy narratives were no exception for most form critics.[5] Bultmann had earlier asserted strongly, "Controversy dialogues are all of them imaginary scenes."[6] He does not necessarily doubt that Jesus, for example, healed on the Sabbath or said some of the things attributed to him by groups such as scribes and Pharisees. But the influence of the early church in fabricating some traditions and reshaping others for purposes of "apologetic and polemic" renders such inquiries secondary at best and, for all practical purposes, out of the historian's reach.[7] For Bultmann, the early church simply could not resist "the increasing tendency . . . to clothe its dominical sayings, its views and its fundamental beliefs in the form of the controversy dialogue."[8] In this sense, P. Winter was simply restating Bultmann's earlier conclusion: "In the form in which we have them the controversy dialogues are imaginary scenes illustrating in some concrete occasion a principle which the Church ascribed to Jesus."[9] Technically, Bultmann distinguished between the "conflict and didactic sayings" of Jesus on the one hand and "controversy dialogues" and "scholastic dialogues" on the other hand.[10] He regarded some of the sayings to be possibly authentic but their narrative frames generally to be artistic constructions.[11] As to the dialogues, he regarded the "imaginary character of the scholastic dialogues" to be less certain than the completely fabricated controversy dialogues, but still cast doubt on any attempts to affirm their historicity.[12] After Bultmann and others, Harvey would claim in 1980 that the idea that the controversy narratives reflected later Christianity's debates with Judaism was an "assured result" of form criticism.[13]

Paul Winter and Bultmann are not alone in this opinion, however, and this general skepticism is not limited to form critics. Twelve years after P. Winter's

5. One must be wary of painting the form critics with too broad a brush on the issue of historicity, however. Dibelius was less certain in this regard than Bultmann (see Dibelius, *From Tradition*, 68), a fact that Bultmann himself addressed as a point of disagreement between the two (*History*, 5). Also Taylor affirmed the historicity of the controversy narratives (Vincent Taylor, *The Formation of the Gospel Tradition* [London: Macmillan, 1960]).

6. Bultmann, *History*, 40; cf. also 41, 54.

7. Ibid., 40–41. Likewise, 54: "It is in itself highly probable that Jesus was asked questions about the way to life, or about the greatest commandment, but it is quite another thing to ask whether the scenes which relate those questions to us are historical reports or not. They are such only in the sense that the Church formulated such scenes entirely in the spirit of Jesus."

8. Ibid., 51.

9. Ibid., 41.

10. Ibid., 39–61.

11. Ibid., 12–27.

12. Ibid., 54–55; quotation from 54 with emphasis removed.

13. A. E. Harvey, *Jesus and the Constraints of History* (London: Duckworth, 1982), 49n69. The lectures in this volume were delivered in 1980.

work, Maccoby assessed the accounts of hostilities between Jesus and the Pharisees in a similar manner: "These passages in the Gospels are unhistorical, and arose out of the later history of the Christian church, which *at the time the Gospels were written* . . . was in a state of enmity with the Pharisees."[14] Similarly, in his 1985 *Jesus and Judaism*, Sanders pronounced against the historicity of the controversy narratives. Sanders is not a form critic and was even critical of form criticism at times in this study, but generally followed Bultmann's insistence upon the "imaginary" character of the controversy narratives.[15] He surmised, "All the scenes of debate between Jesus and the Pharisees have more than a slight air of artificiality."[16] Sanders's argument is important, and I will return to it shortly.

Continuing this line of thought, in 1988 Mack claimed, "It is . . . most improbable that Jesus had a running battle with Pharisees in Galilee"[17] and summarized what he considered the "scholarly consensus":

> There is general agreement that (1) the Jesus of the stories is the Jesus as early Christians came to see him; (2) the issues addressed were Christian issues, matters of importance for the social formation of early Christian groups; and (3) the challenge to Jesus that invites his address in the stories reflects in general the actual challenge that other Jewish movements posed for these early Christian communities.[18]

In the 2011 translation of his 2005 Spanish book on Jesus, Puig i Tàrrech similarly claimed, "The writings of the New Testament generally reflect situations of tension and conflict, or even open hostility, between the Jews who would not acknowledge Jesus' legitimacy and the Jews who had become Christians. . . . These differences are often reflected back on to Jesus' life."[19] In 2012, Cook

---

14. Hyam Maccoby, *Revolution in Judaea: Jesus and the Jewish Resistance* (New York: Taplinger, 1973), 106 (emphasis original). He later repeats these views in *Jesus the Pharisee*, for example, 11. Cf. similarly, concerning the concentration on the Pharisees in the Matthean controversy narratives, Boris Repschinski, *The Controversy Stories in the Gospel of Matthew: Their Redaction, Form and Relevance for the Relationship between the Matthean Community and Formative Judaism*, FRLANT 189 (Göttingen: Vandenhoeck & Ruprecht, 2000), 344.

15. Sanders, *Jesus*, 13–18 (criticism and affirmation of form criticism), 265, 291 (following form critics).

16. Ibid., 265.

17. Burton Mack, *A Myth of Innocence: Mark and Christian Origins* (Philadelphia: Fortress, 1988), 44.

18. Ibid., 177.

19. Puig i Tàrrech, *Jesus*, 280; cf. also his comments on Matt. 23 (283). Puig i Tàrrech is inconsistent in practice, however, since he consistently cites controversy stories as indicative of the life of Jesus. For example, in addition to reflecting concerns between Christianity and Judaism, he claims that the question of authority in Mark 11:28//Matt. 21:23//Luke 20:2 "concerns

revamped P. Winter's 1961 study and came to the same conclusion concerning Mark as had Bultmann and P. Winter already: "I do not deny that Jesus engaged in controversies with Jewish authorities. Assuredly, however, we cannot confidently accept as historically accurate the disputations as Mark himself narrates them."[20]

In various periods of biblical scholarship, then, scholars have advocated the view that, if the controversy narratives reflect any historical set of circumstances, it is the circumstances of later Christians crafting the narrative and not the life of Jesus. Even under the theoretical possibility that Jesus did say and do some of the things that the controversy narratives attribute to him, this approach considers affirmations of these possibilities permanently stalled in light of the early church's reformulation of the tradition.

Although some readers of the Bible may balk at these scholars' treatments of the controversy narratives, this narrative dynamic whereby a storyteller narrates an event of the past and imbues it with present realities is too familiar to dismiss. One example from pop culture is *M*A*S*H*, a dark comedy about a wartime military surgical unit and one of the most popular shows in the 1970s and 1980s in the United States. Formally, the narrative was set in the Korean War of the 1950s; but this wartime backdrop simply enabled the writers of the show to use it as an allegory about the contemporary Vietnam War of the 1970s. To this day, when I am discussing the narrative dynamics of the Gospels, I will often ask the question "What war is *M*A*S*H* about?" The answer from students of varying ages is typically "the Korean War." Then I will ask, "Yes, but what war is *M*A*S*H really* about?" This time the answer returns as "the Vietnam War." Audiences of *M*A*S*H* intuitively understand how the narrative of the show works by using a story about the past to speak to the present. On the not infrequent occasion when students answer "the Vietnam War" to the first question, they simply witness to the success of the show's writers in employing this narrative dynamic. And *M*A*S*H* is one example among myriads that one could cite from pop culture or the Bible.[21]

---

the very heart of Jesus the person, and . . . is the fundamental sticking point between the rabbi of Nazareth and the other rabbis."

20. Michael J. Cook, "The Distribution of Jewish Leaders in the Synoptic Gospels: Why Wariness Is Warranted," in *Soundings in the Religion of Jesus: Perspectives and Methods in Jewish and Christian Scholarship*, ed. Bruce Chilton, Anthony Le Donne, and Jacob Neusner (Minneapolis: Fortress, 2012), 79.

21. As only two examples, one can point to the books of Chronicles and the Letters of the apostle Paul. The chronicler rewrites the books of Samuel from a present perspective that is much more favorable toward the Davidic monarchy. Paul frequently tells stories from the Old Testament for the sake of his current audience; among many other examples, see 1 Cor. 10:1–6; Gal. 4:22–31.

Many of us are therefore quite familiar with the ability of stories to relay the past for the sake of speaking to the present.

And yet, that narratives about the past can speak to the present does not lead automatically to the conclusion that this is all that they do; or the conclusion that they were fabricated wholly in the present; or the conclusion that, under the possibility that a tradition was inherited from the past and not fabricated, present interests swallowed the past to the extent that its impact no longer remains. Much less does this observation lead automatically to the conclusion that historical inquiries into Mark's Gospel or any of the other Gospels are inherently incongruent with the tradition and its formation, although it may mean that pursuing those inquiries is more complex than it initially seems.[22] From this perspective, the problem with this view is not that it is entirely false. The problem is that it is only half true. For this reason, I introduced the memory approach in chapter 3, which acknowledges the interpretive role of present interests, but foregrounds them as the means by which the impact of the past persists into the unfolding present. Thus, even though one may wholeheartedly agree that the present realities of the authors impacted their retellings of the Jesus story to various degrees—and there is no reason to doubt this as a condition of storytelling in general—the tradition being influenced by the contexts of the tradition-handlers is not the same as being "devoid of roots in the circumstances of Jesus."[23] While we are therefore justified in not dismissing these opinions uncritically, we are equally justified in not accepting them uncritically. The perspectives of Mark and the other Gospel authors are not what prohibits historical work on the texts. They are what enables it.

For these reasons and others, it is also significant that a long stream of scholarship finds the broad strokes of the controversy narratives essentially

22. I can say it no better than T. W. Manson, *Studies in the Gospels and Epistles*, ed. Matthew Black (Manchester: Manchester University Press, 1962), 7–8:

> I find myself, after a good deal of labour in this field, being gradually driven to the conclusion that much that passes for historical study of the life of Jesus consists not in asking of any story in the tradition: "Is it credible in itself?" but: "What motive could the Church have had for telling this tale?"—which can easily become the question: "What motives led the Church to invent it?" The danger is that what is entitled "Life of Christ" or the like should turn out to be in fact a psychological novel about a large number of anonymous members of the primitive Church. . . . I venture to think that this kind of thing has gone on too long. It may be granted that the stories in the Gospels have forms. It may also be granted that the early Church found the stories useful for all kinds of purposes. It may even be granted that the Church might have invented them. But it is a long way from what the Church might have done to what the Church in fact did. (emphasis removed)

23. P. Winter, *On the Trial*, 175. For further criticism of this "presentist" perspective in Gospels studies, see Keith, "Memory," 168–77; repr. in *Jesus' Literacy*, 50–70; Le Donne, *Historiographical*, 41–92; Rodríguez, *Structuring*, 53; Schwartz, "Christian Origins," 43–56.

credible on historical grounds. Prior to the onset of form criticism's dominance in the early twentieth century, Albertz attributed a high degree of historical reliability to the controversy narratives.[24] Following Albertz, and in dialogue with Bultmann and Dibelius, Taylor, the great voice of form criticism in the English-speaking world, also pronounced in favor of the historicity of the controversy narratives in 1960. According to Taylor, "We ought . . . to esteem them [the controversy narratives] among the strongest and most stable elements in the Gospel tradition."[25] Ten years later, Dodd likewise affirmed,

> That he did upon occasion set his teaching in deliberate opposition to that of other rabbis cannot be doubted. Nor, whatever allowance be made for overcoloring in the course of controversy, is it possible to doubt that he did deliberately criticize them, and sometimes in trenchant terms. . . . A growing opposition is a feature of the record which cannot be set aside.[26]

After Taylor and Dodd, and working from within a form-critical framework, in 1979 Hultgren likewise rejected an entirely skeptical perspective. He asserted that "all of the conflict stories are Christian compositions," but nevertheless claimed, "It cannot be said that the creative impulse for the conflict story form of presentation originated purely in the conflicts of church and synagogue. Behind the process of conflict story formation stands the personality of Jesus himself as it was remembered by those who knew him."[27] Harvey ultimately took a very similar position in 1980: "The evangelists may have had an interest in adapting his teaching to the terms of the controversies in which their own churches were involved, and some of the controversial settings of the sayings may be contrived. But it is hardly conceivable that the whole picture of an on-going controversy between Jesus and the sages of his time is fictional."[28] Borg claimed in 1984: "Yet a close examination of the tradition demonstrates that the conflict was real."[29]

In 2007, Pickup made the important point that the theory of wholesale creation fails to account for the fact that the controversies in the Gospels do

24. Martin Albertz, *Die synoptischen Streitgespräche: Ein Beitrag zur Formengeschichte des Urchristentums* (Berlin: Trowitzsch & Sohn, 1921), 57–80. Bultmann, *History*, 40n2, was critical of Albertz for continuing to affirm the historicity of the controversy narratives despite acknowledging the creative contributions of the early church in shaping the tradition.

25. Taylor, *Formation of the Gospel Tradition*, 87.

26. C. H. Dodd, *The Founder of Christianity* (New York: Macmillan, 1970), 69–70.

27. Arland J. Hultgren, *Jesus and His Adversaries: The Form and Function of the Conflict Stories in the Synoptic Tradition* (Minneapolis: Fortress, 1979), 198. Hultgren's affirmation in this regard is similar to Bultmann's less confident assessment of the (non)historicity of the "scholastic dialogues."

28. Harvey, *Jesus*, 51.

29. Borg, *Conflict*, 153. The first edition was published in 1984.

not always match the controversies in the early church. If the early church leaders were fabricating stories to meet their own needs, they often failed at the task. He observed, for example, "There is no evidence to suggest that the early church had controversies over healing on the Sabbath, or plucking grain on the Sabbath, or hand-washing before meals, or matters pertaining to Corban."[30] On this basis, Pickup concluded:

> The evangelists' accounts of disputes between Jesus and the Pharisees could, of course, be used hortatively within the church; applications to current problems could be extrapolated. But it makes little sense to assert that these encounters between Jesus and the Pharisees were concocted out of whole cloth to address contemporary church issues, when in so many instances, Jesus' disputes and the church's disputes do not coincide.[31]

In 2009, Meier affirmed that "the first and second generation of Christians selected, reformulated, created, and probably deleted sayings of Jesus on the Law," but equally affirmed that "to sweep away almost all the 'legal material' in the Gospels as inauthentic or as not representing Jesus' truest intentions strikes one from the start as an unlikely, not to say a desperate, solution."[32] Regarding the Sabbath controversies in particular, and acknowledging that "we necessarily deal with degrees of probability rather than absolute certitude," Hagner argued in 2009 that "the evidence warrants acceptance of these accounts as highly probable, trustworthy history."[33] Also with appropriate caveats acknowledging the interpretive influence of later Christians on the controversy narratives asserted and also in 2009, Keener claimed, "The substance of these accounts is likely authentic."[34] After reflecting on the "narrativized" nature of the controversy narratives, Le Donne claimed in 2011, "Nothing in the Gospels is more historically plausible than hostility among like-minded fellows."[35] Casey's book on Jesus from 2010 also consistently affirmed the historicity of hostilities between Jesus and scribal elite teachers.[36]

As this brief and incomplete survey makes clear, scholarly opinion is divided over the historicity of the controversy narratives and has been for some time. Although some scholars doubt wholesale their historical value, other

---

30. Martin Pickup, "Matthew's and Mark's Pharisees," in *Historical*, 111.
31. Ibid., 112.
32. Meier, *Marginal*, 4:40–41, 2, respectively; cf. also 2:140–41; 4:652.
33. Donald A. Hagner, "Jesus and the Synoptic Sabbath Controversies," in *Key Events*, 270.
34. Keener, *Historical*, 225.
35. Anthony Le Donne, "The Jewish Leaders," in *Jesus among Friends and Enemies*, 208.
36. Casey, *Jesus*, 313–52; also 253–56 on the role of Jesus's exorcisms in the conflict.

scholars affirm the historical value of the general portrait of the conflict while acknowledging the early church's necessary interpretive role.

The Nature of the Controversy in Previous Scholarship

In addition to debating the historicity of the Gospels' portrayals of conflict between Jesus and the scribal elite, scholars have also debated the conflict's nature. More specifically, they have debated whether it was an in-house conflict. Of course the conflict was "in-house" if by that one means it was an "intra-Jewish" conflict.[37] Some scholars, however, have further proposed that the controversy narratives reflect intra-Pharisaical debates. On the one hand, that Jesus's teachings occasionally comport with the Pharisees' teachings, such as his similar belief in resurrection (Mark 12:25//Matt. 22:30//Luke 20:35), could suggest this possibility. On the other hand, a few similarities in the midst of other significant differences (over the law, purity, fasting, table fellowship, and Sabbath, for example) may indicate only that Jesus and the Pharisees were "religious/ideological relatives."[38] As we have already seen, however, for some scholars those significant differences between Jesus and the Pharisees are creations of a later time. Among these scholars, some have proposed that those later creations cover up the reality that Jesus *was* a Pharisee.[39] What one sees in the controversy narratives, according to this theory, is a distorted Christian view of a controversy that originally involved Pharisees disagreeing with one another from the same platform with regard to scribal authority. Maccoby even claims, "There can be no doubt that Jesus was educated as a Pharisee."[40] Further, his association with Pharisees was not limited to his education: "Jesus was not only a Pharisee; he remained a Pharisee all his life."[41]

37. Keener, *Historical*, 231.
38. Le Donne, "Jewish Leadership," 217.
39. Falk, *Jesus the Pharisee*, 8–9; Maccoby, *Jesus the Pharisee*, 180; idem, *Revolution*, 105–6; P. Winter, *On the Trial*, 186. Klausner, *Jesus*, 274, 335, too proposes that Jesus was a Pharisee. In light of these scholars, it is strange that Sanders criticizes Harvey by saying, "No one has proposed that Jesus was a Pharisaic teacher" (Sanders, *Jesus*, 400n71); stranger still since Sanders himself notes earlier that Klausner proposed that Jesus was a Pharisee (51).
40. Maccoby, *Revolution*, 105. Some scholars propose that Jesus's education was superior to that of the Pharisee Paul. See David Flusser with R. Steven Notley, *The Sage from Galilee: Rediscovering Jesus' Genius*, 4th English ed. (Grand Rapids: Eerdmans, 2007), 12; repeated in David Flusser, "Jesus, His Ancestry, and the Commandment of Love," in *Jesus' Jewishness: Exploring the Place of Jesus in Early Judaism*, ed. James H. Charlesworth, SGJC 2 (New York: Crossroad, 1991), 161; Brad H. Young, *Jesus the Jewish Theologian* (Peabody, MA: Hendrickson, 1995), xxxiv. This opinion has not won assent, and one should note that Young was Flusser's student.
41. Maccoby, *Revolution*, 106.

Puig i Tàrrech does not believe that Jesus was a Pharisee,[42] but he does seem to see the conflict between Jesus and various scribal-literate groups as a battle between equally competent rabbis.[43] This affirmation is consistent with his view that Jesus was a scribal-literate person who could read and write.[44] For Puig i Tàrrech, the central conflict in the narratives is Jesus's sense of authority and the fact that he did not "justify his views by calling on those other rabbis."[45] According to these various theories, although there was controversy, it existed between equally or similarly qualified authorities.

Other scholars take the perspective that this debate was not between equals. For example, Dodd claims, "Although superior persons in Jerusalem dismissed him as 'this untrained man,' he appears to have been quite capable of meeting scholars learned in the Scriptures upon their own ground."[46] Significant in Dodd's observations is that Jesus bested them despite the fact that he was not one of them. Other scholars argue similarly. For example, throughout a study of Jesus's usage of riddles, Thatcher argues that he used this technique in order to compensate for his lack of academic credentials.[47] A central feature of much of Horsley's work on Jesus is that he was outside the scribal elite.[48] Along similar lines, Snyder observes that Jesus's very presentation of himself as a "text-broker," an authoritative interpreter, "contributed to his troubled relationship with the established guild of interpreters."[49]

Thus, in arguments similar to those over the historicity of the conflict between Jesus and scribal authorities, scholars have also debated the nature of the conflict. Demonstrating a connection between theories of the conflict's historicity and theories of its nature, some scholars have asserted that the controversy narratives are an early Christian smear campaign to cover up the fact that Jesus was, in reality, one of the scribal authorities as a Pharisee. Other theories do not assert such a connection between issues of historicity and issues of the nature of the conflict.

42. Puig i Tàrrech, *Jesus*, 285.
43. Ibid., 279–92.
44. Ibid., 184–92. He interprets the questions of the Jews of John 7:15 and the Nazareth synagogue in Mark 6:3//Matt. 13:55 in the context of Jesus's not having pursued an advanced rabbinical education (188–89). Others have argued similarly (see Keith, *Jesus' Literacy*, 13–16, and rebuttal on 115–16). As chap. 2 demonstrated, the Greek of John 7:15 specifically references the acquisition of scribal literacy.
45. Puig i Tàrrech, *Jesus*, 283–85; quotation from 283.
46. Dodd, *Founder*, 120.
47. Thatcher, *Jesus*, 102, 107, 110, 112, 117.
48. See especially Horsley, "Prophet," 172–90.
49. Snyder, *Teachers*, 222.

The Historicity and Origin of the Conflict

Rather than engaging each of the aforementioned theories, in what follows I will show how the preceding chapters of this study support the historicity of conflicts between Jesus and scribal-literate teachers over Scripture and authority and suggest a particular nature for the conflict in line with the suggestion of Dodd and others. I will do so by foregrounding two historical likelihoods that almost all previous studies have overlooked: first, Jesus was not a scribal-literate teacher; second, some of his audiences thought he was. I have already argued (chap. 4) that Jesus's public debates with scribal-literate authorities perpetuated the conviction among some of Jesus's contemporaries that he was a scribal-literate authority. This argument already assumed the existence of such debates, and it is this issue that I must now address. How did Jesus initially arouse their attention in a manner that warranted their questioning him? My proposal accounts for the rise of conflict independently of additional factors such as the content of Jesus's teaching on the law, table practice with sinners, or his reputation as a miracle worker, exorcist, or healer. It is, however, fully compatible with these and other possible catalysts for hostility.

The Synagogue as a Point of Origin

At least one concrete scenario in the first-century Galilean context of Jesus's ministry would have raised initial questions about him concerning Scripture and authority: his teaching in synagogues, a feature of the Gospel texts that is beyond a reasonable historical doubt (see chap. 1). Here it is worth noting once more that Mark 6:3//Matt. 13:55 is the sole example in the entire historical record of a member of the manual-labor class functioning as a teacher in synagogue. It is also notable that precisely this irregularity results in Jesus's rejection in the narratives. As chapter 4 argues, when Jesus took it upon himself to function as an authoritative teacher in synagogue, this very action would inevitably have brought to the fore questions about his scribal-literate status and authority to function in that capacity. These questions would have come from the crowd of Galileans who knew him as a carpenter, including, especially in Nazareth, his family members and friends. They also would have come from the scribal-literate teachers who typically read and expounded the text in synagogue (per the rest of the historical record outside Mark 6:3// Matt. 13:55). If incongruence between Jesus's social class and pedagogical actions raised questions about his authority as a synagogue teacher, the authorities (and others) naturally would have followed up and asked questions about precisely those issues. And, although I am concentrating upon Jesus's synagogue activities, Jesus clearly did not teach only in synagogues. Some of these other contexts also could have led to questions about him as a teacher, such as his teaching near the temple during a major festival, since the temple was a center of scribal activity. Separately from his public engagement with scribal-literate authorities, if Jesus publicly criticized those authorities before the crowds or his disciples, regardless of whether it was in a synagogue, this action also could have raised questions about his own authority for offering such criticisms. In general, as Meier observes, "Any Jew who chose to mount the public stage in early 1st-century Palestine and present himself as a religious teacher . . . would have to discuss and debate the Torah both as a whole and in its parts."[50]

In addition to how initial concerns regarding Jesus, Scripture, and authority could have arisen, however, the other important question is why the scribal-literate authorities did not simply ignore those concerns or dismiss them once they had arisen. And even further, how did those initial concerns develop into full-blown hostilities? With regard to why the authorities could not simply ignore Jesus, I refer again to the historical likelihood that, although some of Jesus's audiences rejected him as a scribal-literate teacher, many also accepted him as one. For some of the populace, Jesus's teachings, including any possible criticisms of the scribal-literate authorities, radiated from within the circle of scribal-literate authority itself. Simply by occupying social positions reserved for scribal-literate teachers, the threat that Jesus presented to the scribal-literate authorities was that Jesus's teachings appeared, at least occasionally, to come from the same authoritative position as their own. In this case, one cannot limit the nature of the threat that Jesus posed in the early period of his ministry simply to the fact that his teachings differed from those of the scribal-literate teachers, the fact that he criticized them, or the fact that his fame grew as the result of his reputation as a miracle worker. The core problem was not that Jesus said and did these things; the problem was that his chosen social contexts for saying and doing them occasionally placed him too close to the category of scribal-literate authority for those who truly held that position to ignore him. Their need to act would only have been heightened if his pedagogical program undermined their own to any degree.

To build upon this point, the proposal that scribal-literate authorities initially questioned Jesus concerning Scripture and his authority specifically because his actions and identity raised questions offers a plausible explanation for why the subsequent growing hostilities between Jesus and the scribal elite featured precisely Scripture and authority. In other words, if my earlier

50. Meier, *Marginal*, 4:648–49.

arguments concerning Jesus's scribal-literate status and the mixed perception of that status are persuasive to any degree, then one has already acknowledged an important source of the origins of the conflict over Scripture and authority. Not only is a theory of wholesale fabrication of controversies over Scripture and authority entirely misguided from this perspective, the opposite perspective is warranted. Scholars should fully expect that conflict between Jesus and scribal-literate teachers would have featured Scripture and authority.

A Plausible Scenario

In general, then, I propose the following historical development as likely. Jesus's presentation of himself socially at times in the position of a scribal-literate teacher, and especially his public teaching in synagogues, was a catalyst for initial questions about his authority as a teacher of Scripture. These questions stemmed particularly from the fact that he was not a scribal-literate teacher. Scribal-literate authorities' (and others') initial questions may have been innocuous or hostile. Regardless, such questioning in public was an honor challenge in Jesus's culture (see "The Nature of the Conflict" below) and thus exposed Jesus to the real possibility of public shame. Both parties had reputations to earn, establish, or defend, and this process of question and answer quickly turned into full conflict. Like an older sibling pushing on a younger sibling's bruise because the older knows that pressure on this tender spot will hurt, the scribal-literate authorities focused precisely on Scripture and authority in their further challenges because that was where Jesus, the carpenter from Nazareth, was most vulnerable. Jesus continued to respond in kind by seeking to undermine the scribal-literate authority from which they undermined his authority. The content of his teaching, as well as miracles, exorcisms, and healings, may have augmented these efforts at simultaneously establishing his own authority in the eyes of his audiences and diminishing his opponents' authority.

Along these lines, one may note the irrelevance of familiar scholarly rejections of the Gospel claims that scribal-literate authorities from Jerusalem came to Galilee to check on Jesus (Mark 3:22; Mark 7:1//Matt. 15:1).[51] I personally find no good reason to doubt this claim. It was just as possible for scribal-literate authorities to travel from Jerusalem to Galilee as it was for nonscribal people to travel from Galilee to Jerusalem (John 4:45). Furthermore, we have non-Christian first-century evidence for the authorities in Jerusalem sending

---

51. Bultmann, *History*, 18; Sanders, *Jesus*, 265, 273; cf. 292. Cf. also T. A. Burkill, "Anti-Semitism in St. Mark's Gospel," *NovT* 3 (1959): 39n3; Cook, "Distribution," 64.

envoys, including Pharisees and priests, to Galilee.[52] Journeys of scribal-literate authorities from Jerusalem to Galilee were not unprecedented or topographically impossible. Some scholars who doubt this claim say that there was no genuine conflict between Jesus and the authorities over the law, and thus nothing for them to check. As we will see in the discussion of Sanders below, this unnecessarily narrows the parameters of the conflict to Jesus's opinions on the law.

Regardless, in terms of the initial stages of the conflict, it does not matter whether scribal-literate authorities came from Jerusalem to question Jesus. Some scribal-literate authorities who typically ran synagogues in Galilee would have taken note of Jesus and also had these concerns, especially if the scribal-literate class capable of reading and expounding Torah in the synagogues was as restricted as the evidence suggests it was (see chap. 1). At least some of the scribal-illiterate crowds also would have had these concerns since Jesus crossed the scribal-literate line that divided classes.[53] Questions over the identity and qualifications of this new person teaching in synagogues in Galilee arose naturally from the fact that Jesus took it upon himself to stand in the stead of a scribal-literate teacher. Therefore, as far as the origins of the conflict are concerned, one need look no further than a carpenter in Galilean synagogues who was acting unlike other carpenters on record, and doing so occasionally with success.

Thatcher, Snyder, and Jesus's Social Position

Insofar as my proposal highlights the ways in which Jesus's actions relate to his social position in scribal culture, it builds upon and forwards prior insights in the work of Thatcher and Snyder. In *Jesus the Riddler*, Thatcher argues persuasively for Jesus's employment of ambiguity and riddles in his teaching. Most important among Thatcher's contributions is his demonstration that Jesus used this particular debate technique for "social posturing."[54] In other words, in addition to what Jesus was teaching, Thatcher focuses upon the ways in which Jesus self-consciously situated himself among the scribal authorities of his day and navigated those power matrices. Jesus used riddles and ambiguity as "a rhetorical device . . . to position himself and his message."[55] He concludes, "One may therefore confidently conclude that Jesus used riddles to display his wit, and that he did this in order to posture and credentialize

---

52. Josephus, *Life*, 38–39 §§189–98; 60 §309.
53. Hengel, *Charismatic*, 50.
54. Thatcher, *Jesus the Riddler*, xxi.
55. Ibid., 113.

himself as a rabbi/teacher."[56] This emphasis upon Jesus's pedagogy as a means of social posture is a significant contribution to a line of scholarship that typically overlooks it in favor of focusing upon the content of Jesus's teachings. By building upon it, my proposal broadens Thatcher's beyond Jesus's stylistic affinity for riddling to consider a wider set of phenomena in the scribal culture of Jesus and his contemporaries. It also offers full argumentation for why Jesus needed to make use of riddles as a means of establishing pedagogical credentials—he otherwise had none, as his opponents knew.

In a similar manner, Snyder lays the groundwork for a point that I have developed throughout this study. He says,

> Jesus probably did present himself as a text-broker, and it was this interpretive activity on Jesus' part . . . that contributed to his troubled relationship with the established guild of interpreters. We need not presume that Jesus offered radically different interpretations of scripture, though he may have done so at points. But the simple fact that Jesus set himself up as an alternative point of access to authoritative texts would have been alarming to those who controlled the means of interpretation.[57]

Therefore, to a certain extent, and without claiming the necessary absence of any additional factors, the source of the conflict between Jesus and other teachers was quite simply that Jesus carried himself on some occasions as a teacher like them. My proposal affirms Snyder's by proposing further reasons for why those who controlled the interpretation of the law would have been alarmed by Jesus. Specifically, Jesus's own lack of scribal-literate authority, combined with his presumption to teach in synagogues and his positive reception in some of them, disrupted their control of authoritative interpretation of the Scripture.

The Overly Skeptical E. P. Sanders

The contribution of my argument may be most clear when contrasted with E. P. Sanders's incredibly influential *Jesus and Judaism*. In this wide-ranging study, Sanders approaches the historicity of the controversy narratives from the larger question of Jesus's views on the law. This is a crucial factor in understanding his perspective because, throughout the study, Sanders argues that, with the possible exception of the command to let the dead bury their own

---

56. Ibid., 116. Similarly, referring to Jesus's teaching in the temple in the story of the woman caught in adultery (John 7:53–8:11), Thatcher notes: "Jesus is posturing himself as an expert on the Law" (99).

57. Snyder, *Teachers*, 222.

dead (Matt. 8:22//Luke 9:60),[58] Jesus never transgressed the law in a manner that would have bothered Pharisees or others. In support of his thesis, Sanders puts his finger on a problem with assuming that Jesus's views on the law were the catalyst of controversy:

> If he opposed the validity of the Mosaic code, his doing so would account for his meeting opposition during his ministry, it might well account for an opposition to the death . . . , and it would account for a new sect which broke with Judaism. The trouble with this thread is that the apostles in Jerusalem apparently did not know that the Torah had been abrogated: that was the contribution of Paul and possibly other Gentiles.[59]

Likewise, he says later,

> If Jesus had declared all foods clean, why did Paul and Peter disagree over Jews eating with Gentiles (Gal. 2.11–16)? Or, put in terms of Acts rather than Galatians, why did it take a thrice-repeated revelation to convince Peter (or, rather, to leave him puzzled and on the way to conviction) (Acts 10.9–17)? And if Jesus consciously transgressed the Sabbath, allowed his disciples to do so, and justified such action in public debate, how could Paul's Christian opponents in Galatia urge that the Sabbath be kept (Gal. 4.10)?[60]

As the first quotation indicates, Sanders acknowledges that the theory that Jesus opposed the law has a certain degree of explanatory power, but ultimately believes that the evidence from the early church is "fatal to the view that Jesus openly and blatantly opposed the law."[61] He reiterates both these points later: "The theory of explicit opposition may make hostility towards Jesus easier to account for, but it makes the controversies in the early church incomprehensible."[62] For these reasons, Sanders considers the controversy narratives in general to be unreliable, imaginary even, and products of the later church.[63] He thus asserts that Jesus never opposed the law.[64] Ultimately, for Sanders, historical knowledge about Jesus's pre-crucifixion career, and

58. Sanders, *Jesus*, 252–55, 267.

59. Ibid., 56.

60. Ibid., 250; see also 261, 266, 268.

61. Ibid., 246. Likewise, "This great fact, which overrides all others, sets a definite limit to what can be said about Jesus and the law" (268).

62. Ibid., 246.

63. Ibid., 250, 260–69, 272.

64. Ibid., 269, 272, 275. He later claims in E. P. Sanders, *The Historical Figure of Jesus* (London: Penguin, 1993), 223: "Very likely the smoke (the passages in the gospels) arose from the real fire (disputes in Christian churches after Jesus' lifetime)."

especially the emergence of conflict with authorities in that career, begins with his demonstration in the temple.[65]

The sharp end of Sanders's criticism is that the type of Jesus shown in the controversy narratives is incapable of explaining his own aftermath. And significantly, that aftermath also complicates any attempts to run the logic in reverse and claim that Jesus clearly spoke in favor of the law rather than opposed it. Sanders claims, "If Jesus was really on record as saying that absolutely all the law must be kept, Paul could hardly have persuaded James and Peter to sanction his mission."[66]

The end product of this argument is untenable. Jesus cannot have spoken positively of the law because of the controversy in the early church. Jesus also cannot have spoken negatively of the law because of the controversy in the early church. Here we have a historical Jesus who was a thoroughly Jewish first-century teacher and yet said nothing inherently positive or negative about the law[67] (despite the fact that, on Sanders's own proposal, Scripture was at the core of Jewish identity, Jesus cared deeply about Scripture, and "disputes over the law were part and parcel of Jewish life")[68] and a group of later Christians who cared enough about him to fabricate some teachings on the law on his behalf but not enough to make them cohere with one another.

Sanders's effort to connect the historical Jesus to the aftermath of his life is appropriate and in line with the memory approach I outlined in chapter 3. But the tensions in his theory emerge from his efforts to connect that aftermath to a nice and tidy historical Jesus who had one and only one opinion on the law and expressed it consistently with complete clarity.[69] If we do not demand a historical Jesus who spoke univocally about the law and was always understood without confusion, another conclusion lies close to hand. This conclusion accounts for why some members of the early church continued to observe the law and others began to break with it, and all of them continued to claim Jesus as their authority. In short, Jesus did not have *a* view of the law or *an* approach to the law. Perhaps, as the Gospels claim, Jesus's teachings were

65. Sanders, *Jesus*, 268: "It is only the action and saying against the temple which had ascertainable results." Cf. also 11, where Sanders lists "almost indisputable facts" about Jesus. No conflict is associated with Jesus's career until number 5 on the list: "Jesus engaged in a controversy about the temple."

66. Ibid., 261.

67. Sanders ultimately forwards the nuanced thesis that Jesus did not oppose the law but viewed the Mosaic dispensation as "not final" (ibid., 252, 269) and thus the Mosaic law as inadequate for the eschatological era (255, 260; cf. 250, 267–69).

68. Sanders, *Historical*, 205.

69. Sanders, *Jesus*, 268, rules out the notion that the disciples might have misunderstood Jesus: "These are matters of concrete behaviour which the disciples could not have missed."

more complex than a black-and-white statement on the continuing validity
of the law and were context-specific.[70] Perhaps he was sometimes perceived
as someone who upheld the law (Matt. 5:17–18) and sometimes perceived
as someone who abrogated or circumvented the law (Mark 10:3–9//Matt.
19:4–9; Matt. 8:22//Luke 9:60; Matt. 12:3–8//Luke 6:3–5). Sanders grants that
the apostle Paul approached the law in a manner that sometimes looked like
upholding it and sometimes looked like dismissing or altering it, as did the
Qumran community, as did later scribal authorities in the post-70 CE rabbinic
tradition.[71] Why Jesus could not have had an equally complex approach to
the law is not clear to me.

But this is not a monograph on Jesus and the law; neither is it an attempt to
address Sanders's entire thoughts on an issue whose complexities far surpass
the attention I can give them here.[72] Furthermore, my goal is not to argue for
the historicity of every controversy narrative, or any one in particular. I have
no doubt that the early church took interpretive license with many of the
traditions and sometimes may have taken great interpretive license. Narrating from "the shadow of the Cross,"[73] and thus the perspective of the fully
matured conflict between Jesus and the authorities, early Christians sometimes
attributed to all Pharisees, scribes, and other groups in general what may have
been the opinions of only a few, attributed words or actions to one group in
one Gospel and another group in another Gospel,[74] and escalated the tension
in light of later Jewish-Christian relations (particularly Matthew and John).[75]

My goal in engaging the work of Sanders on this multifaceted issue is to
note the manner in which one of the facets that Sanders overlooks—Jesus's
status—informs our thinking about his interactions with other teachers and
the Gospels' accounts of those interactions. In this sense, it is quite important

70. Cf. Meier, *Marginal*, 4:653: "In Jesus' *hālākâ* (as far as we can know it), one cannot discern
any moral or legal 'system' containing some organizing principle or center that makes sense of
the whole. . . . The historical Jesus . . . in his legal pronouncements shows no . . . concern for
system-building." He earlier notes, "I do not think that even Sanders's approach does full justice
to the complexity of the data" (4:3).

71. Sanders, *Jesus*, 57, 248 (rabbis), 249 (Qumran), 262 (Paul). He rightly notes that these
interpretations "were not considered by those who practised them to be denials of the law, nor
to call into question its adequacy" (248, emphasis removed).

72. As an example of just how complex the issue of Jesus and the law is, note that Meier's
recent treatment of the topic (*Marginal*, vol. 4) is 735 pages! He concludes: "The question of
Jesus and the Law refuses to be answered by one neat solution with no ends" (4:652).

73. P. Winter, *On the Trial*, 162.

74. Overman, *Matthew's Gospel*, 115, notes that Matthew often (but not always) omits
the scribes from Jesus's opposition of scribes and Pharisees in Mark's Gospel. Matthew also
sometimes adds scribes to the Pharisees, however (for example, Mark 8:11//Matt. 12:38). More
fully, see the chart of P. Winter, *On the Trial*, 171–73.

75. A fact acknowledged even by Keener, *Historical*, 223.

that Sanders limits the possibility of controversy between Jesus and scribal-literate teachers to whether Jesus opposed the law; that is, to *what* Jesus taught about the law. Note this emphasis in the following quotation:

> It may be argued, to be sure, that "where there is smoke there is fire"; that is, that the accounts of disputes do not *describe* debates between Jesus and the Pharisees, but that they preserve the memory that Jesus fell into conflict with the Pharisees on the law. I think that further consideration of the evidence, however, will lead to the conclusion that there was no substantial conflict between Jesus and the Pharisees with regard to Sabbath, food, and purity laws.[76]

His oversight of the issue of Jesus's status should now be obvious. This oversight is unfortunate since elsewhere in the study Sanders comes very close to allowing it its due. For example, he refers to Jesus as "an untutored Galilean";[77] observes rightly that the Jewish authorities would have dismissed Jesus's claims to speak for God because "they would not, after all, suppose that Jesus actually knew";[78] and says that, from their perspective, Jesus "would have been only one more *'am ha-arets* ["people of the land"] among many."[79] Despite these insights, he entirely overlooks the possibility that the conflict hinged not on Jesus's opinion *about* the law but rather on whether he had the right to speak that opinion publicly and authoritatively.[80] Jesus considered himself someone whose views on the law and other aspects of Jewish identity mattered and occasionally chose to voice those views in scribal-literate venues. In and of itself, this could have drawn the ire of the authorities. If, in response, one were to say that we have no other example of scribal-literate authorities giving concentrated attention to a teacher for such issues, I can only agree and point to the obvious: We also have no other example of a person outside scribal-literate culture taking on the roles of scribal-literate authorities in the synagogue.

No doubt the foregoing argument is a variant of the "Where there's smoke there's fire" conclusion that Sanders dismisses.[81] It is true that smoke does not always require fire. It is also true, however, that sometimes there is smoke because there is fire. Sanders does not entirely escape this argument himself,

---

76. Sanders, *Jesus*, 265 (emphasis original).
77. Ibid., 56.
78. Ibid., 288.
79. Ibid., 291.
80. Vermes, *Jesus and the World of Judaism*, 11, observes, "And it was in this respect that he cannot have been greatly loved by the Pharisees: in his lack of expertise, and perhaps even interest, in halakhic matters." He goes on to attribute further conflict to Jesus's emphasis of ethical law over ritual law, a dichotomy that is difficult to maintain (Meier, *Marginal*, 4:43–47).
81. Sanders, *Jesus*, 265, 292; cf. 3; cf. also *Historical*, 216, 223.

which is clear in a caveat he holds in common with Bultmann, P. Winter, and Cook. Despite their skepticism, each of them claims that he does not in principle deny that Jesus did some of the things that the controversy narratives claim he did; rather, they doubt the reliability of the text making that claim.[82] Sanders even affirms the reality of opposition and its likely source in Jesus's claims to be God's spokesman: "Exegesis indicates that there were *specific issues* at stake between Jesus and the Jewish hierarchy, and that the specific issues revolved around a *basic question*: who spoke for God?"[83] My arguments reinforce this particular aspect of Sanders's arguments as they also reveal his mistake in separating this basic issue too quickly from the controversy narratives. Chapter 3 argues that scholars should not relegate the early church's interpretive categories to the sidelines of historical-critical discourse, but rather should make every effort to explain them where possible. The caveats of Bultmann, P. Winter, Cook, and Sanders lean in this direction, suggesting that thoroughgoing skepticism toward the historicity of the controversy narratives is much less warranted than they otherwise claim. In contrast to such skepticism, I affirm "a link between the present and the past"[84] in the controversy narratives. Later Christians undoubtedly modified the narratives in various ways, but the texts' reflections of Jesus and scribal-literate authorities engaged in conflict over Scripture and authority are accurate. The origins of the conflict are traceable to the life of Jesus and, indeed, to Jesus himself.

The Nature of the Conflict

The relevance of the previous discussion for the nature of the conflict should be clear, but it will be useful to spell it out briefly in four points. First, in contrast to some of the suggestions mentioned earlier, the controversy narratives do not reflect intra-Pharisaical debates or debates between parties with the same social standing as Scripture authorities. The conflict was between scribal-literate authorities and a scribal-illiterate carpenter.

Second, in terms of the goals of the respective parties in this debate of unequal standing, the public critiques and challenges were calculated rhetorical ploys designed to upstage and humiliate the other party. Initial questions concerning Jesus's authority as a Scripture teacher may have been sincere. Furthermore, one need not assume that all interactions between Jesus and

82. Bultmann, *History*, 40, 54; P. Winter, *On the Trial*, 160; Sanders, *Historical*, 205, 223; Sanders, *Jesus*, 262, 264, 265, 267, 280; Cook, "Distribution," 79.
83. Sanders, *Jesus*, 281 (emphasis original).
84. Schröter, "Jesus of Galilee," 38.

scribal-literate authorities in his career were necessarily hostile. As the conflict grew, however, the interactions that were hostile were attempts on the part of the scribal-literate elite to expose Jesus publicly as an imposter to the position of scribal-literate authority. And even the possibly innocuous confrontations would have had a hostile edge as honor challenges. This is precisely why they challenged his authority and his status as an interpreter of Scripture. "They choose . . . to attack Jesus where he is most vulnerable, and certainly most inferior to themselves: he does not possess official academic credentials."[85] He was, again, an imposter from their perspective, and if the general public did not realize this, the official teachers would make it clear for them. To say it another way, questions like "By what authority are you doing these things?" (Mark 11:28) on the part of the scribal-literate authorities were not honest content-seeking queries but rhetorical questions with the implied answer "You have no authority to do these things." There is therefore likely truth in the texts that claim that scribal-literate authorities attempted to trap Jesus (Mark 8:11//Matt. 16:1//Luke 11:16; Mark 10:2//Matt. 19:3; John 8:6; cf. Mark 12:15//Matt. 22:18).

Jesus, on the other hand, was attempting to defend his reputation against the carefully crafted interpretive traps of the authorities and, even more, trying to turn the tables on them and further his reputation as a teacher in his own right. Frequent questions from him like "Have you never read what David did?" (Mark 2:25) were not neutral invitations to consider and discuss texts but strategic jabs designed to undermine the very source of his enemies' social authority—their ability to read the texts. Scholars who insist that these texts indicate that *Jesus* could read the Scriptures have missed this crucial point.[86] The question assumes (1) that Jesus knows what is in the text and (2) that Jesus's opponents, the scribal-literate individuals, had read the text. Jesus is here at his sarcastic best. In asking "Have *you* not read?" Jesus uses precisely this fact to shame his opponents and upstage them. Likewise, a heavy dose of sarcasm should be read in his question to Nicodemus, who is able to search the text himself (John 7:52), "Are you not a teacher of Israel?" (John 3:10 AT).

Third, the conflict between Jesus and the scribal elite reveals the degree to which Jesus's career reflected the honor/shame culture in which he carried it out. Honor and shame were not feelings but near-tangible social realities that one could gain and lose. In Jesus's world, as in some cultures today, "Maintenance of honor—for one's self, one's family, and one's larger groups—is absolutely

85. Thatcher, *Jesus the Riddler*, 102.
86. Casey, *Jesus*, 161–62; Dunn, *Jesus*, 314; Evans, "Jewish," 50; Puig i Tàrrech, *Jesus*, 191.

vital to life."[87] Many biblical texts reflect the cultural currency of these values. Luke's portrayal of Elizabeth's elation at her pregnancy is an example. According to Elizabeth, her pregnancy removed "my shame [or "disgrace," *oneidos*] among the people" that stemmed from barrenness (Luke 1:25). The Old Testament account of Hannah's infertility and eventual pregnancy with Samuel reflects a similar connection. Her rival shames her into tears on account of her barrenness (1 Sam. 1:6–8). Barrenness and childbirth were only two of many cultural events where honor and shame were on display, however. In reality, almost any social interchange in Jesus's context was an opportunity to gain or lose honor, and this was especially the case for public debates over Scripture and authority.[88]

This point is important because it underscores my argument about the nature of the conflict. Controversies over Scripture and authority between Jesus and the scribal-literate authorities were honor challenges, what some scholars refer to as "challenge and riposte." The goal of such verbal spats was not necessarily to make the best point or be the best interpreter in some quantifiable way. That was not the goal because honor was not quantifiably assessed; it was assessed by public opinion. "The judge . . . is, ultimately, the audience."[89] The goal, then, was to upstage one's opponent, be accepted as the winner of the challenge, and walk away with honor.[90] By occupying the social space in which scribal-literate authorities enjoyed esteem in the community, Jesus essentially made a bid for their honor or at least attempted to share in it. In response, the scribal-literate authorities, by exposing Jesus as lacking in status to be a teacher, aimed to shame him publicly and solidify that scribal-literate Torah authorities do not share honor with scribal-illiterate carpenters. If Jesus is able to turn the tables on his antagonists, however, he not only successfully defends himself against their challenge but also takes honor from them, leaving them shamed. Chapter 4 established the likelihood that, at least on occasion, audiences concluded that Jesus was the victor. In narrating

---

87. K. C. Hanson and Douglas E. Oakman, *Palestine in the Time of Jesus: Social Structures and Social Conflicts* (Minneapolis: Fortress, 1998), 6.

88. Further on this topic, see Jo-Ann A. Brant, *Dialogue and Drama: Elements of Greek Tragedy in the Fourth Gospel* (Peabody, MA: Hendrickson, 2004), 123–39; Jerome H. Neyrey, "The Trials (Forensic) and Tribulations (Honor Challenges) of Jesus: John 7 in Social Science Perspective," in his *The Gospel of John in Cultural and Rhetorical Perspective* (Grand Rapids: Eerdmans, 2009), 191–226; repr. from *BTB* 26 (1996): 107–24.

89. Brant, *Dialogue*, 139.

90. If one considers the dynamics at work in rap battles, such as those portrayed in the movie *8 Mile*, one is close to understanding this point. The battling rappers consistently offer hyperbolic statements. No one in the audience would object to a particular insult because it is not logically possible. The point is not necessarily to be "right" or "correct" but simply to upstage one's opponent in the public eye.

victorious results of Jesus in a conflict story, Luke refers to the shaming of his opponents and the transfer of honor to Jesus: "When he said this, all his opponents were put to shame; and the entire crowd was rejoicing at all the wonderful [or "honored," *endoxois*] things that he was doing" (Luke 13:17).

Conclusions

In addition to affirming the historical plausibility of conflicts between Jesus and the scribal elite, this chapter asserts a particular nature for the conflict they reflect. After a possible initial stage of genuine curiosity or inquiry, the conflict grew into a more hostile interchange between Jesus and the scribal-literate authorities. Concerned that Jesus was treading too closely upon their carefully guarded and scribal-literacy-undergirded social positions, they attempted to demonstrate publicly that Jesus was not a scribal-literate authority. At least occasionally, however, Jesus was perceived as having won the honor challenge. This only perpetuated the mixed perceptions of Jesus as both a scribal-literate and scribal-illiterate teacher. Equally, it perpetuated the scribal-literate authorities' need to engage him publicly again in order to regain their honor and to shame him. The conflict between Jesus and scribal-literate authorities eventually grew into issues much larger than Jesus's scribal-literate status. Sanders is undoubtedly correct about the crucial role that Jesus's sayings and actions concerning the temple played in escalating this controversy ever closer to the cross. As this chapter has shown, however, there are good reasons to affirm that conflict between Jesus and Jewish authorities existed in the early period of Jesus's career as well, and that it centered on Scripture, authority, and Jesus.

Concluding Remarks

The Beginning, the End, and the
Beginning of the End

Then they sent to him some Pharisees and some Herodians to trap him in what he said. (Mark 12:13)

After that no one dared to ask him any question. (Mark 12:34)

In this study, I have argued that conflict between Jesus and the scribal elite arose in light of how various groups within Second Temple Judaism would have perceived Jesus, a scribal-illiterate carpenter, upon his occasionally occupying the position of a scribal-literate authority. Throughout I have insisted that, although this proposal for the origins of the conflict is not dependent upon other possible catalysts for controversy, such as Jesus's identity as a miracle worker, a healer, an exorcist, the Messiah, or a/the prophet, it is in no way incompatible with those factors. The interrelation between questions over these aspects of Jesus's identity and questions over Jesus's status as a teacher is an avenue for future research. In that sense, this study is simply one step in that direction.

This step makes contributions of its own, however. It is the first book to approach the controversy narratives in terms of how Jesus's early career led to the emergence of the conflict rather than how the conflict, once in full bloom, led eventually to Jesus's crucifixion. Following the lead of the Gospel narratives, modern scholarly inquiries of Jesus frequently treat the beginning of his career as a short preface en route to the weightier matters surrounding the end of his career. There is, of course, nothing wrong with this typical focus, but its side effect is that students of Jesus and the Gospels often receive scant discussion of the very earliest stages of a process that took Jesus from being just one among a myriad of Second Temple Jews to being the figurehead of a new sect of Judaism that went on to become a major world religion. My humble hope is that this book, as one of the very few studies to focus on the early stages of Jesus's ministry, has demonstrated that these stages are interesting in their own right.

Related to this point, I have made no sustained effort to connect the beginning of the conflict between Jesus and scribal authorities to the end of that conflict. This is for a simple reason. In my view, the evidence does not permit historians to draw an unswerving line of connection between the origins of the controversy and the resolution of the controversy on the cross. To state it another way, we do not need to assume that the authorities first paid attention to Jesus for the same reasons that they eventually killed him. Furthermore, we do not need to assume that there was one homogenous group of authorities that were responsible for both events. The Gospels portray the Pharisees as largely falling out of the picture once the conflict shifts to Jerusalem and Passover week. Likewise, Roman authorities play essentially no role in the early stages of the conflict, whereas the order to crucify Jesus comes from a Roman provincial governor. These aspects of the Gospel narratives are historically credible. Pharisees would have been more concerned with scribal authority and who can speak officially about Scripture; Romans would not have cared about the interpretation of Jewish Scripture but would have cared about unrest in Jerusalem during Passover. More important, though, these claims indicate a shift in both the parties and the tone of the conflict. Jesus was not crucified because of confusion over scribal literacy and scribal authority.

The inability of historians to draw an unswerving line of connection between the beginning of the conflict and the end of the conflict is not the same as an inability to draw any line of connection at all, however. In accounting for why Jesus was someone the authorities deemed it necessary to kill, one must account for how Jesus came to be worthy of their attention in the first place. My contribution, therefore, is that, in addition to other possibilities, confusion over Jesus's scribal-literate status accounts for how Jesus came to be on scribal authorities' radars initially and offers a plausible launching pad for additional hostilities, especially since the confrontations occurred publicly in an honor/shame culture. Along these lines, perhaps the most important contribution of this study is its argument that one can trace the conflict plausibly to Jesus's ministry and, indeed, to Jesus himself. This argument stands in direct contrast to the theory that the controversy narratives are the fabrications of early Christians crafting the Gospels against non-Christian Jews. The theory that early Christians influenced the tradition is correct, but only to an extent. The correct observation of the inherently hermeneutical process of transmitting the Jesus tradition does not lead directly to the conclusion that the Gospels are disconnected from the past; it simply points to the complex ways in which they are connected. In addressing these complexities, I have argued instead that the Gospels are correct in claiming that the conflict that ended on a Roman cross in Jerusalem began in synagogues in Galilee.

In light of the preceding comments, one last observation remains that has often gone entirely unnoticed in scholarly discussions of the conflict between Jesus and the scribal elite. This observation concerns neither the beginning nor the end of the conflict but the beginning of the end, the escalation of the conflict from initial questioning to outright hostility. When the scribal-literate authorities engaged Jesus in debates over Scripture and authority in order to expose him as a pretender to the position of scribal-literate teacher, there was an interesting and ironic contrast between the intended effects of those engagements and their actual effects. By admitting Jesus to public dialogue, they enabled some audiences to come to a conclusion that was precisely opposite from the one they had intended when, at least on occasion, Jesus was perceived as the winner of the debate. This made exponentially worse the very problem that the scribal authorities had sought to remedy and thus perpetuated their need to engage him publicly in order to expose him. In these situations, the scribal elite attempted to put out a fire with gasoline.

Bibliography

Primary Sources

Aland, Barbara, et al., eds. *Novum Testamentum Graece*. 28th ed. Stuttgart: Deutsche Bibelgesellschaft, 2012.

The Ante-Nicene Fathers. Edited by Alexander Roberts and James Donaldson. 1885–87. 10 vols. Repr., Peabody, MA: Hendrickson, 1994.

The Apostolic Fathers: Greek Texts and English Translations. Edited by Michael W. Holmes. 3rd ed. Grand Rapids: Baker Academic, 2007.

Book of Mormon. London: West European Mission, 1959.

Charlesworth, James H., ed. *The Old Testament Pseudepigrapha*. 2 vols. Garden City, NY: Doubleday, 1983–85.

Cicero. *Letters to Atticus*. Translated by E. O. Winstedt. 3 vols. Loeb Classical Library. London: William Heinemann, 1912–18.

Clement of Alexandria. *Christ the Educator*. Translated by Simon P. Wood. Fathers of the Church 23. Washington, DC: Catholic University of America Press, 2001.

Cureton, W., ed. and trans. *Ancient Syriac Documents Relative to the Earliest Establishment of Christianity in Edessa and the Neighbouring Countries, from the Year after Our Lord's Ascension to the Beginning of the Fourth Century*. London: Williams & Norgate, 1864. Repr., Eugene, OR: Wipf & Stock, 2004.

The Dead Sea Scrolls: A New Translation. Translated by Michael O. Wise, Martin G. Abegg Jr., and Edward M. Cook. New York: HarperOne, 2005.

Elliger, K., and W. Rudolph, eds. *Biblia Hebraica Stuttgartensia*. Revised by A. Schenker. 5th ed. Stuttgart: Deutsche Bibelgesellschaft, 1997.

Eusebius. *The Ecclesiastical History*. Translated by Kirsopp Lake and J. E. L. Oulton. 2 vols. Loeb Classical Library. Cambridge, MA: Harvard University Press, 1957–59.

García Martínez, Florentino, and Eibert J. C. Tigchelaar, trans. *The Dead Sea Scrolls: Study Edition*. 2 vols. Grand Rapids: Eerdmans, 1997–98.

159

Hock, Ronald F., trans. "The Infancy Gospel of Thomas." Pages 380–96 in *The Complete Gospels*. Edited by Robert J. Miller. Santa Rosa, CA: Polebridge, 1994.

Howard, George, trans. *The Teaching of Addai*. Society of Biblical Literature Texts and Translations 16 / Early Christian Literature Series 4. Chico, CA: Scholars Press, 1981.

Josephus. Translated by H. St. J. Thackeray et al. 12 vols. Loeb Classical Library. Cambridge, MA: Harvard University Press, 1926–81.

Justin Martyr. *Writings of Saint Justin Martyr*. Translated by Thomas B. Falls. Fathers of the Church 6. Washington, DC: Catholic University of America Press, 1948.

Lewis, Naphtali, Yigael Yadin, and Jonas C. Greenfield, eds. *The Documents from the Bar Kokhba Period in the Cave of Letters: Greek Papyri*. Judean Desert Studies. Jerusalem: Israel Exploration Fund, 1989.

Libanius. *Selected Works*. Translated by A. F. Norman. 3 vols. Loeb Classical Library. London: Heinemann, 1977.

Lucian. *The Works of Lucian*. Translated by A. M. Harmon. 8 vols. Loeb Classical Library. London: Heinemann, 1977.

Minucius Felix. *The Octavius of Marcus Minucius Felix*. Translated by G. W. Clarke. Ancient Christian Writers 39. New York: Newman, 1974.

The Nag Hammadi Library in English. Edited by Marvin W. Meyer. Translated by members of the Coptic Gnostic Library Project of the Institute for Antiquity and Christianity. Leiden: Brill, 1977.

The Nicene and Post-Nicene Fathers, Series 1. Edited by Philip Schaff. 14 vols. 1886–89. Repr., Peabody, MA: Hendrickson, 1994.

The Nicene and Post-Nicene Fathers, Series 2. Edited by Philip Schaff and Henry Wace. 14 vols. 1890–1900. Repr., Peabody, MA: Hendrickson, 1994.

Origen: Contra Celsum. Translated by Henry Chadwick. Cambridge: Cambridge University Press, 1965.

Patrologia graeca. Edited by J.-P. Migne. 162 vols. Paris, 1857–86.

Patrologia latina. Edited by J.-P. Migne. 217 vols. Paris, 1844–64.

Philo. Translated by F. H. Colson and G. H. Whitaker. 10 vols. Loeb Classical Library. Cambridge, MA: Harvard University Press, 1929–62.

Quintilian. *Institutio Oratoria: Books I–III*. Translated by H. E. Butler. Loeb Classical Library. Cambridge, MA: Harvard University Press, 1920.

Rahlfs, Alfred, ed. *Septuaginta: Editio altera*. Revised by Robert Hanhart. Stuttgart: Deutsche Bibelgesellschaft, 2006.

Vermes, Geza, trans. *The Complete Dead Sea Scrolls in English*. New York: Penguin, 1997.

Secondary Sources

Albertz, Martin. *Die synoptischen Streitgespräche: Ein Beitrag zur Formengeschichte des Urchristentums*. Berlin: Trowitzsch & Sohn, 1921.

Alexander, Loveday. "Memory and Tradition in the Hellenistic Schools." Pages 113–53 in Kelber and Byrskog, *Jesus in Memory*.

Allison, Dale C., Jr. *Constructing Jesus: Memory, Imagination, and History*. Grand Rapids: Baker Academic, 2010.

———. *The Historical Christ and the Theological Jesus*. Grand Rapids: Eerdmans, 2009.

———. "How to Marginalize the Traditional Criteria of Authenticity." Vol. 1, pages 3–30 in *Handbook for the Study of the Historical Jesus*. Edited by Tom Holmén and Stanley E. Porter. Leiden: Brill, 2010.

———. "It Don't Come Easy: A History of Disillusionment." Pages 186–99 in Keith and Le Donne, *Jesus, Criteria, and the Demise of Authenticity*.

———. *Jesus of Nazareth: Millenarian Prophet*. Minneapolis: Fortress, 1998.

———. *The New Moses: A Matthean Typology*. Edinburgh: T&T Clark, 1993.

———. *Resurrecting Jesus: The Earliest Christian Tradition and Its Interpreters*. London: T&T Clark, 2005.

———. *Studies in Matthew: Interpretation Past and Present*. Grand Rapids: Baker Academic, 2005.

Bagnall, Roger S. *Reading Papyri, Writing Ancient History*. Approaching the Ancient World. New York: Routledge, 1995.

Barbour, R. S. *Traditio-Historical Criticism of the Gospels*. Studies in Creative Criticism 4. London: SPCK, 1972.

Barclay, William. *The Mind of Jesus*. New York: Harper & Row, 1961.

Bauckham, Richard. "Monotheism and Christology in the Gospel of John." Pages 239–52 in *The Testimony of the Beloved Disciple: Narrative, History, and Theology in the Gospel of John*. Grand Rapids: Baker Academic, 2007. Repr. from pp. 148–66 in *Contours of Christology in the New Testament*. Edited by R. N. Longenecker. Grand Rapids: Eerdmans, 2005.

Beard, Mary, Alan K. Bowman, Mireille Corbier, Tim Cornell, James L. Franklin Jr., Ann Hanson, Keith Hopkins, and Nicholas Horsfall. *Literacy in the Roman World*. Journal of Roman Archaeology: Supplementary Series 3. Ann Arbor, MI: Journal of Roman Archaeology, 1991.

Beavis, Mary Ann. *Mark*. Paideia Commentaries on the New Testament. Grand Rapids: Baker Academic, 2011.

Beilby, James K., and Paul Rhodes Eddy, eds. *The Historical Jesus: Five Views*. Downers Grove, IL: IVP Academic, 2009.

Blomberg, Craig L. "The Authenticity and Significance of Jesus' Table Fellowship with Sinners." Pages 215–50 in Bock and Webb, *Key Events in the Life of the Historical Jesus*.

Bock, Darrell L. "The Historical Jesus: An Evangelical View." Pages 249–81 in Beilby and Eddy, *The Historical Jesus*.

Bock, Darrell L., and Robert L. Webb, eds. *Key Events in the Life of the Historical Jesus: A Collaborative Exploration of Context and Coherence*. Grand Rapids: Eerdmans, 2009.

Bockmuehl, Markus. *This Jesus: Martyr, Lord, Messiah*. Downers Grove, IL: InterVarsity, 1994.

Bond, Helen K. *The Historical Jesus: A Guide for the Perplexed.* T&T Clark Guides for the Perplexed. London: T&T Clark, 2012.

Borg, Marcus J. *Conflict, Holiness and Politics in the Teachings of Jesus.* New ed. Harrisburg, PA: Trinity, 1998.

Bornkamm, Günther. *Jesus of Nazareth.* Translated by Irene McLuskey, Fraser McLuskey, and James M. Robinson. New York: Harper & Row, 1960.

Bovon, François. *Das Evangelium nach Lukas (Lk 1,1–9,50).* Evangelisch-katholischer Kommentar zum Neuen Testament 3.1. Zurich: Benziger, 1989.

Brant, Jo-Ann A. *Dialogue and Drama: Elements of Greek Tragedy in the Fourth Gospel.* Peabody, MA: Hendrickson, 2004.

Bruce, F. F. *In Retrospect: Remembrance of Things Past.* Glasgow: Pickering & Inglis, 1980.

Bultmann, Rudolf. *The History of the Synoptic Tradition.* Translated by John Marsh. Oxford: Basil Blackwell, 1963.

———. "New Testament and Mythology." Pages 1–44 in *Kerygma and Myth.* Edited by Hans Werner Bartsch. Translated by Reginald H. Fuller. Rev. ed. New York: Harper Torchbooks, 1961.

Burge, Gary M. *Jesus, the Middle Eastern Storyteller.* Ancient Context, Ancient Faith. Grand Rapids: Zondervan, 2009.

Burkill, T. A. "Anti-Semitism in St. Mark's Gospel." *Novum Testamentum* 3 (1959): 34–53.

Byrskog, Samuel. *Jesus the Only Teacher: Didactic Authority and Transmission in Ancient Israel, Ancient Judaism and the Matthean Community.* Coniectanea biblica: New Testament Series 24. Stockholm: Almqvist & Wiksell, 1994.

Cadoux, C. J. *The Life of Jesus.* Gateshead on Tyne: Pelican, 1948.

Calderini, Rita. "Gli ἀγράμματοι nell'Egitto greco-romano." *Aegyptus* 30 (1950): 14–41.

Carr, David M. "Literacy and Reading." Pages 888–89 in Collins and Harlow, *Eerdmans Dictionary of Early Judaism.*

———. *Writing on the Tablet of the Heart: Origins of Scripture and Literature.* New York: Oxford University Press, 2005.

Carter, Warren. "The Disciples." Pages 81–102 in Keith and Hurtado, *Jesus among Friends and Enemies.*

Casey, Maurice. *Jesus of Nazareth: An Independent Historian's Account of His Life and Teaching.* London: T&T Clark, 2010.

Catto, Stephen K. *Reconstructing the First-Century Synagogue: A Critical Analysis of Current Research.* Library of New Testament Studies 363. London: T&T Clark, 2007.

Charlesworth, James H., and Petr Pokorný, eds. *Jesus Research: An International Perspective.* Grand Rapids: Eerdmans, 2009.

Chatman, Seymour. *Story and Discourse: Narrative Structure in Fiction and Film.* Ithaca, NY: Cornell University Press, 1978.

Chilton, Bruce. *Rabbi Jesus: An Intimate Biography.* New York: Doubleday, 2000.

Chilton, Bruce, Darrell Bock, Daniel M. Gurtner, Jacob Neusner, Lawrence H. Schiffman, and Daniel Oden, eds. *A Comparative Handbook to the Gospel of Mark:*

Comparisons with Pseudepigrapha, the Qumran Scrolls, and Rabbinic Literature. The New Testament Gospels in Their Judaic Contexts 1. Leiden: Brill, 2010.

———. "Rabbi as a Title for Jesus." Pages 561–67 in Chilton et al., *A Comparative Handbook to the Gospel of Mark.*

Collins, Adela Yarbro. *Mark.* Hermeneia. Minneapolis: Fortress, 2007.

Collins, John J., and Daniel C. Harlow. *The Eerdmans Dictionary of Early Judaism.* Grand Rapids: Eerdmans, 2010.

Cook, Michael J. "The Distribution of Jewish Leaders in the Synoptic Gospels: Why Wariness Is Warranted." Pages 61–79 in *Soundings in the Religion of Jesus: Perspectives and Methods in Jewish and Christian Scholarship.* Edited by Bruce Chilton, Anthony Le Donne, and Jacob Neusner. Minneapolis: Fortress, 2012.

Craffert, Pieter F., and Pieter J. J. Botha. "Why Jesus Could Walk on the Sea but He Could Not Read or Write." *Neotestamentica* 39.1 (2005): 5–35.

Crenshaw, James L. *Education in Ancient Israel: Across the Deadening Silence.* Anchor Bible Reference Library. New York: Doubleday, 1998.

Cribiore, Rafaella. *Gymnastics of the Mind: Greek Education in Hellenistic and Roman Egypt.* Princeton: Princeton University Press, 2001.

Crook, Zeba A. "Collective Memory Distortion and the Quest for the Historical Jesus." *Journal for the Study of the Historical Jesus* 11.1 (2013): 53–76.

Crossan, John Dominic. *The Birth of Christianity: Discovering What Happened in the Years Immediately after the Execution of Jesus.* New York: HarperCollins, 1998.

———. *The Essential Jesus: What Jesus Really Taught.* New York: HarperCollins, 1994.

———. *Jesus: A Revolutionary Biography.* New York: HarperCollins, 1994.

Davies, W. D., and Dale C. Allison Jr. *A Critical and Exegetical Commentary on the Gospel of Matthew.* 3 vols. International Critical Commentary. Edinburgh: T&T Clark, 1988–97.

Dibelius, Martin. *From Tradition to Gospel.* Translated by Bertram Lee Wolf. Scribner Library 124. New York: Charles Scribner's Sons, 1934.

Dobschütz, Ernst von. "Matthew as Rabbi and Catechist." Translated by Robert Morgan. Pages 27–38 in Stanton, *Interpretation of Matthew.* Repr. from *Zeitschrift für die neutestamentliche Wissenschaft* 27 (1928): 338–48.

Dodd, C. H. *The Founder of Christianity.* New York: Macmillan, 1970.

Douglass, Frederick. *Narrative of the Life of Frederick Douglass, An American Slave.* 6th ed. London: H. G. Collins, 1851.

Dunn, James D. G. "Altering the Default Setting: Re-envisaging the Early Transmission of the Jesus Tradition." Pages 79–125 in *New Perspective on Jesus.* Repr. from *New Testament Studies* 49 (2003): 139–75.

———. *Jesus Remembered.* Christianity in the Making 1. Grand Rapids: Eerdmans, 2003.

———. *A New Perspective on Jesus: What the Quest for the Historical Jesus Missed.* London: SPCK, 2005.

Edwards, James R. *The Gospel according to Mark.* Pillar New Testament Commentary. Grand Rapids: Eerdmans, 2002.

Esler, Philip F., ed. *Modelling Early Christianity: Social-Scientific Studies of the New Testament in Its Context*. London: Routledge, 1995.

Evans, C. Stephen. *The Historical Christ and the Jesus of Faith: The Incarnational Narrative as History*. New York: Oxford University Press, 1996.

Evans, Craig A. *Jesus and His World: The Archaeological Evidence*. London: SPCK, 2012.

———. "Jewish Scripture and the Literacy of Jesus." Pages 41–54 in *From Biblical Criticism to Biblical Faith: Essays in Honor of Lee Martin McDonald*. Edited by William H. Brackney and Craig A. Evans. Macon, GA: Mercer University Press, 2007.

Evans, Craig A., and Donald A. Hagner, eds. *Anti-Semitism and Early Christianity: Issues of Polemic and Faith*. Minneapolis: Fortress, 1993.

Eve, Eric. *Behind the Gospels: Understanding the Oral Tradition*. London: SPCK, 2013.

———. "Meier, Miracle, and Multiple Attestation." *Journal for the Study of the Historical Jesus* 3 (2005): 23–45.

Falk, Harvey. *Jesus the Pharisee: A New Look at the Jewishness of Jesus*. New York: Paulist Press, 1985.

Fitzmyer, Joseph A. "The Languages of Palestine in the First Century AD." *Catholic Biblical Quarterly* 32 (1970): 501–30. Repr. as pages 29–56 in *A Wandering Aramean: Collected Aramaic Essays*. Combined ed. in *The Semitic Background of the New Testament*. Biblical Resource Series. Grand Rapids: Eerdmans, 1997.

Flusser, David. "Jesus, His Ancestry, and the Commandment of Love." Pages 153–76 in *Jesus' Jewishness: Exploring the Place of Jesus in Early Judaism*. Edited by James H. Charlesworth. Shared Ground among Jews and Christians 2. New York: Crossroad, 1991.

Flusser, David, with R. Steven Notley. *The Sage from Galilee: Rediscovering Jesus' Genius*. 4th English ed. Grand Rapids: Eerdmans, 2007.

Foster, Paul. "Educating Jesus: The Search for a Plausible Context." *Journal for the Study of the Historical Jesus* 4.1 (2006): 7–33.

———. "Memory, Orality, and the Fourth Gospel: Three Dead-Ends in Historical Jesus Work." *Journal for the Study of the Historical Jesus* 10 (2012): 191–202.

France, R. T. *The Gospel of Mark*. The New International Greek Testament Commentary. Grand Rapids: Eerdmans, 2002.

Fredriksen, Paula. *From Jesus to Christ: The Origins of the New Testament Images of Jesus*. New Haven: Yale University Press, 1988.

Freedman, David Noel, ed. *Eerdmans Dictionary of the Bible*. Grand Rapids: Eerdmans, 2000.

Fuller, Reginald H. "The Criterion of Dissimilarity: The Wrong Tool?" Pages 42–48 in *Christological Perspectives: Essays in Honor of Harvey K. McArthur*. Edited by Robert F. Berkey and Sarah A. Edwards. New York: Pilgrim, 1982.

Funk, Robert W., and the Jesus Seminar. *The Acts of Jesus: The Search for the Authentic Deeds of Jesus*. New York: HarperCollins, 1998.

Gamble, Harry Y. *Books and Readers in the Early Church: A History of Early Christian Texts*. New Haven: Yale University Press, 1995.

Geldenhuys, Norval. *The Gospel of Luke*. New International Commentary on the New Testament. Grand Rapids: Eerdmans, 1951.

Glasson, T. Francis. *Moses in the Fourth Gospel*. Studies in Biblical Theology 40. London: SCM, 1963.

Gnilka, Joachim. *Das Evangelium nach Markus (1,1–8,26)*. Evangelisch-katholischer Kommentar zum Neuen Testament 2.1. Zurich: Benziger, 1978.

Goodacre, Mark. "Criticizing the Criterion of Multiple Attestation: The Historical Jesus and the Question of Sources." Pages 152–69 in Keith and Le Donne, *Jesus, Criteria, and the Demise of Authenticity*.

Goodman, M. D. "Texts, Scribes and Power in Roman Judaea." Pages 99–108 in *Literacy and Power in the Ancient World*. Edited by Alan K. Bowman and Greg Woolf. Cambridge: Cambridge University Press, 1994.

Green, Joel B. *The Gospel of Luke*. New International Commentary on the New Testament. Grand Rapids: Eerdmans, 1997.

Häfner, Gerd. "Das Ende der Kriterien? Jesusforschung angesichts der geschichtstheoretischen Diskussion." Pages 97–130 in *Historiographie und fiktionales Erzählen: Zur Konstruktivität in Geschichtstheorie und Exegese*. By Knut Backhaus and Gerd Häfner. Biblisch-theologische Studien 86. Neukirchen-Vluyn: Neukirchener, 2007.

Hagner, Donald A. "Jesus and the Synoptic Sabbath Controversies." Pages 251–92 in Bock and Webb, *Key Events in the Life of the Historical Jesus*.

Haines-Eitzen, Kim. *Guardians of Letters: Literacy, Power, and the Transmitters of Early Christian Literature*. New York: Oxford University Press, 2000.

Hanson, K. C., and Douglas E. Oakman. *Palestine in the Time of Jesus: Social Structures and Social Conflicts*. Minneapolis: Fortress, 1998.

Haran, Menahem. "On the Diffusion of Literacy and Schools in Ancient Israel." Pages 81–95 in *Congress Volume: Jerusalem, 1986*. Edited by J. A. Emerton. Supplements to Vetus Testamentum 40. Leiden: Brill, 1988.

Harris, William V. *Ancient Literacy*. Cambridge, MA: Harvard University Press, 1989.

Hartmann, Lars. "Mk 6,3a im Lichte einiger griechischer Texte." *Zeitschrift für die neutestamentliche Wissenschaft und die Kunde der älteren Kirche* 95 (2004): 276–79.

Harvey, A. E. *Jesus and the Constraints of History*. London: Duckworth, 1982.

Hays, Richard B. *Echoes of Scripture in the Letters of Paul*. New Haven: Yale University Press, 1989.

Head, Peter M. *Christology and the Synoptic Problem: An Argument for Markan Priority*. Society for New Testament Studies Monograph Series 94. Cambridge: Cambridge University Press, 1997.

Healy, Mary. *The Gospel of Mark*. Catholic Commentary on Sacred Scripture. Grand Rapids: Baker Academic, 2008.

Henderson, Ian H. "Memory, Text and Performance in Early Christian Formation." Pages 157–84 in *Religion und Bildung: Medien und Funktionen religiösen Wissens in der Kaiserzeit*. Edited by Christa Frateantonio and Helmut Krasser. Potsdamer Altertumswissenschaftliche Beiträge 30. Stuttgart: Franz Steiner, 2010.

Hengel, Martin. *The Charismatic Leader and His Followers*. Edited by John Riches. Translated by James C. G. Greig. Edinburgh: T&T Clark, 1981.

―――. *Judaism and Hellenism: Studies in Their Encounter in Palestine during the Early Hellenistic Period*. Translated by John Bowden. 2 vols. Philadelphia: Fortress, 1974.

Hezser, Catherine. *Jewish Literacy in Roman Palestine*. Texte und Studien zum antiken Judentum 81. Tübingen: Mohr Siebeck, 2001.

―――. "Private and Public Education." Pages 465–81 in *The Oxford Handbook of Jewish Daily Life in Roman Palestine*. Edited by Catherine Hezser. Oxford: Oxford University Press, 2010.

Hilton, Allen. "The Dumb Speak: Early Christian Illiteracy and Pagan Criticism." PhD diss., Yale University, 1997.

Hock, Ronald F., trans. "The Infancy Gospel of Thomas." Pages 371–79 in *The Complete Gospels*. Edited by Robert J. Miller. Santa Rosa, CA: Polebridge, 1994.

Holmes, Michael W. Introduction to *The Apostolic Fathers: Greek Texts and English Translations*. 3rd ed. Grand Rapids: Baker Academic, 2007.

Hooker, M. D. "Christology and Methodology." *New Testament Studies* 17 (1970): 480–87.

―――. "In His Own Image?" Pages 28–44 in *What about the New Testament? Essays in Honour of Christopher Evans*. Edited by Morna Hooker and Colin Hickling. London: SCM, 1975.

―――. "On Using the Wrong Tool." *Theology* 75 (1972): 570–81.

Horsley, Richard A. "A Prophet like Moses and Elijah: Popular Memory and Cultural Patterns in Mark." Pages in 172–90 in Horsley et al., *Performing the Gospel*.

Horsley, Richard A., Jonathan A. Draper, and John Miles Foley, eds. *Performing the Gospel: Orality, Memory, Mark*. Minneapolis: Fortress, 2006.

Hultgren, Arland J. *Jesus and His Adversaries: The Form and Function of the Conflict Stories in the Synoptic Tradition*. Minneapolis: Fortress, 1979.

Hurtado, Larry W. *The Earliest Christian Artifacts: Manuscripts and Christian Origins*. Grand Rapids: Eerdmans, 2006.

―――. "Following Jesus in the Gospel of Mark—and Beyond." Pages 9–29 in *Patterns of Discipleship in the New Testament*. Edited by Richard N. Longenecker. Grand Rapids: Eerdmans, 1996.

―――. *Mark*. Understanding the Bible Commentary Series. Grand Rapids: Baker Books, 1989.

―――. "Remembering and Revelation: The Historic and Glorified Jesus in the Gospel of John." Pages 195–226 in *Israel's God and Rebecca's Children: Christology and Community in Early Judaism and Christianity*. Edited by David B. Capes, April D. DeConick, Helen K. Bond, and Troy A. Miller. Waco: Baylor University Press, 2007.

Jensen, Robin M. "The Economy of the Trinity at the Creation of Adam and Eve." *Journal of Early Christian Studies* 7.4 (1999): 527–46.

Jeremias, Joachim. *Jerusalem in the Time of Jesus: An Investigation into Economic and Social Conditions during the New Testament Period*. Translated by F. H. Cave and C. H. Cave. 3rd ed. London: SCM, 1969.

Johnson, Luke Timothy. "Learning the Human Jesus: Historical Criticism and Literary Criticism." Pages 153–77 in Beilby and Eddy, *The Historical Jesus*.

———. "The New Testament's Anti-Jewish Slander and the Conventions of Ancient Polemic." *Journal of Biblical Literature* 108.3 (1989): 419–41.

———. *The Real Jesus: The Misguided Quest for the Historical Jesus and the Truth of the Traditional Gospels*. San Francisco: HarperSanFrancisco, 1996.

Kähler, Martin. *The So-Called Historical Jesus and the Historic Biblical Christ*. Philadelphia: Fortress, 1964.

Kalmin, Richard. "Rabbis." Pages 1132–34 in Collins and Harlow, *Eerdmans Dictionary of Early Judaism*.

Kannaday, Wayne C. *Apologetic Discourse and the Scribal Tradition: Evidence of the Influence of Apologetic Interests on the Text of the Canonical Gospels*. Society of Biblical Literature Text-Critical Studies 5. Atlanta: Society of Biblical Literature, 2000.

Käsemann, Ernst. "The Problem of the Historical Jesus." Pages 15–47 in *Essays on New Testament Themes*. Translated by W. J. Montague. Studies in Biblical Theology 41. London: SCM, 1964.

Keck, Leander E. *Who Is Jesus? History in Perfect Tense*. Studies on Personalities of the New Testament. Columbia: University of South Carolina Press, 2000.

Keener, Craig S. *The Gospel of John: A Commentary*. 2 vols. Peabody, MA: Hendrickson, 2003.

———. *The Historical Jesus of the Gospels*. Grand Rapids: Eerdmans, 2009.

———. *Miracles: The Credibility of the New Testament Accounts*. 2 vols. Grand Rapids: Baker Academic, 2011.

Keith, Chris. "The Claim of John 7.15 and the Memory of Jesus' Literacy." *New Testament Studies* 56.1 (2010): 44–63.

———. "The Indebtedness of the Criteria Approach to Form Criticism and Recent Attempts to Rehabilitate the Search for an Authentic Jesus." Pages 25–48 in Keith and Le Donne, *Jesus, Criteria, and the Demise of Authenticity*.

———. *Jesus' Literacy: Scribal Culture and the Teacher from Galilee*. Library of Historical Jesus Studies 8 / Library of New Testament Studies 413. London: T&T Clark, 2011.

———. "Jesus outside and inside the New Testament." Pages 1–31 in Keith and Hurtado, *Jesus among Friends and Enemies*.

———. "Memory and Authenticity: Jesus Tradition and What Really Happened." *Zeitschrift für die neutestamentliche Wissenschaft* 102.2 (2011): 155–77. Expanded and repr. as pages 27–70 in *Jesus' Literacy: Scribal Culture and the Teacher from Galilee*. Library of Historical Jesus Studies 8 / Library of New Testament Studies 413. London: T&T Clark, 2011.

———. *The* Pericope Adulterae, *the Gospel of John, and the Literacy of Jesus*. New Testament Tools, Studies and Documents 38. Leiden: Brill, 2009.

Keith, Chris, and Larry W. Hurtado, eds. *Jesus among Friends and Enemies: A Historical and Literary Introduction to Jesus in the Gospels*. Grand Rapids: Baker Academic, 2011.

Keith, Chris, with Larry W. Hurtado. "Seeking the Historical Jesus among Friends and Enemies." Pages 269–88 in Keith and Hurtado, *Jesus among Friends and Enemies*.

Keith, Chris, and Anthony Le Donne, eds. *Jesus, Criteria, and the Demise of Authenticity*. London: T&T Clark, 2012.

Kelber, Werner H. *The Oral and the Written Gospel: The Hermeneutics of Speaking and Writing in the Synoptic Tradition, Mark, Paul, and Q*. Voices in Performance and Text. Bloomington: Indiana University Press, 1983.

———. "The Quest for the Historical Jesus from the Perspectives of Medieval, Modern, and Post-Enlightenment Readings, and in View of Ancient, Oral Aesthetics." Pages 75–115 in *The Jesus Controversy: Perspectives in Conflict*, by John Dominic Crossan, Luke Timothy Johnson, and Werner H. Kelber. Rockwell Lecture Series. Harrisburg, PA: Trinity, 1999.

Kelber, Werner H., and Samuel Byrskog. *Jesus in Memory: Traditions in Oral and Scribal Perspectives*. Waco: Baylor University Press, 2009.

Kirk, Alan. "Memory Theory and Jesus Research." Vol. 1, pages 809–42 in *Handbook for the Study of the Historical Jesus*. Edited by Tom Holmén and Stanley E. Porter. Leiden: Brill, 2010.

———. "Social and Cultural Memory." Pages 1–24 in Kirk and Thatcher, *Memory, Tradition, and Text*.

———. "The Tradition-Memory Nexus: Finding the Origins of the Gospel Tradition." In Thatcher, *Keys and Frames*.

Kirk, Alan, and Tom Thatcher. "Jesus Tradition as Social Memory." Pages 25–42 in Kirk and Thatcher, *Memory, Tradition, and Text*.

———, eds. *Memory, Tradition, and Text: Uses of the Past in Early Christianity*. Semeia Studies 52. Atlanta: Society of Biblical Literature, 2005.

Klausner, Joseph. *Jesus of Nazareth: His Life, Times, and Teaching*. Translated by Herbert Danby. London: George Allen & Unwin, 1928.

Kraus, Thomas J. *Ad fontes: Original Manuscripts and Their Significance for Studying Early Christianity—Selected Essays*. Texts and Editions for New Testament Study 3. Leiden: Brill, 2007.

———. "(Il)literacy in Non-literary Papyri from Graeco-Roman Egypt: Further Aspects to the Educational Ideal in Ancient Literary Sources and Modern Times." Pages 107–29 in *Ad fontes*. Repr. from *Mnemosyne* 53 (2000): 322–42.

———. "'Slow Writers'—ΒΡΑΔΕΩΣ ΓΡΑΦΟΝΤΕΣ: What, How Much, and How Did They Write?" Pages 131–47 in *Ad fontes*. Repr. from *Eranos* 97 (1997): 86–97.

Lane, William. *The Gospel according to Mark*. New International Commentary on the New Testament. Grand Rapids: Eerdmans, 1974.

Le Donne, Anthony. "The Criterion of Coherence: Its Development, Inevitability, and Historiographical Limitations." Pages 95–114 in Keith and Le Donne, *Jesus, Criteria, and the Demise of Authenticity*.

———. *Historical Jesus: What Can We Know and How Can We Know It?* Grand Rapids: Eerdmans, 2011.

———. *The Historiographical Jesus: Memory, Typology, and the Son of David*. Waco: Baylor University Press, 2009.

———. "The Jewish Leaders." Pages 199–217 in Keith and Hurtado, *Jesus among Friends and Enemies*.

————. "The Rise of the Quest for an Authentic Jesus: An Introduction to the Crumbling Foundations of Jesus Research." Pages 3–21 in Keith and Le Donne, *Jesus, Criteria, and the Demise of Authenticity*.

————. "Theological Distortion in the Jesus Tradition: A Study in Social Memory Theory." Pages 163–77 in *Memory in the Bible and Antiquity*. Edited by Loren T. Stuckenbruck, Stephen C. Barton, and Benjamin G. Wold. Wissenschaftliche Untersuchungen zum Neuen Testament 212. Tübingen: Mohr Siebeck, 2007.

Lee, Bernard J. *The Galilean Jewishness of Jesus: Retrieving the Jewish Origins of Christianity*. Conversations on the Road Not Taken 1. New York: Paulist Press, 1988.

Lee, Sang-Il. *Jesus and Gospel Traditions in Bilingual Context: A Study in the Interdirectionality of Language*. Beihefte zur Zeitschrift für die neutestamentliche Wissenschaft 186. Berlin: de Gruyter, 2012.

Lemaire, André. *Les écoles et la formation de la Bible dans l'ancien Israël*. Orbis biblicus et orientalis 39. Fribourg: Éditions Universitaires, 1981.

Levine, Lee I. *The Ancient Synagogue: The First Thousand Years*. 2nd ed. New Haven: Yale University Press, 2005.

————. "Synagogues." Pages 1260–71 in Collins and Harlow, *Eerdmans Dictionary of Early Judaism*.

Lightstone, Jack N. "The Pharisees and the Sadducees in the Earliest Rabbinic Documents." Pages 255–95 in Neusner and Chilton, *In Quest of the Historical Pharisees*.

Lippman, Thomas W. *Understanding Islam: An Introduction to the Muslim World*. 2nd. rev. ed. New York: Meridian, 1995.

Luz, Ulrich. *Matthew 8–20*. Translated by James E. Crouch. Hermeneia. Minneapolis: Fortress, 2001.

Maccoby, Hyam. *Jesus the Pharisee*. London: SCM, 2003.

————. *Revolution in Judaea: Jesus and the Jewish Resistance*. New York: Taplinger, 1973.

Macdonald, M. C. A. "Literacy in an Oral Environment." Pages 49–118 in *Writing and Ancient Near Eastern Society: Papers in Honour of Alan R. Millard*. Edited by Piotr Bienkowski, Christopher Mee, and Elizabeth Slater. Journal for the Study of the Old Testament: Supplement Series 426. London: T&T Clark, 2005.

Mack, Burton L. *A Myth of Innocence: Mark and Christian Origins*. Philadelphia: Fortress, 1988.

Malbon, Elizabeth Struthers. "Fallible Followers: Women and Men in the Gospel of Mark." Pages 41–69 in *In the Company of Jesus*. Repr. from *Semeia* 28 (1983): 29–48.

————. *In the Company of Jesus: Characters in Mark's Gospel*. Louisville: Westminster John Knox, 2000.

Mandel, Paul. "Hillel." Pages 742–43 in Collins and Harlow, *Eerdmans Dictionary of Early Judaism*.

————. "Shammai." Pages 1224–25 in Collins and Harlow, *Eerdmans Dictionary of Early Judaism*.

Manson, T. W. *Studies in the Gospels and Epistles*. Edited by Matthew Black. Manchester: Manchester University Press, 1962.

Marshall, I. Howard. *The Gospel of Luke: A Commentary on the Greek Text*. New International Greek Testament Commentary. Grand Rapids: Eerdmans, 1978.

McDonald, Lee Martin. *The Biblical Canon: Its Origin, Transmission, and Authority*. 3rd ed. Peabody, MA: Hendrickson, 2007.

McKnight, Scot. *Jesus and His Death: Historiography, the Historical Jesus, and Atonement Theory*. Waco: Baylor University Press, 2005.

Meier, John P. *A Marginal Jew: Rethinking the Historical Jesus*. 4 vols. Yale Anchor Bible Reference Library. New York: Doubleday; New Haven: Yale University Press, 1991–2009.

Metzger, Bruce M. *A Textual Commentary on the Greek New Testament*. 2nd ed. Stuttgart: Deutsche Bibelgesellschaft, 1994.

Millard, Alan. *Reading and Writing in the Time of Jesus*. Biblical Seminar 69. Sheffield: Sheffield Academic Press, 2001.

Moyise, Steve. *Jesus and Scripture*. London: SPCK, 2010.

Natanson, Joseph A. *Early Christian Ivories*. London: Alec Turanti, 1953.

Neusner, Jacob, and Bruce D. Chilton, eds. *In Quest of the Historical Pharisees*. Waco: Baylor University Press, 2007.

Neyrey, Jerome H. "The Trials (Forensic) and Tribulations (Honor Challenges) of Jesus: John 7 in Social Science Perspective." Pages 191–226 in his *The Gospel of John in Cultural and Rhetorical Perspective*. Grand Rapids: Eerdmans, 2009. Repr. from *Biblical Theology Bulletin* 26 (1996): 107–24.

Oakman, Douglas E. *Jesus and the Economic Questions of His Day*. Studies in the Bible and Early Christianity 8. Lewiston, NY: Edwin Mellen, 1986.

Overman, J. Andrew. *Matthew's Gospel and Formative Judaism: The Social World of the Matthean Community*. Minneapolis: Fortress, 1990.

Paul, Ian. "Introducing the New Testament: New Testament Story." Pages 151–58 in *The IVP Introduction to the Bible*. Edited by Philip S. Johnston. Downers Grove, IL: IVP Academic, 2006.

Perkins, Pheme. *Jesus as Teacher*. Understanding Jesus Today. Cambridge: Cambridge University Press, 1990.

Perrin, Norman. *Rediscovering the Teaching of Jesus*. New York: Harper & Row, 1967.

———. *What Is Redaction Criticism?* Guides to Biblical Scholarship. Philadelphia: Fortress, 1969.

Pickup, Martin. "Matthew's and Mark's Pharisees." Pages 67–112 in Neusner and Chilton, *In Quest of the Historical Pharisees*.

Poirier, John C. "Jesus as an Elijianic Figure in Luke 4:16–30." *Catholic Biblical Quarterly* 71.2 (2009): 349–63.

———. "The Linguistic Situation in Jewish Palestine in Late Antiquity." *Journal of Greco-Roman Christianity and Judaism* 4 (2007): 55–134.

Polkow, Dennis. "Method and Criteria for Historical Jesus Research." Pages 336–56 in *Society of Biblical Literature 1987 Seminar Papers*. Edited by Kent Harold Richards. Society of Biblical Literature Seminar Papers 26. Atlanta: Scholars Press, 1987.

Porter, Stanley E. *The Criteria for Authenticity in Historical-Jesus Research: Previous Discussion and New Proposals*. Journal for the Study of the New Testament: Supplement Series 191. Sheffield: Sheffield Academic Press, 2000.

Powell, Mark Allan. "Do and Keep What Moses Says (Matthew 23:2–7)." *Journal of Biblical Literature* 114.3 (1995): 419–35.

———. *Jesus as a Figure in History: How Modern Historians View the Man from Galilee*. Louisville: Westminster John Knox, 1998.

Price, Robert M. "Jesus at the Vanishing Point." Pages 55–83 in Beilby and Eddy, *The Historical Jesus*.

Puig i Tàrrech, Armand. *Jesus: A Biography*. Translated by David Cullen, Sid Phipps, and Jenny Read-Heimerdinger. Waco: Baylor University Press, 2011.

Repschinski, Boris. *The Controversy Stories in the Gospel of Matthew: Their Redaction, Form and Relevance for the Relationship between the Matthean Community and Formative Judaism*. Forschungen zur Religion und Literatur des Alten und Neuen Testaments 189. Göttingen: Vandenhoeck & Ruprecht, 2000.

Reynolds, Benjamin. *The Apocalyptic Son of Man in the Gospel of John*. Wissenschaftliche Untersuchungen zum Neuen Testament 2.249. Tübingen: Mohr Siebeck, 2008.

Rhoads, David, Joanna Dewey, and Donald Michie. *Mark as Story: An Introduction to the Narrative of a Gospel*. 3rd ed. Minneapolis: Fortress, 2012.

Riesner, Rainer. *Jesus als Lehrer*. Wissenschaftliche Untersuchungen zum Neuen Testament 2.7. Tübingen: Mohr Siebeck, 1981.

———. "Jesus as Preacher and Teacher." Pages 185–210 in *Jesus and the Oral Gospel Tradition*. Edited by Henry Wansbrough. London: T&T Clark, 1991.

———. "Jüdische Elementarbildung und Evangelienüberlieferung." Vol. 1, pages 209–23 in *Gospel Perspectives: Studies of History and Tradition in the Four Gospels*. Edited by R. T. France and David Wenham. Sheffield: JSOT Press, 1980.

Rodríguez, Rafael. "Authenticating Criteria: The Use and Misuse of a Critical Method." *Journal for the Study of the Historical Jesus* 7 (2009): 152–67.

———. "The Embarrassing Truth about Jesus: The Criterion of Embarrassment and the Failure of Historical Authenticity." Pages 132–51 in Keith and Le Donne, *Jesus, Criteria, and the Demise of Authenticity*.

———. *Oral Tradition and the New Testament: A Guide for the Perplexed*. T&T Clark Guides for the Perplexed. London: T&T Clark, 2013.

———. *Structuring Early Christian Memory: Jesus in Tradition, Performance and Text*. Library of New Testament Studies 407. London: T&T Clark, 2009.

Rohrbaugh, Richard L. "Legitimating Sonship—A Test of Honour: A Social-Scientific Study of Luke 4:1–30." Pages 183–97 in Esler, *Modelling Early Christianity*.

Rollston, Christopher A. *Writing and Literacy in the World of Ancient Israel: Epigraphic Evidence from the Iron Age*. Society of Biblical Literature Archaeology and Biblical Studies 11. Atlanta: Society of Biblical Literature, 2010.

Runesson, Anders. "Entering a Synagogue with Paul: Torah Observance in First-Century Jewish Institutions." Paper presented at the annual meeting of the Society of Biblical Literature. Chicago. November 18, 2012.

————. "The Historical Jesus, the Gospels, and First-Century Jewish Society: The Importance of the Synagogue for Understanding the New Testament." In *City on a Hill: Essays in Honor of James F. Strange*. Edited by Daniel Warner and Donald D. Binder. Mountain Home, AR: BorderStone, 2013.

Runesson, Anders, Donald D. Binder, and Birger Olsson, eds. *The Ancient Synagogue from Its Origins to 200 C.E.: A Source Book*. Leiden: Brill, 2010.

Saldarini, Anthony J. *Pharisees, Scribes and Sadducees in Palestinian Society: A Sociological Approach*. Biblical Resource Series. Grand Rapids: Eerdmans, 2001.

Sanders, E. P. *The Historical Figure of Jesus*. London: Penguin, 1993.

————. *Jesus and Judaism*. London: SCM, 1985.

Schams, Christine. *Jewish Scribes in the Second-Temple Period*. Journal for the Study of the Old Testament: Supplement Series 291. Sheffield: Sheffield Academic Press, 1998.

Schnelle, Udo. *Theology of the New Testament*. Translated by M. Eugene Boring. Grand Rapids: Baker Academic, 2009.

Schröter, Jens. "The Criteria of Authenticity in Jesus Research and Historiographical Method." Pages 49–70 in Keith and Le Donne, *Jesus, Criteria, and the Demise of Authenticity*.

————. "The Historical Jesus and the Sayings Tradition: Comments on Current Research." *Neotestamentica* 30.1 (1996): 151–68.

————. "Jesus of Galilee: The Role of Location in Understanding Jesus." Pages 36–55 in Charlesworth and Pokorný, eds., *Jesus Research*.

————. *Jesus von Nazaret: Jude aus Galiläa—Retter der Welt*. 3rd ed. Biblische Gestalt 15. Leipzig: Evangelische Verlagsanstalt, 2006.

————. "Von der Historizität der Evangelien: Ein Beitrag zur gegenwärtigen Diskussion um den historischen Jesus." Pages 163–212 in Schröter and Brucker, *Der historische Jesus*. Repr. as pages 105–46 in his *Von Jesus zum Neuen Testament: Studien zur urchristlichen Theologiegeschichte und zur Entstehung des neutestamentlichen Kanons*. Wissenschaftliche Untersuchungen zum Neuen Testament 204. Tübingen: Mohr Siebeck, 2007.

Schröter, Jens, and Ralph Brucker, eds. *Der historische Jesus: Tendenzen und Perspektiven der gegenwärtigen Forschung*. Beihefte zur Zeitschrift für die neutestamentliche Wissenschaft und die Kunde der älteren Kirche 114. Berlin: de Gruyter, 2002.

Schürmann, H. "Zur Traditionsgeschichte der Nazareth-Pericope Lk 4,16–30." Pages 187–205 in *Mélanges bibliques en hommage au R. P. Béda Rigaux*. Edited by Albert Descamps and André de Halleux. Gembloux: Duculot, 1970.

Schwartz, Barry. "Christian Origins: Historical Truth and Social Memory." Pages 43–56 in Kirk and Thatcher, *Memory, Tradition, and Text*.

————. "Where There's Smoke, There's Fire: Memory and History." In Thatcher, *Keys and Frames*.

Schwartz, Seth. *Imperialism and Jewish Society, 200 BCE to 640 CE*. Jews, Christians, and Muslims from the Ancient to the Modern World. Princeton: Princeton University Press, 2001.

Schweitzer, Albert. *The Quest of the Historical Jesus: A Critical Study of Its Progress from Reimarus to Wrede.* Translated by F. C. Burkitt. Baltimore: Johns Hopkins University Press, 1968.

Segbroeck, Frans van. "Jésus rejeté par sa patrie (Mt 13,54–58)." *Biblica* 48 (1968): 167–98.

Shanks, Hershel. "Is the Title 'Rabbi' Anachronistic in the Gospels?" *Jewish Quarterly Review* 53.4 (1963): 337–49.

Smith, Morton. *Jesus the Magician.* Wellingborough, UK: Aquarian, 1985.

Snyder, H. Gregory. *Teachers and Texts in the Ancient World: Philosophers, Jews and Christians.* Religion in the First Christian Centuries. New York: Routledge, 2000.

Stanley, Christopher D. *The Hebrew Bible: A Comparative Approach.* Minneapolis: Fortress, 2010.

Stanton, Graham N., ed. *The Interpretation of Matthew.* 2nd ed. Studies in New Testament Interpretation. Edinburgh: T&T Clark, 1995.

Stein, Robert H. *The Method and Message of Jesus' Teachings.* Rev. ed. Louisville: Westminster John Knox, 1994.

Strauss, David Friedrich. *The Life of Jesus Critically Examined.* Edited by Peter C. Hodgson. Translated by George Eliot. Lives of Jesus Series. London: SCM, 1973.

Stuckenbruck, Loren T. "'Semitic Influence on Greek': An Authenticating Criterion in Jesus Research?" Pages 73–94 in Keith and Le Donne, eds., *Jesus, Criteria, and the Demise of Authenticity.*

Sullivan, Kevin P., and T. G. Wilfong. "The Reply of Jesus to King Abgar: A Coptic New Testament Apocryphon Reconsidered (P.Mich. Inv. 6213)." *Bulletin of the American Society of Papyrologists* 42 (2005): 107–23.

Taylor, Vincent. *The Formation of the Gospel Tradition.* London: Macmillan, 1960.

———. *The Gospel according to St. Mark.* London: Macmillan, 1963.

Thatcher, Tom. *Jesus the Riddler: The Power of Ambiguity in the Gospels.* Louisville: Westminster John Knox, 2006.

———, ed. *Keys and Frames: Memory and Identity in Ancient Judaism and Early Christianity.* Semeia Studies. Atlanta: Society of Biblical Literature, forthcoming.

Thatcher, Tom, Chris Keith, Raymond Person, and Elsie Stern, eds. *Dictionary of the Bible and Ancient Media.* London: T&T Clark, forthcoming.

Theissen, Gerd. *The Gospels in Context: Social and Political History in the Synoptic Tradition.* Translated by Linda M. Maloney. Minneapolis: Fortress, 1991.

———. "Jesus as an Itinerant Preacher: Reflections from Social History on Jesus' Roles." Pages 98–122 in Charlesworth and Pokorný, eds., *Jesus Research.*

Theissen, Gerd, and Dagmar Winter. *The Quest for the Plausible Jesus: The Question of Criteria.* Translated by M. Eugene Boring. Louisville: Westminster John Knox, 2002.

Thompson, Marianne Meye. *The God of the Gospel of John.* Grand Rapids: Eerdmans, 2001.

Toit, David S. du. "Der unähnliche Jesus: Eine kritische Evaluierung der Entstehung des Differenzkriteriums und seiner geschichts- und erkenntnistheoretischen Voraussetzungen." Pages 88–129 in Schröter and Brucker, *Der historische Jesus.*

Toorn, Karel van der. *Scribal Culture and the Making of the Hebrew Bible*. Cambridge, MA: Harvard University Press, 2007.

Tucker, W. Dennis, Jr. "Rabbi, Rabboni." Pages 1105–6 in Freedman, *Eerdmans Dictionary of the Bible*.

Tuckett, Christopher. "Form Criticism." Pages 21–38 in Kelber and Byrskog, *Jesus in Memory*.

VanderKam, James C. Foreword to *Pharisees, Scribes and Sadducees in Palestinian Society: A Sociological Approach*, by Anthony J. Saldarini. Biblical Resource Series. Grand Rapids: Eerdmans, 2001.

Vermes, Geza. *Jesus and the World of Judaism*. London: SCM, 1983.

———. *Jesus the Jew: A Historian's Reading of the Gospels*. Philadelphia: Fortress, 1973.

Walzer, Richard. *Galen on Jews and Christians*. Oxford Classical and Philosophical Monographs. London: Oxford University Press, 1949.

Watson, Francis. *Paul and the Hermeneutics of Faith*. London: T&T Clark, 2004.

Webb, Robert L. "The Historical Enterprise and Historical Jesus Research." Pages 9–93 in Bock and Webb, *Key Events in the Life of the Historical Jesus*.

Winter, Dagmar. "Saving the Quest for Authenticity from the Criterion of Dissimilarity: History and Plausibility." Pages 115–31 in Keith and Le Donne, *Jesus, Criteria, and the Demise of Authenticity*.

Winter, Paul. *On the Trial of Jesus*. Edited and revised by T. A. Burkill and Geza Vermes. 2nd ed. Studia judaica 1. Berlin: de Gruyter, 1974 [1961].

Witherington, Ben, III. *The Jesus Quest: The Third Search for the Jew of Nazareth*. 2nd ed. Downers Grove, IL: InterVarsity, 1997.

Wright, N. T. *The New Testament and the People of God*. Christian Origins and the Question of God 1. Minneapolis: Fortress, 1992.

Young, Brad H. *Jesus the Jewish Theologian*. Peabody, MA: Hendrickson, 1995.

Youtie, Herbert C. "Βραδέως γράφων: Between Literacy and Illiteracy." Pages 629–51 in his *Scriptiunculae II*. Amsterdam: Hakkert, 1973. Repr. from *Greek, Roman, and Byzantine Studies* 12.2 (1971): 239–61.

Scripture and Ancient Writings Index

Luke

Author Index

183

Subject Index

Abgar legend 92

Babatha 25, 27n43

carpenter 13, 31n53, 45, 47, 61, 150. *See also* Jesus: as carpenter/manual laborer
Celsus 21, 54–56, 94–95, 97
chief priests. *See* priests
controversy narratives xi, 7–9, 14, 111–26
   historicity 129–42
   nature 137–38, 148–51
criteria of authenticity/criteria approach 70, 73–84
crucifixion/cross 3, 6, 8, 9n15, 26, 54, 69, 125, 144, 146, 151, 155–56

education. *See* literacy: literate education
8 Mile 150n90

form criticism 74–78, 80, 82, 111n1, 129–32, 135

Galilee 9, 33, 44, 47–48, 50, 57, 98, 104, 108, 132, 141–42, 156

Hanina ben Dosa 12n29, 19
Hillel 11, 19, 31n53, 46
historical positivism 71, 76–77, 80
Honi the Circle Drawer 12n29, 19
honor/shame xii, 4, 32, 36, 44, 51, 59, 64, 107, 116, 121–22, 129, 141, 149–51, 156

Jerusalem 3, 6, 8–9, 12, 22n26, 23n29, 26, 35, 73, 94, 104–5, 85n108, 115, 119, 121, 138, 141–42, 144, 156

Jesus
   as carpenter/manual laborer 13, 44–65, 69, 91, 94, 96–97, 108, 139, 141–42, 148, 150, 155
   death of. *See* crucifixion/cross
   as exorcist 9–13, 48, 50, 112, 126, 136n36, 139, 141, 155
   as healer 9–10, 11, 13, 48, 50, 123–24, 126, 136, 141
   as Messiah 112
   as miracle worker 3, 10–12, 51, 62, 83n52, 112, 139–41, 155
   as prophet 4, 19, 44, 50, 59, 62, 64, 87, 103, 105, 112, 155
   as rabbi 4, 17–19, 57, 87n2, 88, 89n13, 133n19, 135, 138, 143
   reputation as teacher 11–12, 14, 50, 141, 149
   and sarcasm 149
   scribal-literate status 13, 31–32, 37, 41–65, 69–70, 84, 87, 89–98, 105, 107–8, 125, 129–30, 138–43, 147–51, 155–57
   as synagogue teacher 13, 43–64, 69, 91, 139–42
Jesus ben Ananias 19
John the Baptist 11, 18, 62, 121
Josephus 23, 28, 30–31, 33–34, 46, 100

law. *See* Torah/the law
Le Donne, Anthony xii
literacy. *See also* Jesus: scribal-literate status
   grapho-literacy 25, 27, 88, 92
   literate education 6, 14, 21–24
   multilingualism 26–27
   percentages 21, 90
   perception 21, 32–33, 85–108, 141, 151